Birder's Eye View
Savannah & the Low Country

Diana Churchill

© 2012 by Diana Churchill
All rights reserved.

Book design by Skipping Stones Design

Publisher: Chimney Creek Press
P.O. Box 30025
Savannah, GA 31410

Printed in the United States of America
by Lewis Color, Inc. Statesboro, GA

ISBN-13: 978-0-9827491-0-4

Library of Congress Control Number: 2011919586

All photographs are by Diana Churchill
except where noted in the photo credits.

Cover Photo: *Great Egret, breeding plumage, in Wax Myrtle*

www.dianachurchillbirds.com

*This book is dedicated to my grandmother,
Estelle Erwin Kandel, who loved reading and words
and passed that love on to all her children and grandchildren,
and to my parents,
Bob and Phillippa Paddison,
educators "par excellence" whose lifetime of love and caring
has helped this book take flight.*

To Patsy
Good Birding!
Diana Churchill

FOREWORD

The land that we call the Low Country was celebrated in the first detailed, illustrated account ever published on birds of the Americas. An Englishman named Mark Catesby had lived for a time in Charleston, South Carolina, and had traveled throughout the coastal areas of Georgia, the Carolinas, and nearby states, and had fallen in love with the birdlife there. His multi-volume *Natural History*, featuring his own written descriptions and hand-colored illustrations, started off with five sections treating 100 different kinds of birds. The first of these was published in 1729. Nearly half a century before the United States became a nation, nearly a century before the appearance of John James Audubon's *Birds of America*, scholars in Europe were fascinated by Catesby's depictions of Low Country birds.

The birdlife of this region has been inspiring fascination ever since. I have been fortunate enough to visit the Low Country many times; after every visit, I have come away simply astonished by the sheer numbers and variety of birds.

On the beaches and tidal flats around the innumerable islands and estuaries, swarms of sandpipers and plovers from the Arctic may stand next to flocks of terns from the Caribbean. In the groves of graceful live oaks, in the cypress stands draped with Spanish moss, flocks of colorful songbirds abound at all seasons. In the magnificent stretches of salt marshes – reduced to scraps elsewhere on the Atlantic Coast, but still thriving here – flocks of herons, egrets, ibises, and other wading birds cavort in the shallows. This is a wonderland of birds. The 200-mile stretch of coastline centered on Savannah, Georgia, should be recognized as one of the great birding destinations of North America. But some who are blessed to live in the area may almost take the local abundance of birds for granted.

One who definitely does not take the birds for granted is Diana Churchill. After growing up in Savannah, she lived and traveled in other states for twenty-five years before moving home to Georgia in 1999. Since 2001, she has been writing about birds for the *Savannah Morning News*, illustrating her column with her own photographs, and attracting legions of followers to take note of the natural world.

Now the finest of those columns have formed the basis for this beautiful book, which leads us season by season through the avian delights of this region. Diana Churchill's writing – graceful and warm and inviting, like the land that it celebrates – provides the perfect invitation for all of us to discover anew the amazing and beautiful birdlife of the Low Country.

Kenn Kaufman

TABLE OF CONTENTS

FOREWORD BY KENN KAUFMAN iv

FIRST ONE TO SEE A KINGFISHER 1

WELCOME TO THE LOW COUNTRY 3

LOW COUNTRY HABITATS
    Maritime Forest 9
    Coastal Scrub 10
    Longleaf Pine Forest 11
    Slash & Loblolly Pine Forest 12
    Floodplain Forest & Swamp 13
    Urban & Suburban Park 14
    Open Field 15
    Early Successional Shrub 16
    Lake, Pond, & Lagoon 17
    Freshwater Marsh 18
    Salt Marsh 19
    Tidal Creek & River 20
    Tidal Sandbar & Mudflat 21
    Sandy Beach 22
    Near-shore Ocean 23
    Pelagic 24

YEAR-ROUND BIRDS OF THE LOW COUNTRY 25

WINTER: AN OVERVIEW 29
    December
        Here a Duck, There a Duck 33
        The Secrets of the Salt Marsh 35
        What's So Crazy About a Loon? 38
        The *Grinches* 40
    January
        Talking to Owls 43
        National Bird Watching 45
        Oystercatchers Among Us 49
        The Martins Are Coming! 52

TABLE OF CONTENTS

February
- Watching Warblers in Winter 55
- Keep Your Eyes Upon the Sparrows 58
- Beware the Berry Bandits...61
- Buzzard Bait 63

SPRING: AN OVERVIEW 67

March
- The Three-Ring Circus of Spring 71
- The Return of the Mafia 73
- What a Bird Guy Will Do to Get a Gal! 76
- Tuning Your Ears to Bird Song 79

April
- Nesting Box Blues 82
- Cheerio the Vireos 84
- Rhapsody in Blue...87
- Fish Hawks Make Good Neighbors 90

May
- Look Out for the Lord of the Flies 93
- Bunting Fever 96
- Disturbing the Peace 98
- Get Thee to a Rookery 100

SUMMER: AN OVERVIEW 107

June
- All Those Begging Babies...111
- All Hail the Brown Thrasher 114
- Mud Hens & Swamp Chickens 117
- How Much Wood Could a Woodpecker Peck? 119

July
- It's a Stick! It's a Snake! It's a BIRD?? 123
- Chimney Swifts Take Life on the Wing 125
- The Marvelous Tale of the Clapper Rail 128
- A Visit to the Breakfast Club 131

August
- Why Do Hummingbirds Hum?......................................134
- Let's Go Spy a Kite 136
- Making a Living at Low Tide..139
- To Everything, Tern, Tern, Tern…..................................142

Fall: An Overview 147
- **September**
  - Migration Is the Spice of Life 151
  - Beautyberry and the Birds 154
  - The Shriek of the Shrike 156
  - Are You a Lover of Plovers? 158
- **October**
  - May There Always Be Pelicans 162
  - Tree Swallows & More Tree Swallows 165
  - Dance of the Black Skimmers 168
  - Keep Your Eyes on the Skies for Raptors! 171
- **November**
  - The Changing of the Guard 175
  - What's So Purple About a Sandpiper? 178
  - The Yellow-rumps Are Back! 180
  - Has Anybody Seen My *Icterid*? 183

In Your Yard
- Attracting Birds to Your Yard 187
- Which Birds Eat Which Food? 190
- The Pleasures of the Bath 191
- Becoming a Birdlord 193
- Oh, Those Pesky Squirrels 196

Quick Reference Photo Guide 199

Low Country Bird Watching Locations 205

Glossary of Terms 218

Resources 220

Checklist 224

Acknowledgments & Photo Credits 227

Index 228

About the Author 233

First One to See a Kingfisher

Belted Kingfisher perched on wire

When someone asks me how I got started with bird watching, I blame it, naturally, on my parents.

There were those long rides from Savannah to Tybee back when U.S. 80 to the beach was the longest palm-lined drive in the country. The bridge over the Bull River was so narrow that we prayed fervently we would encounter no oncoming traffic.

Three of us were packed in the back of the Pontiac, jostling and squabbling over something.

"First one to see a kingfisher gets a nickel," my Dad would offer from the front seat. Our bickering forgotten, all eyes went to the power lines, eager for a glimpse of that distinctive silhouette. The shape of the belted kingfisher is unmistakable, even seen from a moving vehicle at 50 miles an hour. There the crest, the squat, hunched body, and the long bill as the bird leans forward, watching intently for the silvery shimmer of fish in the water below.

Except during nesting season, kingfishers are solitary creatures. We

Female Belted Kingfisher on piling

would find them at discreet intervals, staked out above likely fishing territor

Kingfisher in flight

To see one or two during the 15 mile drive to Tybee was typical. Five or more was a red-letter day.

Only the first one was worth money, but by that time we were engrossed in the game.

To this day, the kingfisher remains one of my favorite birds. It can be seen throughout the United States, anywhere there is a river, pond, stream, brook, ocean or lake. Listen for the loud, dry rattle of its call as it flies down the creek, or watch one hover, helicopter-like, above the water before plummeting with a splash to emerge with a wriggling fish.

Adding to its uniqueness, the belted kingfisher is one of the few species where the female is more colorful than the male. He has a blue-gray band spanning his chest. She sports a reddish band below the blue one, giving her a jaunty distinction.

When spring comes, the kingfishers disappear from the creeks and rivers around Tybee as they retreat further inland to find a suitable nesting site – a dirt mound or river bank that won't flood at high tide.

Once on the breeding grounds, the male kingfisher abandons his "you catch your fish, I'll catch mine" attitude, and begins offering his beloved tasty morsels. If she finds his tidbits to her liking, they mate and set up housekeeping. Like a sensible modern couple they share in burrow digging, egg sitting, and chick feeding. The parents spend three weeks on the nest, another four feeding the nestlings, and three more tending the fledglings – ten weeks total and no saving for college!

Usually, by August, the familiar shape reappears on the wires along U.S. 80 – once again solitary as each bird sets up its own territory.

In the summer, with the kingfishers busy elsewhere, my Dad's offer changed. "First one to see a willet gets a nickel." But that's another story.

Belted Kingfishers courting

WELCOME TO THE LOW COUNTRY

Aerial view of the Low Country

If you ask a dozen people "What is the Low Country?" you are likely to get a dozen different answers. Some will claim that it relates to coastal South Carolina with Charleston as its capital. In the book *Drives of a Lifetime,* National Geographic offers "Low Country: South Carolina and Georgia" and traces a route south from Charleston through Edisto Island, Beaufort, St. Helena Island, Hunting Island, and Pinckney Island National Wildlife Refuge, ending in Savannah.

An advertising supplement on Boston.com urges New Englanders to get a jump on spring with a trip to the Georgia Low Country. The itinerary calls for flying to Jacksonville, renting a car, and heading north, with stops at St. Mary's, Cumberland Island, Jekyll Island, St. Simon's Island, and finally Savannah.

I grew up in Savannah, so naturally I think of Georgia's first city, founded by Gen. James Edward Oglethorpe in 1733, as the center of the Low Country. Geographically speaking, if you drive two plus hours north from Savannah, you get to Charleston, South Carolina. Drive two hours south and you'll come to Jacksonville, Florida. These two cities could be considered the bookends of a unique two-hundred-mile stretch of the east coast of North America.

When people think about the mountains, they usually think of rocks. Mention a desert, and most people envision sand. In the Low Country, the defining element is water. For starters, the country is "low" because the elevation of this area that begins at the ocean and extends inland for some

25 miles, is basically "sea level." When my friend Buck helped me move back to Savannah at the end of 1998, we drove through the rolling hills of Virginia and North Carolina, and then entered the South Carolina coastal plain. As we crossed river after river, and began seeing large stretches of golden marsh, Buck intoned, like a litany, "it's so flat."

There are three main water sources in the area. First, and most obvious, is the salt water of the Atlantic Ocean. Because these 200 miles of coastline enjoy the distinction of being the furthest west on the east coast, the ocean water is funneled into the area with dramatic regularity. Low Country rhythms are governed by the relentless ebb and flow of the tides. Every newspaper in the area prints – on the same page with the weather, sunrise, and sunset — the time and height of that day's high and low tides. There are two high tides and two low tides during every 24-hour period. High tides range from 6 to 9 feet, depending on the phase of the moon. At new and full moon, high tides are higher and

Periwinkle Snails on Smooth Cordgrass

low tides are lower.

Knowing the tides is important for boaters, but also for birdwatchers. Low tide, when the mudflats, sandbars, shell rakes, and rock jetties are exposed, is feast time for shorebirds. At high tide, when the buffets are closed, the birds can be found resting in large numbers on any high ground – usually area beaches.

Very few plants can tolerate being inundated by salt water twice a day. The one best adapted to survive these harsh conditions is marsh grass, scientifically known as smooth cordgrass or *spartina alterniflora*. Because of how far inland the water surges with each high tide, nearly one third of the salt marsh of the entire east coast of North America can be found along the 200 miles of Low Country coastline.

The second major source of water has its origin hundreds of miles inland, in the mountains of north Georgia and western South Carolina. When it rains, fresh water

High tide at Chimney Creek

flows down the mountains and begins a slow march to the sea, carried along by an assortment of alluvial rivers with strange names, like Edisto, Ashepoo, Combahee, Ogeechee, and Altamaha. When the rivers reach the flat coastal plain, they settle into a series of lazy, curving pathways, carving a meandering route through the salt marsh and intervening land to get to the sea. In the process, they create a series of bodies of water known as sounds, and an assortment of short, fat, barrier islands, bounded on the east or "front" side by the Atlantic Ocean, and on the "back" or west side by rivers, tidal creeks and salt marsh.

Blue Crab

The area where the salt water from the ocean meets the fresh water from the rivers is known as the estuary. This area contains high levels of nutrients and is one of the most productive natural habitats in the world, serving as a nursery for the shrimp, crabs, fish, and oysters that form the basis of Low Country cuisine.

All this seafood is harvested both commercially and recreationally. Each coastal community has its fleet of shrimp boats that can be seen dragging their nets through the creeks, rivers, and into the ocean, pursued by flocks of gulls, terns, pelicans, and often bottlenose dolphins. These marine mammals are real Low Country entertainers. Seeing a fin, a tail, or an entire dolphin leap from the water brings a thrill matched only by the rare eye-to-eye encounter.

Blue crabs are another of the Low Country's tasty treats. Commercial crabbers bait large wire traps and drop them to the river bottom, marking their locations with colored floats. I use simple traps made of concentric metal rings connected with mesh netting. I bait them with chicken necks, and tie them to the dock railing. By diligently checking the traps throughout the day, I may end up with enough crabs for supper.

When the tide comes in from the ocean, it actually pushes the rivers upstream. The early colonists discovered that rice would grow well in these swampy lowlands, and they found a way

Shrimp boat enters Lazaretto Creek

to harness the power of the tides. They created impoundments, bordered by elevated dikes, and a series of trunk gates that could be raised and lowered to bring in the fresh water being pushed upstream by the tides. Rice production began in the early 1700s and continued until the early 1900s. Many of these former rice plantations are now freshwater marsh habitats, managed either publicly or privately for wildlife, including ducks, shorebirds, wading birds, and alligators.

American Alligator basks on river bank

Bottlenose Dolphin

The American alligator can occasionally be found in salt or brackish water, but is more abundant in freshwater ponds, sloughs, and marshes. On cool, sunny days, they can be found sunbathing at the water's edge. Alligators provide valuable community service by digging "gator holes" during times of drought. They also act as unwitting security guards below heron rookeries, discouraging climbing predators from reaching the nests and eating eggs or chicks.

The third source of water in the Low Country is critical but not immediately visible. Much of the water used for drinking and by industry comes from underneath our feet. The Floridan aquifer underlies an area of about 100,000 square miles including all of Florida and parts of coastal Georgia, Alabama, and South Carolina.

Groundwater is contained under pressure by a confining bed of connected carbonate rocks, mostly limestone and dolomite. Around 3 million gallons of water a day are extracted from the Floridan aquifer for household, industrial, and agricultural uses.

All this water is responsible for one of the less pleasant aspects of Low Country living – humidity. Summer in the Low Country is typically hazy, hot, and humid – perfect for the growth of one of our signature plants – Spanish moss. It is neither Spanish nor a moss, but no picture of the Low Country would be complete without the image of a southern live oak, liberally adorned with the lacy gray strands of this flowering air plant. Spanish moss is not a parasite. It doesn't live off the trees, but traps moisture and nutrients from the air around it.

Another word that comes to mind when people think about the Low Country is "swamp." In general, a

Spanish Moss on Live Oaks

swamp is a forested, rather than an open wetland. These areas are also referred to as floodplain forests, or bottomland hardwood forests.

Signature trees are bald cypress with its buttressed trunk and spreading system of "knees," water tupelo, black gum, and red maple. The water in these areas turns dark, stained by the tannins that are leached out of decaying vegetation. Paddling a kayak or canoe along one of the Low Country's "blackwater" rivers can be a near-mystical experience.

Put simply, the Low Country is a terrific place for birds. Taking into account year-round residents, winter visitors, and Neotropical migrants, some 250 species can be regularly found here. The Savannah Area Christmas Bird Count usually reports more than 150 species present in late December or early January. There are birds to watch during every season of the year, although fall, winter, and spring are more pleasant for birdwatchers.

The key to finding birds in the Low Country is getting to know where and when they usually hang out – habitat and timing. The text and photos that follow are designed to familiarize you with this unique area of the country, and help you follow the movements of our feathered friends through four seasons of Low Country living.

An old rice trunk gate on the Savannah River

Low Country Habitats

Maritime Forest

Maritime Forest

Maritime forest is mixed pine and hardwood forest found along the coast, generally adjacent to beach or salt marsh. It is composed of more than 50 percent live oak trees with the balance being a mixture of pine, palmetto, red bay and wax myrtle. Spanish moss is a signature plant in maritime forest.

Yellow-throated Warbler

Specialty Birds of Maritime Forests
Blue-gray Gnatcatcher – year-round
Yellow-throated Warbler – year-round
Black-and-white Warbler – migration, winter
Summer Tanager – summer
Painted Bunting – summer
Northern Parula – summer

Blue-gray Gnatcatcher

COASTAL SCRUB

Coastal Scrub

This habitat is the brushy area found on the edges of many coastal habitats. Plants typical in this habitat include wax myrtle, yaupon holly, saw palmetto, catbrier, and sparkleberry.

Painted Bunting

Common Yellowthroat, juvenile male

Specialty Birds of Coastal Scrub
Eastern Towhee – year-round
Common Yellowthroat – year-round
Blue-gray Gnatcatcher – year-round
Yellow-rumped Warbler – winter
Gray Catbird – migration, winter
Ruby-crowned Kinglet – winter
Painted Bunting – summer

LONGLEAF PINE FOREST

Longleaf Pine Forest

Longleaf pine trees dominate this type of forest, with a diverse understory including wiregrass, saw palmettos, turkey oaks, and reindeer moss. Once prevalent in the southeastern United States, longleaf pine forest is now found only in isolated Low Country locations, including Ft. Stewart, the Okefenokee, and Webb Wildlife Management Area. The timber industry generally replaced longleaf pines with faster growing slash and loblolly pines.

Bachman's Sparrow

Specialty Birds in Longleaf Pine Forests
Red-cockaded Woodpecker – year-round
Bachman's Sparrow – year-round
Pine Warbler – year-round
Brown-headed Nuthatch – year-round

Red-cockaded Woodpecker

Slash & Loblolly Pine Forest

Slash & Loblolly Pine Forest

Slash and loblolly pines are faster growing than longleaf pines and not as fire resistant. They have been planted in many locations by the timber industry. Slash pine occurs primarily in the coastal plain, while loblolly pine is prevalent throughout the state. When fire is suppressed in a longleaf pine forest, slash and loblolly pines encroach and alter the course of the habitat.

Pine Warbler

Brown-headed Nuthatch

Specialty Birds in Slash & Loblolly Pine Forests
Pine Warbler – year-round
Brown-headed Nuthatch – year-round
Brown Creeper – winter
Prairie Warbler – summer

Floodplain Forest & Swamp

Floodplain Forest

The bottomland hardwood forests of the Low Country are sometimes referred to as "swamps." This flooded or wet forest is found adjacent to waterways, and is dominated by bald cypress, water tupelo, and swamp gum trees which are sur-

Barred Owl

rounded by water during the wetter months of the year.

Specialty Birds of Floodplain Forest & Swamps
Barred Owl – year-round
Winter Wren – winter
Prothonotary Warbler – summer
Acadian Flycatcher – summer
Yellow-billed Cuckoo – summer

Prothonotary Warbler

Urban & Suburban Park

Forsyth Park, Savannah, Georgia

The Low Country is noted for the stately live oaks, southern magnolias, and assorted hardwood trees that grace both urban and suburban parks, creating wonderful habitat for birds. Although house sparrows and rock pigeons are common urban residents, a diverse assortment of other birds can be found year-round. Spring and fall migration bring a surprising number of warblers, tanagers, vireos, orioles, buntings and grosbeaks.

American Robin

Specialty Birds of the Urban & Suburban Parks
House Sparrow – year-round
Rock Pigeon – year-round
Northern Mockingbird – year-round
American Robin – year-round
Brown Thrasher – year-round
Red-bellied Woodpecker – year-round
Chimney Swift – spring, summer
Great Crested Flycatcher – spring, summer

House Sparrow

OPEN FIELD

Grassy Field

Fields in the Low Country can be grassy or cultivated. This habitat can include golf courses, ball parks, agricultural fields, and sod farms.

Eastern Meadowlark

American Pipit

Specialty Birds of Grassy Fields
Killdeer – year-round
Chipping Sparrow – winter
Savannah Sparrow – winter

Field Sparrow – winter
American Pipit – winter
Eastern Meadowlark – winter

Specialty Birds of Moist Agricultural Fields
Killdeer – year-round
Pectoral Sandpiper – migration
American Pipit – winter
Least Sandpiper – migration, winter
Wilson's Snipe – winter

Early Successional Shrub

Early Successional Shrub

This habitat is a transitional habitat dominated by shrubs or young trees. If left unmowed, grassy fields will become early successional habitat. Often fire is used to maintain this habitat, as it will eventually turn into forest if growth continues unchecked.

Yellow-breasted Chat

Specialty Birds of Early Successional Shrub
Pine Warbler – year-round
Yellow-breasted Chat – summer
Indigo Bunting – summer
Blue Grosbeak – summer
Prairie Warbler – summer

Indigo Bunting

Lake, Pond & Lagoon

Herons and egrets feed at the edge of a pond

This habitat type refers to any small, permanent body of water, generally fresh. Many of these are man-made in subdivisions, golf courses, or community parks.

Specialty Birds of Lake, Pond & Lagoon
Anhinga – year-round
Common Gallinule – year-round
Wood Duck – year-round
Belted Kingfisher – year-round
Pied-billed Grebe – winter
American Coot – winter
Hooded Merganser – winter
Spotted Sandpiper – migration
Green Heron – summer

Spotted Sandpiper

Pied-billed Grebe

FRESHWATER MARSH

Freshwater marsh at Bear Island Wildlife Management Area, SC

This habitat is found along the edges of rivers, ponds, and artificially created wetlands. Numerous former rice plantations have converted to freshwater marsh. Plants found here include cattail, lizard's tail, wild rice, water-hyacinth, pickerelweed, and water-lily.

Black-necked Stilt

Sora

Specialty Birds of Freshwater Marsh
Common Yellowthroat – year-round
King Rail – year-round
American Bittern – winter
Virginia Rail – migration, winter
Sora – migration, winter
Purple Gallinule – summer, in areas with water lilies
Black-necked Stilt – summer

Salt Marsh

Salt Marsh

This specialized habitat is found only along the coast where salt or brackish water meets land. Because the Low Country regularly records six to nine foot high tides,

Seaside Sparrow

coastal Georgia and South Carolina boast more than one third of the salt marsh found along the entire east coast of the United States. The dominant plant of the low marsh is smooth cordgrass – *spartina alterniflora*. At the edges or high marsh, look for *spartina patens,* glasswort, saltwort, needle rush, and sea ox-eye. The salt marsh serves as a nursery for a wide diversity of invertebrates, fish, shrimp and crabs and is great source of food for herons, egrets, storks, gulls, terns, and shorebirds.

Specialty Birds of the Salt Marsh
Clapper Rail – year-round
Seaside Sparrow – year-round
Marsh Wren – year-round
Nelson's Sparrow – winter
Saltmarsh Sparrow – winter

Marsh Wren

Tidal Creek & River

Water birds on a shell rake at low tide

These are medium-sized to large bodies of flowing water that originate in the northern part of the state and meander through the coastal plain to the ocean. Many are salt or brackish where they intersect with ocean tides.

Bufflehead, female

Hooded Merganser, male

Specialty Birds of Tidal Creeks & Rivers
Brown Pelican – year-round
American Oystercatcher – year-round
Hooded Merganser – winter
Red-breasted Merganser – winter
Bufflehead – winter
Common Loon – winter
Horned Grebe – winter

Tidal Sandbar & Mudflat

Shorebirds, gulls and terns rest on sandbar

These low-lying areas are alternately exposed and submerged as the Low Country tides rise and fall. There are two high tides and two low tides in each twenty-four hour period. Also included in this habitat type are oyster rakes where American oystercatchers can be found feeding.

Specialty Birds of Sandbars & Mudflats

American Oystercatcher – year-round

Short-billed Dowitcher – migration, winter

Black-bellied Plover – migration, winter

Marbled Godwit – migration & winter

Reddish Egret – mid- to late summer

Marbled Godwits

Reddish Egret

SANDY BEACH

Shorebirds gather on the north end of Tybee Island at high tide

The sandy beaches and dunes along the coast are constantly being shaped by wave and wind action. Shorebirds, gulls, terns, skimmers, and pelicans use this habitat

Short-billed Dowitcher

extensively during all seasons of the year. Where humans have installed rock jetties, small shorebirds such as ruddy turnstones, sanderlings, and the uncommon purple sandpiper can be found.

Specialty Birds at the Beach
Willet – year-round
Black Skimmer – year-round
Sanderling – migration, winter
Ruddy Turnstone – migration, winter, near rock jetties
Purple Sandpiper – winter near rock jetties
Piping Plover – migration, winter
Red Knot – migration, winter
Wilson's Plover – summer, rare winter

Sanderling

Near-shore Ocean

Flock of gulls feeds just offshore in the ocean

Royal Tern with its meal

Northern Gannet soars

For this narrative, ocean refers to the shallow areas of the Atlantic Ocean along the coast of Georgia and South Carolina. Birds that spend most of their time in the ocean can be seen by scanning from shore, either with binoculars or a spotting scope.

Specialty Birds of Near-shore Ocean
Brown Pelican – year-round
Royal Tern – year-round
Northern Gannet – winter
Black Scoter – winter
Common Loon – winter
Red-throated Loon – winter
Red-breasted Merganser – winter

Pelagic

Greater Shearwater flying over the open ocean

The term *pelagic* refers to the open ocean. The best pelagic birding is generally found

Flock of Wilson's Storm Petrels

where the colder water from near the coast meets the warm water of the Gulf Stream. To reach this habitat from Georgia or South Carolina, you generally have to travel some fifty miles offshore.

Specialty Pelagic Birds
Northern Gannet – winter
Wilson's Storm Petrel – summer
Cory's Shearwater – summer
Greater Shearwater – summer
Sooty Tern – summer
Bridled Tern – summer

Cory's Shearwater

Year-Round Birds in the Low Country

IN YOUR YARD

Northern Cardinal
Carolina Chickadee
Tufted Titmouse
House Finch

Rock Pigeon
Red-bellied Woodpecker
Downy Woodpecker
Red-headed Woodpecker
Northern Flicker
Pileated Woodpecker
Eastern Towhee
Red-winged Blackbird
Brown-headed Cowbird
Boat-tailed Grackle
Common Grackle
House Sparrow
American Crow
Fish Crow
Carolina Wren
Brown Thrasher
Northern Mockingbird
American Robin
Eastern Bluebird
Pine Warbler

Blue Jay at a feeder

Brown-headed Nuthatch
White-breasted Nuthatch
Blue Jay
Mourning Dove
Eurasian Collared-Dove

LONG-LEGGED WADING BIRDS

Wood Stork
White Ibis
Glossy Ibis
Great Blue Heron
Little Blue Heron
Tricolored Heron
Green Heron – rare winter
Great Egret
Snowy Egret
Cattle Egret – rare winter
Black-crowned Night-Heron
Yellow-crowned Night-Heron
Roseate Spoonbill – uncommon

Glossy & White Ibis

AT THE BEACH
Brown Pelican
Black Skimmer
Royal Tern
Laughing Gull – summer nester
Ring-billed Gull – uncommon summer
Herring Gull – uncommon summer
Double-crested Cormorant –
    uncommon summer
Wilson's Plover – rare in winter
Willet*
Killdeer
Ruddy Turnstone – uncommon
    summer
Belted Kingfisher – retreats inland
    summer

BIRDS OF PREY
Bald Eagle
Red-tailed Hawk
Red-shouldered Hawk
Cooper's Hawk
Osprey – uncommon winter
Great Horned Owl
Barred Owl
Eastern Screech-Owl
Barn Owl
Turkey Vulture
Black Vulture

IN THE SALT MARSH
Marsh Wren
Clapper Rail
Seaside Sparrow
Belted Kingfisher –
    retreats inland summer
Boat-tailed Grackle
Common Grackle
Red-winged Blackbird
Double-crested Cormorant –
    uncommon summer

Ring-billed Gull

* Although Willets are found year-round in the Low Country, there are two distinct populations. The summer nesters move south in the winter and are replaced by birds from the western population.

Marsh Wren

IN FIELDS OR ON WIRES
Northern Bobwhite
Wild Turkey
Loggerhead Shrike
Northern Mockingbird
Eastern Bluebird

IN LONGLEAF PINE FOREST
Red-cockaded Woodpecker
Bachman's Sparrow
Eastern Towhee
Pine Warbler
Brown-headed Nuthatch
Northern Bobwhite
Wild Turkey

Loggerhead Shrike

IN FRESHWATER WETLANDS
Anhinga
Boat-tailed Grackle
Red-winged Blackbird
Belted Kingfisher
Wood Duck
Common Gallinule
American Coot – uncommon summer
Double-crested Cormorant – uncommon summer

Common Gallinule family

Winter

Winter - An Overview

I have organized this book according to the human delineation of seasons. However, the birds that spend time in coastal Georgia and South Carolina don't regulate their lives by our calendar. Some of our "winter" birds arrive here as early as September and many remain in the area until early April. This would make them actually fall, winter and spring birds. Usually, these birds are easiest to find and here in the greatest numbers during December, January and February.

Wood Ducks on a dock

Winter is generally quite pleasant for watching birds in the Low Country. Our temperatures are moderate, we rarely have snow, and the bugs aren't biting. With our diversity of habitats and a bit of work, you can routinely tally more than 60 species in a day of birding.

Here are some of the birds to look for during the winter.

DUCKS
More than twenty species can be found on lakes, rivers, lagoons, canals, freshwater wetlands, and in the ocean.

Dabblers
Blue-winged Teal
Green-winged Teal
Northern Shoveler
Mallard
American Wigeon
Gadwall
Northern Pintail
Mottled Duck
Wood Duck

Divers
Ruddy Duck
Ring-necked Duck
Lesser Scaup
Greater Scaup
Canvasback
Hooded Merganser
Red-breasted Merganser
Common Goldeneye
Bufflehead
Redhead

Sea Ducks
Black Scoter
Surf Scoter
White-winged Scoter

Rare Ducks
Common Eider
Long-tailed Duck
Harlequin Duck
Cinnamon Teal

Once Rare But Now Regular and Nesting
Black-bellied Whistling-Duck

GEESE
Canada Goose
Snow Goose – uncommon winter visitor
Greater White-fronted Goose – rare visitor

LOONS AND GREBES
Common Loon – common in creeks, river and ocean
Red-throated Loon – common off the coast, occasional in creeks
Pied-billed Grebe – common in lagoons and creeks
Horned Grebe – uncommon to common in creeks and rivers
Eared Grebe – rare

SPARROWS AND THEIR ALLIES
Some twenty species can be found, many in specialized habitats.
House Sparrow – non-native, year-round
Seaside Sparrow – year-round in salt marshes
Bachman's Sparrow – elusive year-round in long-leaf pine forest; easily seen in spring
Chipping Sparrow – abundant; flocks eat white millet at feeders
White-throated Sparrow – abundant; on ground or platform feeders
Savannah Sparrow –abundant; open, grassy habitats
Swamp Sparrow – abundant; wet, marshy areas
Song Sparrow – abundant; variety of habitats
Saltmarsh Sparrow – common; salt marshes
Nelson's Sparrow – common; salt marshes
Field Sparrow – uncommon; overgrown fields
Grasshopper Sparrow – uncommon; overgrown fields
Vesper Sparrow – uncommon; weedy fields and open areas
Fox Sparrow – uncommon; thick, wooded areas, often near water
Henslow's Sparrow – rare; damp weedy fields
Le Conte's Sparrow – rare; fields with broom sedge
Lark Sparrow – rare in migration
Clay-colored Sparrow – rare in migration
Dark-eyed Junco – uncommon on coast
Eastern Towhee – common; brushy habitat and backyards

Seaside Sparrow

SMALL SONGBIRDS
Ruby-crowned Kinglet
Golden-crowned Kinglet
Blue-gray Gnatcatcher
Blue-headed Vireo
Yellow-rumped Warbler
Black-and-white Warbler
Pine Warbler
Palm Warbler
Orange-crowned Warbler
Yellow-throated Warbler
Common Yellowthroat
White-eyed Vireo
House Wren
Winter Wren
Sedge Wren
Yellow-bellied Sapsucker
Brown Creeper
Tree Swallow

WINTER FINCHES
American Goldfinch
Purple Finch
Pine Siskin

IN THE FIELDS
Eastern Meadowlark
American Pipit
Eastern Phoebe
Loggerhead Shrike

EATING BERRIES
Cedar Waxwing
Gray Catbird
Hermit Thrush
American Robin
Eastern Towhee
Northern Mockingbird

CHANGING PATTERNS: Over the past ten years, we are seeing an increase in the number of hummingbirds wintering in the Low Country. Some of these are ruby-throated, but there are a number of western hummingbirds coming east for the winter, including black-chinned, rufous, calliope, broad-tailed, and broad-billed. Recent reports have even included buff-bellied.

Also, we are seeing increasing numbers of Baltimore orioles staying for the winter. They are often found in yards with blooming camellias, in pecan orchards, and will visit feeders for nectars, fruit and jelly.

Bald Eagle hunting coots

RAPTORS
Bald Eagle – nests late fall/winter
Sharp-shinned Hawk
Great Horned Owl – nests in winter
Short-eared Owl – rare visitor
Peregrine Falcon
Merlin
American Kestrel
Northern Harrier

IN FRESHWATER WETLANDS

American Bittern
American Coot
Common Gallinule
Sora
Virginia Rail
King Rail
Wilson's Snipe
Boat-tailed Grackle
Red-winged Blackbird
Belted Kingfisher
Anhinga
Double-crested Cormorant

AT THE BEACH, SALT MARSH & TIDAL CREEKS

Royal Tern – common
Forster's Tern – common
Black Skimmer – year-round
Sandwich Tern – uncommon
Caspian Tern – uncommon
Herring Gull – common
Ring-billed Gull – common
Laughing Gull – common
Great Black-backed Gull – uncommon
Lesser Black-backed Gull – uncommon
Bonaparte's Gull – regular visitor
Brown Pelican – common
Belted Kingfisher
Tree Swallow
Northern Gannet

Bonaparte's Gull

SHOREBIRDS

Sanderling
Western Sandpiper
Least Sandpiper
Dunlin
Short-billed Dowitcher
Long-billed Dowitcher – uncommon
Red Knot
Ruddy Turnstone
Purple Sandpiper
Marbled Godwit
Stilt Sandpiper
American Oystercatcher – more in winter
Semipalmated Plover
Black-bellied Plover
Piping Plover
American Avocet
Greater Yellowlegs
Lesser Yellowlegs
Long-billed Curlew – uncommon
Wilson's Plover – uncommon winter
Wilson's Snipe
American Woodcock
Willet

Winter title page features a male Ruddy Duck (winter plumage), a Barred Owl and a Cedar Waxwing, pictured top to bottom.

HERE A DUCK, THERE A DUCK...

Blue-winged Teal, female and male

It might be possible for non-bird watchers to go through life never seeing or hearing about warblers, alcids, or grebes. Ducks, however, are another story. These waddling waterfowl have found their way into our language, our stories, and our pillows – not to mention our stomachs! We have "lame ducks," "lucky ducks," "ugly duck-

A frequent sight when observing ducks!

lings," and "great weather for ducks." While snuggled under eiderdown comforters, we read *Make Way for Ducklings*, chow down on "Peking Duck," and listen to Ernie on *Sesame Street* croon, *"Rubber ducky I'm awfully fond of you!"* Old MacDonald wasn't kidding when he said "here a duck, there a duck, everywhere a duck, duck!"

That's how it is in the Low Countr – at least in the winter. Find a lagoon, a pond, a canal, a lake, a river, or an ocean, and you are almost certain to find a duck – or two or three or a hundred or a thousand. Ducks are social creatures and hang out together in flocks. They have webbed feet, dens waterproof plumage, and they spend much of their time swimming.

Duck-watching would be a cinch if all we had to contend with were a single barnyard variety of quacker. Instead, a confusing twenty-five differen species find their way to the Low Country. We can't complain that we lack variety, but it does provide for challenges where identification is concerned. Ducks have mastered the art o

Hooded Mergansers, 3 females and male

standing way out in the middle of large bodies of water, far enough from shore so that even with binoculars they still look like colorless, dark, floating shapes. When they fly, it's almost always "away" with their short, rounded wings pumping furiously.

Ask a duck hunter what he relies on for identification. Most often, he will tell you, it is not the fine, colorful details so beautifully rendered in field guides. At dawn, when most hunters are out, it's too dark for details. Hunters rely on silhouette, bill shape, and flight style. The heavy, spatulate bill of a northern shoveler is distinctive, as are the long tail and neck of a pintail.

It is possible, however, to get a good look at ducks. One thing that helps is a spotting scope. This long-distance spying device is mounted on a tripod and brings images 15 to 60 times closer. A scope makes it possible to scan resting or feeding flocks for key features, such as the white crescent patch on the face of a male blue-winged teal or the blue bill of a lesser scaup.

By watching ducks in action, you can sort them by their feeding style. Puddle ducks, such as mallards, shovelers and teal, are known as "dabblers" – picking up food on or near the surface. They are often seen with necks underwater and rumps to the sky, "upending" to scrounge for vegetation on pond bottoms. "Divers" – such as canvasbacks, ring-necked ducks, ruddy ducks, buffleheads and mergansers – disappear completely below the water's surface,

Northern Shoveler, male

using their feet for propulsion to forage in deeper water.

Ducks dine on a range of vegetable and animal matter, including seeds, aquatic grasses, underground tubers, tiny invertebrates and fish. What they eat can have an impact on how likely they are to get eaten – at least by humans. The hooded and red-breasted mergansers eat a lot of fish and taste like it – putting them low on the hunters' lists. Mallards, along with gadwalls, wigeons, pintails and black ducks are rated to have excellent flavor by *North American Game Birds*. Shovelers

Red-breasted Merganser, female

Wood Ducks, male

and bufflehead get mixed reviews because of their strong-tasting meat.

When spring approaches, almost all of these ducks desert the Low Country for breeding grounds up north. Until recently, only the wood ducks and the domestic mallards and muscovy ducks actually raised their families in the Low Country. Now we can find mottled ducks breeding in the freshwater wetlands. An exotic newcomer to the duck scene, the black-bellied whistling-duck, now breeds in several South Carolina locations as well as around the Altamaha Wildlife Management area in Georgia.

One unusual feature of ducks, particularly the males, is the way they molt or lose their feathers. In late summer, after breeding season, male ducks replace all their flight feathers at once, moving to a duller, eclipse plumage. For the month or so that this process takes, they are unable to fly, and literally become "sitting ducks."

To learn more and improve your duck ID skills, join your local birding group for a winter visit to Savannah, Harris Neck, or Pinckney Island National Wildlife Refuges, the Altamaha Wildlife Management Area, Lake Mayer, or any body of water near you. Happy Quacking!

The Secrets of the Salt Marsh

*Ye marshes, how candid and simple and nothing-withholding and free
Ye publish yourselves to the sky and offer yourselves to the sea!*
— from "The Marshes of Glynn" by Sidney Lanier

Sometimes it's easy to take for granted the things that are right under our noses, the familiar backdrops of daily existence, like salt marsh. I drive past it almost every day traveling back and forth from Tybee to Savannah. Sometimes, at the top of the bridge over Lazaretto Creek, I get behind a car poking along at 25 miles an hour. Annoyed, I glance at the West Virginia license plate.

"Tourists," I snort to myself. Then I try to take a deep breath, curb my impatience, and look with fresh eyes at the vast expanse of marsh before me, fading now to brown and gold. I glance at the winding creek and see the exposed mud flats. It's low tide.

A "marsh hawk," or Northern Harrier

White Ibis feeding in the marsh

"Will those visitors know," I wonder, "that the marsh is showing but one of its many faces? Will they stay long enough to see the inexorable incoming tide cover all the mud? Will they hear any of the stories that the salt marsh has to tell?"

A keen observer might glimpse, from the top of the bridge, a dark brown shape patrolling back and forth, low over the marsh. One look at its white rump patch, and anyone with marsh savvy will recognize the "marsh hawk," or northern harrier. With its wings held at an angle, teetering like a turkey vulture, it scans the marsh for rodents, frogs, snakes, small birds, and insects.

Whizzing by at 55 miles an hour, a traveler might not see a group of white shapes probing in the mud with bright red, downward curved bills. He wouldn't stop to ask the flock of white ibis what the attraction was in all that mud. The ibis, for their part, wouldn't have the words to rave about the marine worms, snails, frogs, small fish, and 500,000 fiddler crabs an acre that turn the salt marsh into a delectable buffet of unparalleled diversity.

If a visitor took the time to sit on a dock in the early morning surrounded by salt marsh, he might be treated to the tinkling trill of the marsh wren, or the bold raspy rattle of the belted kingfisher. At low tide he might witness a clapper rail, familiarly called a marsh hen, stealing down to the water's edge for a vigorous morning bath. He might spy a snowy egret using its "golden slippers" to trouble the waters in pursuit of breakfast.

If this traveler were clever enough to get out of the car, off the dock, and into a boat, he would enjoy the salt marsh from a different angle. Low tide

> *One look at its white rump patch and anyone with marsh savvy will recognize the "marsh hawk," or northern harrier.*

Snowy Egret troubles water

would reveal the irregular mounds of oyster bars, where American oystercatchers with sturdy orange bills never have to pay for a dozen on the half-shell. From a boat, a fortunate observer might get to watch bottlenose dolphins swimming, playing or even "mudding" – a behavior unique to South Carolina and Georgia dolphins, where the mammals work together to herd fish onto a mud flat, slide onto the mud to eat the stranded fish, and then slide back into the water.

A glance across the expanse of the marsh would reveal lush coastal hammocks covered with live oaks, magnolias, red cedar, wax myrtle, palmettos, and red bay. A careful look would reveal roosting wood storks, or an osprey perched on a dead snag, gripping a fish in its talons.

An explorer trained to read the book of the marsh would know to steer clear of the tidal creeks and the marsh grass (*spartina alterniflora*) when searching for high ground. He would look instead for areas where needle rush, sea ox-eye, and glasswort predominate. This knowledge comes in handy when searching for elusive seaside, Nelson's, and saltmarsh sparrows. At flood tide the sparrows are forced out of the marsh and take refuge in the vegetation that isn't under water. There's a clump of sea ox-eye just past the entrance to Ft. Pulaski, where I stop on my way to work if the tide is high. I drive up, roll down the window, make smacking sounds, and watch while the curious sparrows hop to the tops of the stalks to investigate. Easy as pie if you know the secret.

Yet even for the initiate, the marsh retains an element of mystery. Any of us might wish, as did Sidney Lanier,

I would I could know what swimmeth below when the tide comes in On the length and the breadth of the marvelous marshes of Glynn.

— from "The Marshes of Glynn" by Sidney Lanier

Nelson's Sparrow in sea ox-eye

What's So Crazy About a Loon?

I sat by the fire one winter evening as Johnny Mercer's lyrics, penned to a skylark, drifted lazily from the radio. "Crazy as a loon?" I thought. "What's so crazy about a loon?"

Every time I get out to the beach or the coastal rivers during the winter, I scan the water for the distinctive, low-slung, hunch-necked shape of the common loon.

"Ah, there it is – oops, it's gone!" With a quick dive the bird vanishes below the surface, emerging up to a minute later grasping a wriggling fish. Float and dive, float and dive – the loon pursues its fishing with a sober purposefulness that seems anything but crazy.

On the lakes of the far north during the summer, loons go about the business of nesting in a manner difficult to fault. Sitting right at the water's edge, the loon gathers nearby plant material to form a hollow mound around its body where two eggs will be laid. Both parents incubate the eggs. Both feed the babies once they hatch, even carrying them on their backs. Loon parents can compress the air out of their bodies, sinking low into the water to enable the chicks to clamber aboard. Babies swim within a day of hatching, but it will be almost three months before they master flight. The same two adults often remain paired year after year. Doesn't seem too crazy to me.

According to scholars, the term "loony" is an abbreviation from the

> *Float and dive; float and dive. The loon pursues its fishing with a sober purposefulness that seems anything but crazy.*

Common Loon

Red-throated Loon

word "lunatic" which came into use during the 13th century. Its root is "luna," the Latin for moon. Even then, mental instability was thought to be related to the phases of the moon. It wasn't until the 17th century that the water bird came to be called a loon. No one quite knows why.

What has earned this bird its reputation for lunacy is its call, given primarily during courtship and nesting. Some years ago in mid-July, my friend Judy and I pitched our small tent beside a lake in Nova Scotia. Tired from a long day of driving and sightseeing, we watched the full moon rise, and then climbed gratefully into our sleeping bags. Several hours later we were startled awake by a moaning yodel echoing eerily across the lake. Groggily, I made sense of the noise.

"Listen to those crazy loons," I laughed in amazement.

Loons have their legs set far back on their bodies, which is great for underwater propulsion but makes them quite awkward on land. They are strong fliers but must "patter" across the water for almost a quarter of a mile in order to take off. If a loon lands on wet asphalt, mistaking its sheen for a lake surface, it will be grounded, unable to get airborne.

Loons dress up for mating in the spring and summer. With jet-black bill, dark iridescent head, red eye, and striking black-and-white neckband and wing feathers, they are a far cry from the gray-bodied, white-necked birds that find their way to the Low Country in winter.

Not every loon we see here is a common loon. The slightly smaller red-throated loon – twenty-five inches compared to the common loon's thirty-two inches – also winters in the Low Country. The best way to tell the two apart is by their posture. The red-throated loon sits more upright in the water with a thinner, upturned bill and speckled back. It nests farther north than the common loon, and is able to take off, either on water or land, without a running start.

If you study a British field guide, you won't find any mention of loons. They refer to this family of birds as "divers." The Brits maintain that "common loon" is a demeaning name for this marvelous bird. They prefer the respectful title "great northern diver."

No matter the name, the bird remains the same. Crazy or not, I am happy that these purposeful divers find their way back to the Low Country each winter.

Common Loon

THE GRINCHES

Almost everybody knows *The Grinch* – the Dr. Seuss creation determined to steal Christmas from all the "Whos down in Whoville." But *grinches* are another matter entirely. Try repeating "goldfinches" very fast about a dozen times and you might get some idea as to why, in my family, goldfinches are affectionately known as *grinches*.

About the same time that *The Grinch* returns to a theater or TV screen near you, bird feeding enthusiasts in the Low Country are asking, "When will the goldfinches (aka *grinches*) arrive?" Folks up north, including north Georgia, may see the American goldfinch at their feeders all year long, but for us they are only a winter visitor.

"A good thing," I sometimes think, since their favorite food – the tiny but costly *nyjer* or thistle seed, imported from India – has rightfully earned the nickname "black gold."

"Good thing your children are all out of college," I tease my dad. "You can afford to feed your *grinches!*"

Unlike the Neotropical birds who return to North America each spring with clock-like regularity, the winter finches are considered to be *irruptive* – likely to appear suddenly and dramatically with no annual pattern. Their movements seem to be tied to the availability of food rather than to cold weather.

The *grinches*, when they come, rarely arrive singly. They descend on feeders in noisy flocks with much chirping, twittering and jostling for position on the perches. Unlike the dainty chickadee, they do not extract a single seed and fly off to a nearby branch to eat it. No, the *grinches* sit there and chow down. A

Male American Goldfinch in breeding plumage

good-sized flock of fifty birds can empty a feeder in a matter of hours.

My dad has the ultimate in finch feeders – three plastic tubes linked by eight long plastic perches, providing an opportunity for 24 goldfinches to feed simultaneously. No self-respecting chickadee or cardinal would be caught dead feeding in such a tumultuous crowd. For the finches, however, it's finch heaven! "All my condominiums are rented," my Dad proudly announces, when his feeder is covered with birds. He figures the *grinches* consumed about 100 pounds of nyjer between mid-January and early May, when they finally headed north to nest.

If you inspect your flock carefully, you may find a bird that doesn't look quite like a goldfinch. Its breast, instead of being clear, is finely streaked like that of a sparrow. Close inspection will reveal a bar of yellow in the wings and some yellow in the tail. This finch cousin, the pine siskin, is an infrequent visitor here on the coast, usually spotted in years when finches are plentiful.

We can't neglect the finches of another color. The house finches, year-round residents, have red-orange heads with streaked brown and red breasts. At least the males do. Females are streaked brown, and are often mistaken for sparrows. The purple finch, sometimes described as raspberry, is a winter visitor to the Low Country. Telling these two finches apart can be tricky. The purple finch is slightly larger with a more horizontal posture. and no brown streaking on the sides. Look for a definite white eye stripe on the female purple finch.

There's one thing *The Grinch* and the *grinches* have in common – transformation. They begin the story or season in one way, and end up another. The mean-spirited *Grinch* at the start of Seuss's tale bears little resemblance to the large-hearted one who carves the "roast beast" at the end. Likewise, the goldfinches that arrive in December do not

Flock of Goldfinches, winter plumage

Pine Siskin with American Goldfinches

look much like the ones that leave in May. In winter, the birds are drab and unremarkable – a dull greenish-gray with dark wings. As spring approaches, the males begin to change. Feather by feather the lusterless color is replaced until the males are dressed in vibrant yellow with a neat black cap to match their now sharply defined black wings.

"Look at me!" the bright color shouts to a female finch. "Am I a catch or what?"

House Finches, male (l) and female (r)

In good years, the goldfinches may extend their stay through winter into spring. If we're lucky, April can bring a true feast of avian color. As the waves of migratory songbirds begin to pour in from Central and South America, bright yellow finches are joined at the feeders by electric-blue indigo buntings, rainbow-hued painted buntings, and stylishly showy rose-breasted grosbeaks. For all us "Birders in Birdville," it's better than Christmas!

Purple Finch, female

The grinches, when they come, rarely arrive singly. They descend on feeders in noisy flocks.

Purple Finch, male

TALKING TO OWLS

Barred Owl

When I visit Oatland Island Wildlife Center, I always talk to the owls. The best part is that they sometimes talk back. Usually the great horned owl is the first to respond. The feathers around his throat blow up like a balloon and he thrusts his head forward to utter a deep, resonant "hoo, hoo hoo, hoooo hoo," phrased like "Who's awake, me tooo." I respond with my best owl call in hopes of striking up a conversation.

The barred owl chimes in next, with a slightly higher "hoo hoo hoo-hoo, hoo hoo hoo-hoooooaw," translated into people-talk as "Who cooks for you, who cooks for you all-l-l?"

The two tiny eastern screech-owls huddle silently on their shelf, unimpressed by my rendition of a descending whinny or my trilled "pirrup, pirrup."

There's something fascinating about owls. Perhaps we look at their round, flattened faces with forward-facing eyes and see a creature like ourselves, but with abilities generally reserved for super heroes – like extra keen night vision and silent, powerful flight. These primarily nocturnal hunters fill the air with eerie, unearthly sounds. Owls have inspired fear, awe and even worship. They have been considered bringers of bad news, messengers from the spirit world, or omens of death. Athena, the Greek goddess of

> *These primarily nocturnal hunters fill the air with eerie, unearthly sounds. Owls inspire fear, awe and even worship.*

wisdom, kept an owl as a companion, as did Merlin the magician and tutor to the legendary King Arthur. In the *Harry Potter* books and films, the owls bring the mail and are considered (along with cats and toads) to be appropriate "familiars" for aspiring wizards.

whistling wing whirr, most owls have what amounts to built in mufflers on their flight feathers. The feather barbs at the front edge are loose and unattached, creating a soft surface that diffuses the rush of air during flight.

Additionally, owls have acutely sensitive hearing. Their shallow, elliptical facial disks capture sound waves and direct them toward the ears. These ears are positioned slightly asymmetrically on either side of the owl's face. Listening to the squeak of a mouse, the owl tilts its head side-to-side and up-and-down until it hears the sound with equal loudness in each ear. The brain processes this data to come up with a mental image of the source of the sound. The barn owl in particular has demonstrated the ability to repeatedly strike within one to two degrees of a target, even in

Eastern Screech-Owl

In this age of science, we can explain things that previously dwelt in the realm of mystery and magic. Studies of owl eyes have revealed extra long light-gathering rods, making their eyes tubular rather than spherical. Owls have expanded night vision but sacrifice the ability to roll their eyes within the sockets, limiting peripheral vision. Thus, the extremely flexible neck that enables an owl to rotate its head nearly 270 degrees in either direction is not an entertaining luxury but an urgent necessity.

Another aspect of the owl mystique is their ability to approach their prey with stealth and silence. Whereas mourning doves take off with a noisy,

Great Horned Owl fledgling

JANUARY

Great Horned Owl

complete darkness.

During the winter, owls get particularly chatty. While most other birds are figuring out how to survive until spring, owls turn their thoughts to love. Great horned owls begin their courtship rituals in late fall with a lot of back and forth hooting. The male woos the female by offering her tasty tidbits. If she finds him to her liking, the couple may spend some time perched close together, indulging in mutual preening. Just before the eggs are laid, owl communications increase in frequency and intensity, even spilling over into daylight hours.

During the 28 to 35 day incubation period, things quiet down. Five weeks after hatching, the young ones depart the nest for the pleasures of branch hopping. It will be at least another month before they venture into flight. When they do, a multitude of perils await. Chief among them is inexperience. The sophisticated skills that help an owl survive are not mastered overnight. Factor in predators, disease, bad weather, and encounters with man-made objects such as automobiles, power lines and shotguns, and it is no wonder that only 30 to 50 percent of young owls make it past their first birthday. Fortunately, skilled rehabbers take in some of the injured birds and they end up in wildlife education centers. There they bring knowledge and delight to thousands of adults and children – particularly those of us with a fondness for talking to owls!

E. Screech-Owl fledglings

NATIONAL BIRD WATCHING

The date is June 20, 1782. The members of the Second Continental Congress of the United States of America have finally settled on a design for the Great Seal of the new nation. Central to the image is an eagle, wings spread wide, bearing 13 arrows in one talon and an olive branch in the other. With its majestic looks, great strength, and longevity, the eagle is deemed a suitable emblem for the fledgling country.

Not everyone is pleased with the choice. Benjamin Franklin is particularly eloquent in his opposition.

He is a bird of bad moral character, he does not get his living honestly, you may have seen him perched on some dead tree, where, too lazy to fish for himself, he watches the labor of the fishing-hawk, and when that diligent bird has at length taken a fish, and is bearing it to its nest for the support of his mate and young ones, the bald eagle pursues him and takes it from him…For a truth, the turkey is in comparison a much more respectable bird, and withal a true original native of America.

While I always enjoy spotting a wild turkey, it simply does not inspire the same ripple of awe as does the sight of a bald eagle in flight, white head and tail glinting in the sunlight.

Adorned with some 7000 feathers, the bald eagle is not bald at all, just white headed. If you happen to be fluent in Greek, you might figure out that *haliaeetus leucocephalus* is an eagle (*aetos*) of the sea (*halos*), with a white (*leucos*) head (*kephalos*).

As befits a sea eagle, the bald eagle's primary food is fish. They aren't as picky as ospreys, and will eat dead as well as live fish. And as Franklin indicated, they are not above stealing the catch of gulls, ospreys, or pelicans. They also dine on waterfowl, gulls, shorebirds, and rabbits.

When humans noticed that the eagle population was plummeting, they passed the Bald Eagle Act in 1940. However, about this time, there was a marked increase in the use of pesticides, including DDT. These chemicals went into the waterways where they accumulated in fish, which in turn were eaten by eagles. Eagles then laid eggs with shells so thin that they broke during incubation, resulting in almost total reproductive failure. In 1970, there was only one active bald eagle's nest in Georgia, this one located on St. Catherines Island. Since the ban of DDT in 1972 and the passage of the Endangered Species Act in 1973, bald eagles have made a steady recovery. In 2010 in Georgia, aerial surveys documented 135 nesting territories, 118 successful nests and 187 young eagles fledged.

Eagle courting can be quite showy, with spectacular aerial displays.

An adult bald eagle, white head and tail glinting in the sunlight, is an awesome sight.

Our magnificent national bird

Bald Eagle carries a big stick

Partners even lock talons high in the air and cartwheel to earth, pulling up just before hitting the ground. Males competing for territory may also engage in high-flying combat. In early November on Skidaway Island, near Savannah, two males got tangled up while airborne, and ended up locked together near a golf course cart path. They remained in this position for several hours until a Georgia DNR wildlife ranger cautiously approached the pair and lifted a wing. The two released each other and flew off.

As is usual for raptors, Mrs. Eagle is about 30 percent larger than her mate. Bald eagles generally maintain a long-term pair bond, and both participate in building huge nests in the tops of tall trees, some 30 to 60 feet above the ground. They often use the same nest year after year, adding sticks and remodeling. In the Low Country, late November and December are the big months for eagle nesting.

Being modern, liberated parents, both male and female share incubation duties for nearly five weeks. Then both participate in feeding the babies for close to three months, when the all-dark young birds finally leave the nest. It will be four years before they acquire the showy white head and tail of adult bald eagles.

Residents on Skidaway Island have taken a proprietary interest in the welfare of one nesting eagle pair, dubbed "Charlie" and "Doris." First observed in 2000, the pair built a large nest but no chicks were fledged. In Year Two they fledged a single chick. Since then, they have generally hatched and raised two young ones.

In 2010, Skidaway Island residents were closely monitoring the progress of two young eaglets. Both had successfully left the nest but one young bird was hanging out on the ground. The residents contacted a local wildlife rehabilitator who was able to capture the bird and transport it to the Raptor Center in Charleston, S.C. Experts there examined the young eagle and found that it was weak and covered with mites. They cleaned her, fed her

An eagle's nest can weigh up to a ton

Bald Eagle harasses a flock of American Coots

and kept her until she showed signs of being able to fly to high perches. Then they brought her back to Skidaway Island where workers from a local tree service were waiting with a bucket truck to return the bird to its nest tree. Amazingly, as we watched, the second young eagle flew into the tree and observed the entire proceedings from a branch high up in the tree. After ten minutes of stretching and flapping her wings, the young eagle took off, soaring over the street and finally landing awkwardly in the top of a tree some three hundred yards away.

In this age of technology, researchers have begun installing web cams in eagle's nests, enabling computer users throughout the world to keep a daily watch on the entire nesting process, from egg to hatchling to fledgling. This intimate look at eagles, as they deliver a variety of food to the nest, tear it into small bits, and carefully feed it to their babies adds to the mystique of these amazing birds. It provides us with a different way to go National Bird Watching.

Juvenile Bald Eagle spreads its wings

Oystercatchers Among Us

What do a curly-haired female birdwatcher and a distinctive black and white shorebird with a heavy orange beak have in common? For one thing, both of them can occasionally be found on the beach. For another, they both have a taste for oysters. The pile of empty shells next to my driveway is a testimony to our family's love of this succulent bivalve. We build fires, heat steel plates, hose down burlap sacks, and purchase sophisticated propane cookers. We eat them raw, steamed, fried, in stew, and even baked with spinach. Following popular wisdom, we generally eat them in months that contain the letter "r."

American Oystercatchers on the oyster bar

For the American oystercatcher, it's much simpler. During all twelve months of the year, they just wait for low tide and hit the bars, the oyster bars that is. With bright, orange-red oyster knives mounted on the front of their heads, oystercatchers deftly extract mollusks from their shells, and probe in the mud for crabs and marine worms. They don't need saltines, melted butter or cocktail sauce – just oysters on the whole shell.

While it can be difficult to sort out the assortment of small brown birds that hang out on the beach, American oystercatchers are refreshingly easy to identify. Look for a heavy-bodied bird about eighteen inches long with a black head and neck, dark brown back, white underparts, pink legs, startling yellow eyes rimmed in red, and that awesome long, orange beak.

When the tide comes in and closes down the bars, oystercatchers head for the beach. One morning in early January, I counted 50 oystercatchers resting together at the water's edge on Tybee's north beach. Every now and then, the rushing water from a ship's wake would rouse the birds from their rest, sending them squawking loudly to land further down the beach and resume their napping.

Oystercatchers are among a handful of shorebird species that opt out of the annual breeding trip to the Arctic tundra. These birds avoid the rigors of long distance flying, but their breeding season is still fraught with peril. In 2003, several scientists working out of the University of Georgia began a two-year project to document the hazards of nesting on sandy beaches. They set up video cameras to do time lapse photography of a number of oyster-catcher nests on Cumberland Island. They found that raccoons, bobcats, and American crows all had a taste for oystercatcher eggs. Even the lowly ghost crab was recorded attacking a young chick. The cameras also detected nest failures caused by tidal overwash, horse trampling, and human disturbance.

In 2002 and 2003, aerial surveys

estimated the wintering population of American oystercatchers on the Atlantic coast at approximately 11,000 birds. In 2004, scientists conducting research on these charismatic birds came together to form the American Oystercatcher Working Group. Oystercatchers are great research subjects because they are large, easy to identify, and relatively long-lived. Participating states adopted a standardized banding protocol, each using a distinct band color – Yellow for Massachusetts; Orange for New Jersey; Black for Virginia; Green for North Carolina; Blue for South Carolina; Red for Georgia. Since oystercatchers spend a lot of time standing on one leg, the large color bands with a two-digit code are placed on both upper legs. One lower leg has a US Fish & Wildlife Service silver band.

I spotted my first banded American oystercatcher on Tybee's north beach in October, 2006. I reported my sighting to Brad Winn at the Georgia DNR. He passed the information along to a researcher in North Carolina, who

American Oystercatchers in flight

shared with me that he, himself, had banded this particular bird in 2003 on Monomoy Island, Massachusetts. The bird had been reported on Tybee each successive winter, returning to Monomoy to nest each summer.

I was hooked. I began making high-tide pilgrimages to the beach to survey the wintering oystercatcher population and look for bands. One of the advantages of banding oystercatchers is that the bands are large enough to read and photograph, without having to recapture the birds. Resight data can be submitted on the Working Group web site.

Some people collect coins. Others

American Oystercatchers rest on the beach at high tide

collect shells. I "collect" banded oystercatchers. To date, (summer 2011) my collection is up to thirty-eight birds. Researchers, many of them graduate students, are a busy lot, but they generously share the stories. "Yellow N4," that I observed and photographed in September 2007, was banded on Nantucket as a breeding adult earlier that same summer. "Black 3U" was

American Oystercatcher takes off

banded on Assawoman Island, VA on July 23, 2006. "Orange Y2" was banded at Barnegat Light, NJ on June 14, 2008. In 2010, it nested at Barnegat Light and fledged two chicks. I spotted it on Tybee in October, 2010.

Why so much effort to study a bird? Why should we care? Many of my early memories involve being out in a small boat in our creeks and rivers, fishing, crabbing, swimming, and observing the world around me. Oystercatchers were always a unique and fascinating part of the landscape. I can't bear to imagine my nieces and nephews telling their children that "once upon a time there used to be these really cool birds with long orange beaks that hung out on the oyster bars and came up on the beach at high tide." On a less poetic note, a healthy oystercatcher population usually means a healthy habitat, for humans as well as birds.

One major problem that all of the beach nesting birds face is that their nesting season, from April to August, exactly coincides with the time most of us humans like to go to the beach. Beachcombers, recreational boaters, and even turtle researchers patrolling the beaches with all-terrain vehicles pose a threat to these birds. The Georgia Department of Natural Resources offers the following suggestions for sharing our world with these beach-nesting birds:
1. Try to avoid nesting beaches from March through August.
2. If you visit, walk below the last high tide line to avoid injuring chicks or eggs.
3. Leave your dog at home. They destroy nests and chase young birds
4. Avoid remote stretches of beach where birds may be nesting.
5. Teach others to appreciate our native beach-nesting birds.

For the oyster lovers among us, winter is a great time to eat them, as well as to see oystercatchers in coastal Georgia and South Carolina. Just check your tide charts and head for the beach or the bars.

Banded American Oystercatchers

The Martins Are Coming!

Lucky people have them. Other people want them. They are discussed endlessly in newsletters, on web sites, forums, and chat rooms. At the center of this commotion is – you guessed it – a bird! They are not

Purple Martin, male (l) and female (r)

majestic like sandhill cranes or vividly multi-colored like painted buntings, but somehow these eight-inch long, iridescent, bluish-purple swallows with a fondness for nesting with family and friends have managed to capture the hearts of countless Americans.

Our largest North American swallow, the purple martin has been tracing a migratory route between North and South America for centuries. Ornithologist Alexander Wilson, writing in the early 1800's, referred to the hollowed-out natural gourds that Native Americans placed near their dwelling places to attract nesting martins. They welcomed these birds for their ability to drive away hawks, crows, and vultures, and for their alarm calls given at the first sign of danger.

What sets the purple martins on their yearly North American pilgrimage is their taste for flying insects. Simply put, they come for our bugs. Previously, the word was that a single martin would eat close to two thousand mosquitoes a day. A nesting colony, it was thought, would provide the lucky landowner with abundant natural pest control. Unfortunately, researchers have since determined that mosquitoes make up only about three percent of the purple martin diet. They much prefer larger insects, such as wasps, ants, flies, beetles, damselflies, moths, butterflies, and dragonflies.

There is no need for feeders or seed to attract martins to your yard. Just give them a home. Originally, martins nested in natural cavities – abandoned woodpecker holes or niches and crannies in rock ledges. A decrease in suitable habitat combined with an increase in nest site competition from European starlings and house sparrows has led the eastern population of purple martins to rely almost entirely on housing

Nestling Purple Martin begs

provided by humans. Only in the desert and western mountains do these birds still nest primarily in natural cavities.

One thing that is amazing about purple martins is their site fidelity. Birds will return to the same place, the same colony, and sometimes even people – within 100 feet of a human habitation is good. They don't generally like trees, structures or other objects closer than forty feet from their house. Houses should be mounted ten to fifteen feet above the ground and should be easy to lower for cleaning and inspection.

Adult male Purple Martin brings nest material

to the same nest compartment that they occupied the previous year. If you succeed in attracting nesting purple martins, your odds of getting them back year after year are high – particularly if you maintain the housing, discourage use of the house by other species, and use baffles to keep out predators.

If you're hoping to attract martins, first consider your habitat. The birds prefer broad open areas with good foraging opportunities such as marshes, bays, swamps, meadows and pastures. They will take to residential areas, particularly if the nest house is placed in the open with a water source nearby. For some reason, martins like to be near

Only adult males are "purple" all over. Adult females have a dark head and back with gray throat and belly. Young males have a few purple feathers on throat and back, while young females are gray.

Female Purple Martin with dragonfly

all over. Generally, it is a pioneering young male that will attempt to start a new colony. He arrives somewhat later than the full adults, identifies a potential home, and then spends time trying to convince a mate and other sub-adult birds to buy into his development.

The first year that I put up a house and gourds on the dock, I returned from a mid-April birding trip to Colorado to discover that about a dozen purple martins had moved in. Now I eagerly await the chirping, clicking and trilling that signal the start of martin season.

There are abundant resources available for anyone ready to take on the job of purple martin landlord. For answers to all your martin questions, try *Enjoying Purple Martins More* by Richard Wolinski or *The Purple Martin Book* by Donald and Lillian Stokes. For $25 you can join the Purple Martin Conservation Association and receive their quarterly update. Visit their web site – www.purplemartin.org – for more information. If you're willing to make the effort, you, too, may one day count yourself among the lucky!

Purple Martin condo with gourds

Our largest North American swallow, the purple martin has been tracing a migratory route between North and South America for centuries.

Purple Martin, nest building

Watching Warblers In Winter

In the spring, watching warblers can be overwhelming. Warblers are tiny, flit about in the treetops, and come in as many flavors as Baskin-Robbins ice cream. Mostly, the 110 species in this songbird family entertain themselves eating insects in the tropics. However, come March, some 50 warbler species hightail it to North America to nest in our forests and eat our bugs. Bird watchers bemoan the challenge of identifying these "butterflies of the bird world."

Yellow-rumped Warbler, winter plumage

Black-and-white Warbler, female

Winter warbler watching is different. For a start, only seven species regularly remain in the southeastern United States during the winter: yellow-rumped, pine, yellow-throated, orange-crowned, black-and-white, palm, and common yellowthroat. Insects are scarce so wintering warblers rely on alternate food sources, including berries, seeds and nuts. They can be enticed from the treetops to backyard feeders if you offer suet, hulled sunflower seed, peanuts, mealworms and nectar.

The most abundant winter warbler is the yellow-rumped, commonly dubbed the "butter-butt." Once upon a time this species was called the "myrtle warbler," due to the birds' fondness for dining on the blue-black berries of the wax myrtle tree.

Yellow-rumps forego the annual trek to South America. In late fall, they leave their nesting territories in the mixed forests of the northern United

Common Yellowthroat, male

Male Pine Warbler visits feeder

States and Canada for the warmer climate of the southern half of North America. You may see one in your yard snacking on suet or taking a quick slurp from the hummingbird feeder. Occasionally, in my yard, an entire flock of yellow-rumps will descend on the birdbath for a vigorous "dip en masse." In late April, the "rumps" head north to nest.

The pine warbler is a year-round resident in the Low Country – at least some of them are. When the weather gets cold, most of the nation's population of pine warblers heads south. Until spring migration, our local pines will be sharing the trees with their northern relations. If you see a glowingly yellow bird at your feeder in January or February snacking on suet or peanuts, it is probably a pine warbler rather than an American goldfinch. The finches don't turn bright yellow until March and April.

While the majority of the population of yellow-throated warblers goes to Florida and points south for the winter, some do remain in the Low Country. Not to be confused with the common yellowthroat – the "masked bandit" warbler found primarily in marshy wetlands – the yellow-throated warbler has a long, very pointed bill that it uses to probe for insects in the crevices of tree bark as well as deep in the grooves of palm fronds. Yellow-throated warblers do occasionally visit feeders during the winter, snacking on suet, sunflower

Yellow-throated Warbler

Orange-crowned Warbler

chips and mealworms.

Dressed in subtle shades of gray and olive green, the orange-crowned warbler will never win any warbler beauty pageants, although it does hide a secret stash of muted yellow beneath its tail. These warblers nest in the western United States, Canada and even into Alaska, with the entire population wintering in the southern United States. They tend to forage in low bushes and small trees, flicking their tails frequently as they poke about in search of insects. Several years ago my parents hosted an orange-crowned at their suet feeder throughout the winter.

The black-and-white warbler behaves like a nuthatch, creeping about on branches and tree trunks, probing for insects in the bark crevices. A small number of these tiny zebra-striped birds spend the winter each year in the Low Country. Come April, they begin announcing their presence with a song that sounds like a car with squeaky brakes. As the temperature rises here on the coast, the black-and-whites pack up and head north.

Unlike the pine warblers, palm warblers are not faithful to the tree whose name they bear. Although the first specimens were found in palm trees in Hispaniola, palm warblers are often found in low brushy areas, feeding on the ground in fields, or wagging their tails while flitting about in a variety of tree species. With their rusty caps, drab brown color and habit of hanging out in flocks, they could easily be confused with sparrows. They do have thin warbler beaks and a bright patch of yellow beneath the tail. The members of the eastern race of palm warblers are more vividly yellow than their western counterparts. Both races show up in the Low Country during the winter, with the western birds being more numerous.

Master these seven warbler species and you'll have a head start when the other thirty species start pouring into North America for the spring and summer!

> *Only seven warbler species regularly remain in the southeastern United States during the winter: yellow-rumped, pine, yellow-throated, orange-crowned, black-and-white, palm, and common yellowthroat.*

Palm Warbler, western race

Keep Your Eyes Upon The Sparrows

As we near the end of winter, many bird lovers begin to anticipate the return of colorful migrants like ruby-throated hummingbirds and painted buntings. Others are busy setting up nesting boxes in hopes of attracting eye-catching eastern bluebirds. Few people pay attention to the oh-so-drab and easy-to-overlook little brown birds that slip into the Low Country late in the fall and spend the winter eating seeds here until, with little fanfare, they move north again for nesting season.

Swamp Sparrow

House Sparrows, female (l) and male (r)

When I was new to bird watching, I was captivated by the herons, egrets and water birds. Later I got hooked on the intricately colorful wood warblers. Next I had a "hawk phase." As far as I was concerned, sparrows were a "default" bird – something to look at if there was nothing else available. When Bill Drummond, one of my birding gurus, said that sparrows were his favorite bird group, I thought him more than a little mad. Gradually though, I too have developed a fondness for the "little brown jobbies" – "LBJs" for short.

Sparrows are an acquired taste -- like oysters and avocados. Learning to identify them takes time and patience. A connoisseur of wine becomes sensitive to refinements of smell and taste that set one vintage apart from another. An accomplished painter knows exactly what shade of green will bring to mind the first budding leaves of spring. An expert on sparrows pays attention to subtle distinctions in shades of brown, facial pattern, tail length, flight pattern, and behavior.

Sparrows have a frustrating habit of appearing briefly and then vanishing again. They do seem to be a curious

Chipping Sparrow, winter plumage

Savannah Sparrow

The chipping sparrow is a regular winter feeder visitor, filling every feeder perch or gathering in large groups on the ground to eat the millet discarded by the sunflower-loving woodpeckers and cardinals. With a clear gray breast and reddish back, its rusty cap and white eyebrow get more prominent as breeding season approaches.

If you take a winter walk along one of the dikes at the Savannah National Wildlife Refuge, you are almost certain to encounter large numbers of sparrows with streaked breasts and a yellowish wash above the eyes. Scotsman Alexander Wilson named the Savannah sparrow in the late 1700s after he collected a specimen near Savannah. This species prefers open fields.

White-throated sparrows do what I call the "hop & scratch." They search for food by hopping forward and back in a kind of dance, attempting to unearth seeds or insects. Their sweet whistled song –

lot, and will pop up to perch briefly on top of a stalk or branch if the observer *pishes* – makes hissing, squeaking, or whistling noises. My fervent hope, when sparrow watching, is that the bird will venture into the open and pose long enough for me to inventory its identifying field marks.

During the winter, sparrows are social creatures. Where there is one sparrow, there will likely be a flock. Sparrows subscribe to the safety-in-numbers theory of self-protection. By feeding close to cover with lots of eyes to keep watch, they hope to escape the marauding cat or hawk that may be lurking about looking for a meal.

Our most abundant sparrow is an import. The house sparrow, actually a weaver finch, was brought to New York in 1850 to help eat cankerworms. As with other such experiments with non-native species, this one resulted in the proliferation of house sparrows that flourish around human habitations – sometimes to the detriment of other cavity nesters like bluebirds and purple martins.

> *Sparrows are an acquired taste — like oysters and avocados. Learning to identify them takes time and patience.*

White-throated Sparrow

Song Sparrow

"Oh Sam Peabody, Peabody, Peabody" is one signal that spring is approaching.

A good time to look for marsh sparrows is at the extra-high tides around the full or new moon. When the marsh is covered with water, birds retreat to the higher clumps of sea oxeye. The large grayish-brown seaside sparrow is one of the few sparrows that nests in the Low Country. Nelson's and saltmarsh sparrows have buffy, orange cheek patches and varying amounts of streaking on their breasts. Both species move further north to nest.

So, I confess. Give me a choice and I'll take warblers any day. Sparrows however, have their own muted beauty. They'll be gone by mid-April. We won't see them leave. Rarely will anyone ask, "When will the sparrows be back?" We'll be busy filling our hummingbird feeders and oohing and ahhing over summer tanagers, indigo buntings, and rose-breasted grosbeaks. Until then, make sure you keep your eyes upon the sparrows.

Saltmarsh Sparrow

Beware The Berry Bandits

It's a good thing that the Police Department is not charged with the task of apprehending berry bandits. We'd have to raise taxes and double the size of the force to contend with the huge numbers of cedar waxwings, American robins, and northern mockingbirds that terrorize area hollies, cherry laurels, pyracantha bushes and mulberry trees in late winter and early spring.

Take a close look at cedar waxwings, and you'll know you've got yourself some robbers. If the jaunty crests weren't enough to tell you they mean mischief, check out the stylish black masks. Don't be deceived by the muted tan colors, pointy wings, or yellow-edged tails. These birds have only

Cedar Waxwing on Yaupon Holly

one thing on their minds – stealing your berries. They swirl about in tight flocks, calling to each other with high-pitched, wheezing chitters. Then, at the sight of a tree with fruit ripe for the picking, they descend in a noisy cloud to begin their nefarious work.

While such behavior is hardly surprising from a waxwing, we expect better from that wholesome icon of song, the American robin. After all, the "red, red, robin" that "comes bob, bob bobbin' along," is up there with baseball, Mom, and apple pie. They announce the arrival of spring, (or fall in the Low Country), feast on worms, and lift our spirits with their sweet singsong melodies. Who would suspect this sterling character of banditry?

I was strolling in Forsyth Park one morning and all the grassy areas were covered with robins – walking, pausing, listening, reaching down to grasp a worm, walking and pausing again. It was all sedate and rather dignified, the

Flock of Cedar Waxwings

kind of behavior you would expect from a robin.

Then, several days later, I parked in downtown Savannah and emerged from the car to a cacophony of sound. I followed the activity to a bare tree that was filled with robins. Further investigation led me to a large, fully-leafed tree that was loaded with blue-black berries. Flying in and out of the tree were literally hundreds of robins. This was feeding at its most frenzied. I heard a steady "plop, plop" as berries and seeds hit the ground.

The tree, I later discovered, was a cherry laurel. The berries are a magnet for birds and wildlife, but are poisonous if ingested by humans. Cherry laurels have proliferated in the southeast, particularly below power lines. Birds sit on the lines to digest their berry treats, depositing large quantities of seed on the ground below them.

The northern mockingbird might best be described as a berry bully. Mockingbirds play the game differently. They disdain all that flock togetherness, opting instead for the solo or paired food stakeout. Wherever you find a healthy crop of berries, there's sure to be at least one mockingbird crying "mine, all mine!" Let a cardinal or titmouse so much as think about approaching the berry source, and the mockingbird is instantly on the attack to drive off the interloper.

Occasionally, this territoriality can even extend to bird feeders. I usually put out a small amount of "treat food" every day - a mix that includes peanuts, almonds, sunflower chips and raisins. One year, a mockingbird staked out all the feeders in the front yard and wouldn't let any other bird come near them. Only the advent of spring courting distracted him from his bullying ways.

Now it may seem like the berry bandits have it made, but there are always risks to a life of crime. First there is gluttony. Occasionally cedar

American Robin in Cherry Laurel

Northern Mockingbird guards berries

waxwings eat themselves into a stupor. They get so stuffed with berries that they have to simply hang out and allow their food to digest before they can fly. During this time, they make an easy target for a passing hawk or cat.

Another hazard is eating fermented berries. While birds may not get hauled in for being drunk and disorderly, the cost for FWI – flying while intoxicated – can be high. In Charleston, SC, cedar waxwings began feasting on fermented holly berries in a courtyard adjacent to a glass-walled office building. Some got so loopy they began falling off the tree branches. Others attempted to fly and got confused by the glass. More than a hundred birds smacked into the windows and dropped to the pavement, some simply stunned, others, unfortunately, dead.

Enjoy these bandits while you may. While some robins do nest in the Low Country, most will head north by mid-March to serve as eagerly awaited harbingers of spring. Then in late April, the waxwings will take their mobile berry bash up to cooler climes, where they will augment their high-carb winter diet with beetles, caterpillars and ants. Only the mockingbirds will remain all summer – courting, nesting, and eating bugs. It'll be easy street for the berry bandit police, at least until next winter.

Buzzard Bait

"There he is. It's Buzzard Bates!" My brother and sister and I stared in fascination at the dark shape soaring overhead, wings slightly raised in a V shape and teetering from side to side.

Now I know "buzzard" is an informal term for a vulture. I don't know how we came by the surname of "Bates." When I posed the question to a friend, his response was immediate.

"It's *buzzard bait*," he asserted. "You ain't good for nothing but *buzzard bait!*"

"That must be it," I chuckled. Anything useless or dead is *buzzard bait*.

Vultures have found their way into our culture in a variety of intriguing ways. They have made it in films. No cowboy movie would be complete without the vultures circling above the hero about to die of thirst in the desert. Then

Black Vulture in flight

Turkey Vulture

...re vultures in the comics. Broomhilda, ...he small, plump, perennially unfortu...ate witch, has for best buddies Nerwin ...he troll, and Gaylord the vulture. ...here are vulture jokes.

Did you hear about the turkey ...ulture that approached the gate at the ...irport carrying three dead raccoons? ...he flight attendant stopped him. "I'm ...orry sir, but each passenger is only ...lowed two carrion."

Vulture enthusiasts at Reed ...ingham State Park in south Georgia ...elebrate Buzzard Day each February ...ith pontoon boat trips through the ...ark to view thousands of wintering ...ultures. There is even a non-profit ...rganization devoted exclusively to the ...-depth study of the turkey vulture.

Actually, vultures and humans have ... thing or two in common. Both ...ecies, excluding the vegetarians ...mong us, eat meat. Both prefer their ...eat fresh but generally do not kill it ...emselves. Humans have the advan...ge of refrigeration. Vultures have a digestive system powerful enough to kill any virus or bacteria should the meat they find be well-aged.

There are two species of vulture that hang out in coastal Georgia. The larger turkey vulture – TV for short – got its name because its featherless red-skinned head resembles the red wattle of a turkey. With a 69-inch wingspan, it soars effortlessly on the thermals, seldom needing to flap its wings. Seen from underneath, turkey vulture wings have a distinctive two-toned pattern – dark toward the forward edge of the wings and silvery white on the flight feathers. Unlike most other birds including their smaller cousin, the black vultures, TVs have a keen sense of smell which they use along with their eyesight to locate food.

Black vultures have short, stubby tails and only a 57-inch wingspan. Their flight pattern can be described as "flap, flap, flap, glide." The wing beats are hurried and the glide is not as sustained as that of the turkey vulture.

Turkey Vulture in flight

> Vultures are friendly
> and co-operative
> by nature.
> They roost together
> at night and let
> each other know
> where the food is.

Black Vultures on post

Since black vultures rely on sight or the observation of other vultures to locate food, they often soar higher for a better view. The large white patches on the underside of each wing tip are an easy aid to identification. Black vultures are reputed to be more aggressive than their larger turkey cousins, sometimes attacking and eating the young of large mammals.

One day I received a call from a friend who had seen more than 50 vultures hanging out near the Bull River bridge on the way to Tybee Island. I went to investigate and found the birds huddled around a deer carcass. According to Bill Kohlmoos, one of the founders of the Turkey Vulture Society, vultures are friendly and co-operative by nature. They roost together at night and let each other know where the food is. When a large food source is found, a message goes out, without cell phones or e-mail – "Ya'll come on over. We've got a big one here!"

Vultures are the clean-up crew of the bird world. With their bare, wrinkled heads and shaggy-looking black and brown feathers, they're not likely to win any beauty pageants. Some of their habits – like regurgitating smelly substances when threatened – are downright repulsive. However, the service they provide is invaluable. They are highly efficient at disposing of one of the unforeseen by-products of modern civilization – road kill.

They don't rate a spot on our coins. They don't get to fly into stadiums against the backdrop of the flag as the national anthem is sung. However, when the spectacle is over, who's there for the dirty work?

I say let's hear it for vultures!

Spring

SPRING - AN OVERVIEW

Spring in the Low Country is buzzing with bird excitement. The first stirrings begin in late January with the arrival of purple martin scouts. In early February, the resident songbirds begin shopping for nest sites, singing, and advertising for mates. March brings the arrival of the first northern parulas and ruby-throated hummingbirds. From mid-March to early May, some 200 species of Neotropical migratory birds including songbirds, shorebirds, wading birds and raptors, will pour into the area, traveling from Central and South America to spend the summer nesting in North America. Some species stay to nest in the Low Country while others just stop off to eat and rest, before continuing their journey to points north.

Semipalmated Sandpiper & Ruddy Turnstone

Long-legged wading birds, most of which are year-round residents, dress up for breeding in elaborate plumes and gather in crowded communities known as "rookeries" to build nests and raise young.

NEOTROPICAL MIGRANTS

Swallows
Purple Martin
Northern Rough-winged Swallow
Bank Swallow
Tree Swallow – leave for summer
Cliff Swallow – rare
Barn Swallow

Vireos
Yellow-throated Vireo
Red-eyed Vireo
Warbling Vireo – rare
Blue-headed Vireo – some remain in winter
White-eyed Vireo – some year-round

Northern Parula

Warblers – Stay to Nest
Northern Parula
Common Yellowthroat
Yellow-throated Warbler
Prothonotary Warbler
Hooded Warbler
Yellow-breasted Chat
Swainson's Warbler
Prairie Warbler
Pine Warbler

Warblers – Migrate Through: Regular in Spring
Louisiana Waterthrush
Northern Waterthrush
Black-and-white Warbler
Ovenbird
Orange-crowned Warbler
Cape May Warbler
Worm-eating Warbler
Palm Warbler
Yellow-rumped Warbler
American Redstart
Blackpoll Warbler
Black-throated Blue Warbler

Northern Waterthrush

Warblers – Migrate Through: Rare in Spring
Black-throated Green Warbler
Blackburnian Warbler
Cerulean Warbler
Chestnut-sided Warbler
Blue-winged Warbler
Golden-winged Warbler
Magnolia Warbler
Canada Warbler
Bay-breasted Warbler

Buntings, Tanagers, Grosbeaks and Orioles
Indigo Bunting – nests
Painted Bunting – nests
Blue Grosbeak – nests
Rose-breasted Grosbeak – migrates through
Scarlet Tanager – migrates through
Summer Tanager – nests
Baltimore Oriole – migrates through; many now winter
Orchard Oriole – nests

Rose-breasted Grosbeak

SPRING - AN OVERVIEW

Flycatchers
Great Crested Flycatcher – nests
Acadian Flycatcher – nests
Eastern Kingbird – nests
Eastern Wood-Pewee – nests
Least Flycatcher – migrates through
Yellow-bellied Flycatcher –
 migrates through

Thrushes
Hermit Thrush – winter, migrates
Wood Thrush – nests
Veery – migrates
Swainson's Thrush – migrates
Gray-cheeked Thrush – migrates
Bicknell's Thrush – migrates

Miscellaneous migrants
Chuck-will's-widow – nests
Whip-poor-will – migrates through
Chimney Swift – nests
Yellow-billed Cuckoo – nests
Black-billed Cuckoo – migrates
Bobolink – migrates through
Common Nighthawk – rarely nests
Ruby-throated Hummingbird – nests
Purple Gallinule – nests

Dunlins wading

Shorebirds
Whimbrel
Lesser Yellowlegs
Greater Yellowlegs
Short-billed Dowitcher
Long-billed Dowitcher
Stilt Sandpiper
Red Knot
Sanderling
Ruddy Turnstone
Marbled Godwit
Long-billed Curlew
Dunlin
Semipalmated Plover
Piping Plover
Black-bellied Plover
American Golden-Plover
Spotted Sandpiper
Solitary Sandpiper
Pectoral Sandpiper
Least Sandpiper
Semipalmated Sandpiper
Western Sandpiper
White-rumped Sandpiper
Buff-breasted Sandpiper – inland, fields
Upland Sandpiper – inland, fields
Willet – some migrate; some nest

Neotropical Raptors
Swallow-tailed Kite
Mississippi Kite

Yellow-billed Cuckoo

OTHER RAPTORS
Northern Harrier – leave by late May
Sharp-shinned Hawk – leave by May
Cooper's Hawk – some nest
American Kestrel – leave by May
Merlin – leave by May
Peregrine Falcon – leave by May

LONG-LEGGED WADING BIRDS
Great Blue Heron
Little Blue Heron
Tricolored Heron
Green Heron
Great Egret
Snowy Egret
Cattle Egret
Roseate Spoonbill – uncommon
White Ibis
Glossy Ibis
Wood Stork
American Bittern – leaves for summer
Least Bittern – summer nester
Black-crowned Night-Heron
Yellow-crowned Night-Heron

Wood Stork & nestling

GULLS, TERNS AND SKIMMERS
Least Tern – nests
Royal Tern – year-round
Sandwich Tern – uncommon winter, summer nester
Common Tern – migrates through
Forster's Tern – leave for summer
Laughing Gull – year-round, more summer
Ring-billed Gull – year-round, uncommon summer
Herring Gull – common winter, uncommon summer
Black Skimmer – year-round

Royal Terns courting

Spring title page features a female Eastern Bluebird, a Great Egret in breeding plumage and Royal Terns courting with fish, pictured top to bottom.

THE THREE-RING CIRCUS OF SPRING

I haven't been to the circus in years – at least not the circus with lion tamers, elephants, clowns, and men on the flying trapeze. However, when it gets to be March in the Low Country, I feel like the bird circus has come to town.

For starters, there's the noise. On the dock, the laughing gulls take on the role of circus barker with gusto. Perched atop every available piling, the gulls have traded in winter's smudgy gray headgear for crisp, black helmets. Hunched forward, they fluff up their wings, open their mouths wide and emit lengthy raucous cackles, letting anyone within earshot know that the show is about to start.

Inside the circus tent, vendors greet you with a background medley of "peanuts, popcorn, cotton candy." In the avian circus, boat-tailed grackles and red-winged blackbirds take on the job. They roam about in noisy flocks, peddling their wares with a non-stop chorus of squawks, clucks, and whistles.

Once you settle into your seat you can focus on the action under the big top. Inevitably, as in any good circus, too many things are happening at once. You constantly have to shift your attention as the spotlight shifts from ring to ring. That's what makes spring a bird circus.

In Ring Number One, the resident songbirds are headed full speed into courting, mating and nesting.

In Ring Number One, the resident songbirds are headed full speed into courting, mating and nesting. Before dawn, the Carolina wren hollers "tea kettle, tea-kettle" while the northern cardinal whistles "what cheer, cheer, cheer." A woodpecker stakes out his territory with a sharp burst of drumming. The brown thrasher croons raspy couplets from the treetop. Bluebirds,

Red Knot, breeding plumage

Eastern Bluebird, female

chickadees, nuthatches, and titmice fight over birdhouses and gather nest material.

In Ring Number Two, the long-legged wading birds are strutting their stuff. Great egrets put on green eye shadow and flounce their nuptial plumes, while tricolored herons don feathery mantles and little blue herons sport fluffy pink boas. Snowy egrets parade in plumes that once were popular hat adornments.

Abandoning their solitary feeding habits, the wading birds begin to gather in an avian commune known as a rookery. They'll spend the next three months laying eggs and raising chicks in strident togetherness.

Ring Number Three features the incoming tourists. As days get longer and the temperature rises, some 200 species of birds ride the winds from their tropical winter homes to nesting territories in

Great Egrets on the nest

North America. A buzzy ascending trill announces the arrival of the tiny northern parula while the great crested flycatcher makes its presence known with an emphatic "wheep, wheep." Bird enthusiasts throughout the area are filling nectar feeders for hummingbirds and millet feeders for painted buntings. Each new arrival brings a thrill of recognition and pleasure. How could I have lived all these months without chimney swifts, chuck-will's-widows, orchard orioles, and purple martins?

Laughing Gull as circus barker!

But wait – there's more. This circus has not three rings but four. With such a hubbub, it is easy to ignore the winter birds. At the beach, there are still ducks and loons in the water. Northern gannets are patrolling the shore. Red knots are actually turning rusty orange and black-bellied plovers are beginning to match their names. Goldfinches, sparrows, hermit thrushes, meadowlarks and snipe all know instinctively that it is too soon to head north. They linger longer, adding to the topsy-turvy, rough-and-tumble, oh-so-entertaining spectacle that here in the coastal Low Country gathers under the arching big top of "spring."

THE RETURN OF THE MAFIA

Mostly I love spring. I love wandering the neighborhood in search of migratory songbirds just back from the tropics. I love watching the chickadees building a nest in my birdhouse. I love planting my garden to attract butterflies and hummingbirds. But there are two things about spring that I greet with mixed emotions – biting insects and boat-tailed grackles. The insects I can rationalize. They are, after all, what bring my beloved warblers. The grackles are another matter.

At a suitable distance, grackles are interesting and even entertaining. If I see them at the Savannah National Wildlife Refuge, I can admire their iridescent blue-purple plumage, bright yellow eyes, and mammoth keel-shaped tails. I can watch them strut and posture with amused detachment. It is only when they start chowing down on my bird food, hogging the birdbath

Common Grackle

Boat-tailed Grackle, male

and bullying all the smaller birds in the yard that I announce despairingly, "the mafia is back in town."

A single grackle wouldn't be so bad. After a winter of almost no birds at the feeders, I am thrilled when the first boat-tailed grackle shows up in late February. The problem is that grackles are naturally gregarious, and one soon turns into many. When winter is over, they return en masse. There is courting to do and nest sites to claim. All of it, for grackles, is noisy business. I wake to an assortment of noisy clacks, gurgles, and whistles.

When it comes to food, grackles are omnivores. They dine on aquatic insects, crayfish, crabs, mussels, shrimp, tadpoles, frogs, small fish, grasshoppers, and caterpillars. Not averse to a little larceny, they steal food from larger birds and raid other nests for eggs and young. It is their fondness for birdseed that I deplore.

When the mafia comes to town, the gang swarms over my feeders, displacing the more desirable and less aggressive cardinals, chickadees and tufted titmice. I do my best to discourage them. I use feeders with cages and feeders with weighted bars. I put out safflower seed that isn't their favorite. Finally, I give up and try to make the best of it.

After all, John James Audubon painted an exquisite verbal picture of

Boat-tailed Grackle, female

the courting male boat-tailed grackle or "great crow blackbird."

Proud of his elegant form and splendid plumage, he alights on the topmost branch of some evergreen oak, droops his wings and tail, swells his breast, and glittering in the bright rays of the sun, which call forth all the variations of tint for which his silken plumes are remarkable, pours forth his loud though not always agreeable song. He watches his rivals as they pass, pursues them with ardent courage, returns to his stand exulting,

Boat-tailed Grackle up close

Boat-tailed Grackle chows down and again pours forth his song.

For male boat-tailed grackles, there is a point to all this posturing. The winner gets the girls. Boat-tailed grackles don't go in for monogamy or lifetime commitments. They spend most of the year in single species flocks, joining the ladies in the spring for procreation. While many males may hang about a breeding colony, only the high-ranking individuals actually get to mate. Each successful male usually claims two to three females. Being liberated, females may mate with more than one male in the course of the season.

The female boat-tailed grackle is less visually showy. She is tawny brown with darker wings and a shorter tail. She also gets stuck with the housework, building a large, bulky nest of twigs, marsh grass, weeds, and mud. She incubates two to four greenish-blue, irregularly speckled eggs for thirteen to fifteen days. When the eggs hatch, she does all the feeding for another two weeks until the young leave the nest.

Grackles do get high marks for fastidiousness. After a morning spent mud-bathing in the marsh, they take full advantage of my birdbath. They drink. They splash. They posture and preen – all noisily of course. They bring their food to water to rinse and soften it.

If you happen to live inland and are not blessed with boat-tailed grackles, do not despair. There is a grackle just for you. The smaller common grackle is found throughout the east and midwest in farmland, towns, groves and streams. It is still gregarious, noisy, and prone to descend on backyards or farms in large flocks.

Unlike the boat-tails, common grackles opt for monogamy. They nest together in colonies of ten to thirty or more pairs. A female common grackle gets a little more help with the kids. She still builds the nest and incubates, but he pitches in with the feeding.

In early spring, I went for a walk around Lake Mayer. There were gnats. The harsh squawks, trills and whistles of grackles filled the air. Never mind. As soon as I hear the ascending buzzy trill of the tiny northern parula, I'll forget all that. Mostly, I love spring!

> *When the grackles start chowing down on my bird food, and hogging the birdbath, I announce despairingly that "the mafia" is back in town.*

Boa-tailed Grackle in birdbath

What a Bird Guy Will Do to Get a Gal!

The sharp, staccato drumming wedged its way into my early morning awareness. My first thought was that construction on the new house next door was starting awfully early. I found my way to the living room just as the noise vibrated down through the metal chimney to the fireplace. "Oh, no," I thought, "it's that time of year again! The red-bellied woodpecker is in the mood for love."

When the symphony of bird song starts up in the spring, the male woodpecker proudly provides the percussion – an emphatic rapping amplified to establish his territory and proclaim his superiority to the available females within range. This is not the relatively quiet and deliberate pecking that characterizes foraging for food or cavity

Great Egret, breeding plumage

excavation. This drumming is showy, dramatic, and above all – loud!

"He's courting," I informed my brother when he complained about the racket at his house.

"Courting a case of lead poisoning," was his less than sympathetic reply.

I am constantly amazed and fascinated by the wide assortment of strategies employed by bird guys in their efforts to win the affection of the female of the species. The males dress up in bright colors, put on fancy plumes, sing from exposed perches, build elaborate structures, dance, strut, bow, preen, or offer tasty tidbits. They pull out all the stops in pursuit of the prize.

Herons and egrets impress potential mates with long, lacy, nuptial plumes. The normally black legs of the cattle egret turn red, as does its yellow bill. Add mustard-colored patches on head, back and breast, and what girl egret

Red-bellied Woodpecker prepares his nest

could resist?

The skin around the eye of the great egret turns bright green. To woo his mate, he will fly in a circular pattern with slow wing beats and neck extended. He may also stretch his neck with bill pointed skyward, or bring it forward and down to show off fancy crown and neck feathers. Opening his bill and then closing it again with an audible "snap" is another move designed to please.

Some birds rely not on their looks but on their vocal abilities to woo the girl of their dreams. The male brown thrasher makes no alteration to his appearance. He simply gives up his ground thrashing ways to take up a vulnerable perch some 20 to 30 feet in the air, from which he serenades his beloved. He favors couplets, performing an incredible diversity of phrases with a slightly raspy tone. If his melodies earn her favor, she may join him for a soft, stirring duet.

At the beach, male gulls and terns use a combination of snappy fresh plumage, vocal prowess and gift giving to woo their beloveds. When searching for the right gift, they follow conventional wisdom – "when in doubt, choose seafood." Small fish make ideal gifts, as do crabs, shrimp and squid.

The male ruby-throated hummingbird has earned a reputation as a feathered Don Juan. He sets up shop on a site with abundant food where he is likely to encounter many females. To impress the ladies, he relies on aerial

Male birds dress up in bright colors, put on fancy plumes, sing, dance, strut, and offer tasty tidbits – all in pursuit of the prize.

Royal Terns courting

acrobatics that involve climbing to a height of 40 to 50 feet and diving steeply in front of his intended. He will also fly back and forth in front of her in a deep "U" pattern, so regular that he seems to be suspended from a wire. For his final sales pitch, he hovers in front of the female, points his bill at her, erects the brilliant feathers of his gorget, and flares his tail – all while maintaining a constant buzzy chatter. If she responds to his advances, they mate. Then she goes off alone to build a nest, lay eggs, and raise the young. He turns his attention to the next conquest.

He does, however, pay a price for his pleasure. Male hummingbirds often become so focused on mating that they forget to eat properly. They can lose as much as twenty percent of their body weight and become ragged and weakened by summer's end. Female ruby-throated hummingbirds regularly live twenty-five percent longer than the hard-courting males.

For many songbirds, colorful plumage is the way to a female bird's heart. Male scarlet tanagers, painted buntings, and rose-breasted grosbeaks run the risk of being more visible to predators, but what's a little risk when compared to the reward of winning the

Ruby-throated Hummingbird, male

bird girl of your dreams. While male buntings, grosbeaks and cardinals stay bright all year, the male scarlet tanager changes in the fall, becoming yellow like the female.

Many shorebirds also dress up for the big dance. During the winter, I feel foolish pointing out black-bellied plovers with white bellies, red knots that are non-descript gray, and ruddy turnstones that are brown and white. Finally, when spring arrives, the birds begin to match their names. With a rust-colored back, black bib, and harlequin face, the male ruddy turnstone is quite a looker. The male black bellied plover knows that in his tuxedo – black face and belly, white shoulders and forehead, and richly patterned back – he will catch the eye of any female plover.

So keep your senses tuned for the sights, sounds, and smells of spring. The flowers are bloomin', the birds are croonin' and the guys are doin' whatever it takes to get their gal!

Black-bellied Plover, breeding plumage

Tuning Your Ears to Bird Song

It's a habit now. I can't walk anywhere – even out to get the paper in the morning – without listening. Each chirp or twitter tells me who's in the neighborhood.

A sweet, whistled "what cheer, cheer, cheer" informs me that the cardinals have begun courting. "Tea-kettle, tea-kettle, tea-kettle," the tiny Carolina wren hollers from the saw palmettos, scolding with a "prrrp, prrrp, prrp," as I walk by. A bubbly, whiny, twittering symphony lets me know that a multitude of goldfinches will soon be swarming all over my feeders.

While I was working at Wild Birds Unlimited, a call came from a Bartlett Middle School teacher. She asked if we carried tapes of bird songs. Several students were preparing for a special examination, and they needed to be able to identify the calls of common birds.

Things seem to have changed since I was a Bartlett student. In the 7th grade, we had a choice of studying French or Spanish. "Bird Song" was not an option. I chose Spanish and studied it all through high school and college, even spending a semester in Spain. I loved the feeling of being able to make sense of sounds that would otherwise be a meaningless jumble of noise.

It was while I was living in Boston that I began to devote concentrated effort to learning bird calls. I tagged along on walks led by members of the Brookline Bird Club and was in awe of the leaders who, without raising their binoculars, called out "titmouse in the oak," "pine warbler overhead," or "great crested flycatcher in the willow." It seemed as if the people who knew the sounds had an advantage when it came to finding the birds.

Northern Cardinal, male

Carolina Wren, the little loudmouth

Northern Mockingbird

Fortunately, I discovered the Peterson *Birding by Ear* recordings made by Richard K. Walton and Robert W. Lawson. Instead of listening to music in my car, I drove around immersed in chirping and twittering. The authors grouped the birds into categories and did an excellent job of comparing and contrasting similar songs.

The "name-sayers" get their names from their calls and obligingly announce their identities. One common feeder visitor – dapper with gray back, white cheek patches and a black cap – usually intones an energetic "chick-a-dee-dee-dee" before it carefully extracts a single sunflower seed to eat on a nearby branch. A small gray flycatcher – the eastern phoebe – has a habit of sitting on snags near water and rhythmically pumping its tail. It happily pronounces, with short raspy syllables, that it's a "phee-be, phee-be, phee-ba-be." Another "name-sayer" arrives each spring to announce with a ringing, repetitive, call heard late at night or before dawn, that the "chuck-will's-widow, chuck-will's-widow" is back in the neighborhood.

The birds with "mimic" calls are an entertaining group. The northern mockingbird, the gray catbird, and the brown thrasher are noted for their ability to imitate the calls of other birds.

Perhaps the most vocally accomplished member of the group, the mockingbird will typically repeat a

Eastern Phoebe sings its name

Carolina Chickadee

In the spring, birds show off their most elaborate vocal repertoires.

Bobolink

phrase three to six times before it changes to a new tune. Scientists don't know if mockingbirds mimic just for the fun of it or if they are trying to set territorial boundaries to keep other birds away from their nests and berry bushes. Some mockingbirds have even been heard to imitate car alarms and backhoes.

Just when you are puzzling over the irregular jumble of notes coming from a dense thicket, a harsh, emphatic "mew" clears up the mystery. The sleek gray catbird with the small, black cap and rusty undertail coverts gets its name from its ability to pass for a feline – at least vocally.

Some birds have relatively simple calls. Great crested flycatchers advertise their presence with a non-musical "wheep, wheep," while white-breasted nuthatches honk like tiny tin horns. Green herons announce their spring arrival with an explosive "skeow."

Birds with complex songs include the American goldfinch, the bobolink and the house wren. These species fill the air with a delightful assortment of bubbling, chirping and twittering.

Spring is the time to tune your ears to bird song. While birds have chip notes and calls that they use year round to communicate with each other, they show off their most elaborate vocal repertoires in the spring. There are girls to impress, rivals to warn off, and territories to establish.

My advice to the eager bird song student is: 1) Start by learning the songs of the common birds. 2) Don't tackle too many birds at once. 3) Keep at it. As the Spaniards would say, *poco a poco se va lejos* – little by little one goes far. The rewards are well worth the effort!

NESTING BOX BLUES

APRIL

You did your homework and bought exactly the right size bluebird box. The entrance hole measures 1 1/2 inches, it's well ventilated, and the side swings up for easy cleaning. After much contemplation you selected the perfect location – an open area in the yard facing away from the afternoon sun and the prevailing wind. You even spent the extra money to pole mount the box with a baffle to keep out raccoons and snakes. The bluebirds came, right on schedule in early March, inspected your box thoroughly, and then settled in the neighbor's newspaper tube.

It's unfathomable! It's outrageous! Can't they read? You stumble inside in a daze. You've just come down with a case of the dreaded Nesting Box Blues.

Working at Wild Birds Unlimited I've heard lots of stories. My aunt put up a screech-owl box. Immediately, a pair of great crested flycatchers moved in. One man put up a wood duck box. His first tenants were screech-owls. Another woman put up four different boxes at her Hinesville home. Chickadees and bluebirds began batting for one of the boxes. When the chickadees brought in nesting material, the bluebirds would carry it out again. Finally, the chickadees moved to another

Eastern Bluebirds check the box

box. The bluebirds, having won the disputed box, lost interest and moved elsewhere.

I had a bluebird box in my yard for two years and no bird came near it blue or otherwise. I moved it to my parents' backyard and within a week the chickadees had built an impressive mossy nest.

Oh, those Nesting Box Blues!

There is something fascinating about new life coming into the world, whatever the species. Finding a nest with eggs in it is like being let in on a special secret. It has to be wondered over and shared in hushed whispers with a child,

Carolina Chickadee nest

Carolina Wren nest in wreath

a parent, or a friend. Curiosity grows. How long until the eggs hatch? When will they *fledge* – leave the nest?

Different species of birds play the nesting game differently. Some – like cardinals, brown thrashers, and mockingbirds – build nests in shrubbery, trees or dense underbrush. Hummingbirds and blue-gray gnatcatchers build a tiny nest that they cover with moss and lichens until it looks like another bump on the branch. Others species – such as woodpeckers, chickadees, titmice, nuthatches, and bluebirds – prefer to build their nests in a tree cavity. These cavity nesters will also use nest boxes. Put up a box and you're a "bird lord," with all the attendant responsibilities, joys, and frustrations – at risk for a case of the Blues.

To keep the blues at bay, we might take a lesson from the Buddhists. Attachment, they say, generates suffering. To avoid suffering, practice non-attachment. In other words, put up your box and take what you get.

I know. We all have our favorites. "But I really wanted bluebirds," you cry when the titmice move in. Guess it's time to put up another box.

Really, the joys usually win out in the end. In Hinesville, the bluebirds

Blue-gray Gnatcatchers at their nest

finally returned to nest in the disputed box. Brown-headed nuthatches, while not as showy as bluebirds, make feisty and entertaining tenants. The thin, high-pitched squeaks from my relocated box tell me the first batch of chickadees has arrived. Bluebirds, after all, nest three or four times in a season so they may get that perfect box the next time around.

"Be gone," I say. "I just ain't got time for those Nesting Box Blues!"

Brown-headed Nuthatch inspects post

CHEERIO THE VIREOS

While hummingbirds and painted buntings get most of the spring publicity, I'd like to put in a plug for an often-overlooked bird family – the vireos. The name comes from the Latin *vireo*, "to be green," and refers to an assortment of small songbirds found only in the Western hemisphere.

Vireos are plain birds with colorful names. They generally conceal themselves within dense foliage, moving deliberately and methodically among the leaves and branches in search of caterpillars, moths, beetles, stink bugs, wasps, bees, and other assorted insects.

While fourteen species of vireo are found in North America, only four species are common in the Low Country. Each has a name that starts with a color – blue-headed, white-eyed, yellow-throated, and red-eyed. As vireos are by nature somewhat secretive, finding one usually takes active looking or listening.

As I walked out to the mailbox one morning in early April, I heard a slightly whiny ascending "here I am," followed by the down-slurred query, "where are you?"

"Ah-hah," I thought. "The blue-headed vireo has come to call." I scanned the tree canopy for small movements, finally resorting to dialing up the song on my iPod. "Here I am, where are you?" called my recorded vireo. Immediately, a small shape flew towards me, landing on a nearby branch and cocking his head to the side in the quizzical fashion characteristic of

White-eyed Vireo

vireos. With binoculars, I could see the distinctive gray-blue head, bold white "spectacles," white underbelly with yellowish wash along the sides, and pair of white wing bars. As I watched, the blue-headed vireo darted into action, grabbing a small orange butterfly. The blue-headed is our winter-only vireo. When spring arrives, they depart for points north, preferring to raise their families in the mountains of north Georgia, the Appalachians, and up into the boreal forests of Canada.

Glancing into a nearby tree, I spied another bird foraging lower in the tangle of leaves and vines. This bird had a greenish back, white underbelly, yellowish flanks, a pale gray head, and two white wing bars. With binoculars I could make out bright yellow "spectacles." I could not see the light colored irises that are supposedly diagnostic for vireo number two – the year-round resident white-eyed vireo.

The white-eyed vireo has a loud, snappy song that sounds to me like

Yellow-throated Vireo

"chick, I'm a veerreo, chick." While its appearance may be unremarkable, the white-eyed vireo is an accomplished vocalist and mimic. A single male may boast a repertoire of more than a dozen songs. He artfully weaves snippets of the calls of other birds into the compositions designed to woo his beloved.

Just as the blue-headed vireos are preparing for the journey north, vireo number three arrives on the scene. The showiest of the bunch, the yellow

Blue-headed Vireo

White-eyed Vireo guards her nest

throated vireo retreats to the tropics for the winter, returning to North America to nest in mature, deciduous woodlands. At first glance, it is easy to mistake a yellow-throated vireo for the slightly smaller pine warbler. The vireo has a heavier bill, yellow "spectacles," and a bright yellow throat. Its sides are unstreaked, and the border between yellow chest and white belly is much crisper than on the pine warbler. Then there is the voice. While pine warblers announce their presence with an even, ringing trill, the yellow-throated vireos offer a variation of the ascending and descending "here I am, where are you?" They pause longer between phrases than the blue-headed vireos and add a Scottish burr to their tones. Their call has been rendered as a raspy "thirty-eight?.....thirty-eight."

Vireo number four also migrates north from the tropics. It is a common and abundant nester throughout the Low Country. With a drab greenish back, gray crown, dark eye line, and white stripe above the eye, the red-eyed vireo is particularly adept at vanishing into the foliage in the tops of the trees, where it forages for insects and the occasional berry. The song of the red-eyed vireo lacks the complexity of his white-eyed cousin, but he wins the prize for sheer endurance. His whistled phrases are quicker and less nasal than those of the yellow-throated vireo – "here-I-am, in-the-tree, look-up, at the top," he intones continually throughout the day.

During April it is possible to win the vireo lottery and find all four species in the Low Country at the same time. They may not be as showy as painted buntings, but these small songsters perform tireless community service, eating many times their weight in "noxious insects."

> *Four species of vireo are common in the Low Country – blue-headed, white-eyed, red-eyed, and yellow-throated.*

Red-eyed Vireo

APRIL

RHAPSODY IN BLUE

"If happy little bluebirds fly beyond the rainbow why, oh why, can't I?"

I listened to this line from "*Over the Rainbow*" sung by more than a few contestants in the Savannah Music Festival vocal competition and wondered about the emotional state of bluebirds. If I confessed to feeling blue, I'd be sad, in need of cheering up. In contrast, a *blue bird* somehow evokes happiness. There's just no sense to it.

But then there's no rational explanation for the way people feel about bluebirds. Why should a small songbird – a thrush to be precise – inspire such wonder, awe, and even devotion? Poems have been written and songs sung. Their color has been deemed celestial, and compared to that of the robe of the Virgin Mary. It's just hard to be matter-of-fact, indifferent, or ho-hum where bluebirds are concerned.

Even other birds seem to be fasci-

Eastern Bluebird, male

nated by bluebirds. One observer reports that in her yard, the house finches and goldfinches follow the bluebirds around like rock star groupies. If the bluebird flies up to the telephone wire, a couple of finches are sure to follow.

Although I have certainly seen my share of bluebirds, they don't visit my yard or my feeders or my birdbath. My coastal hammock with its wealth of live oak, pine, wax myrtle, and palmetto is very attractive to painted buntings, but not to the taste of the open-space-loving bluebirds. They much prefer a golf course, a pasture, or a school playground – particularly if there are plenty of perches from which to scan the grassy lawn for insects.

Mostly, I have to content myself with watching or hearing about other people's bluebirds – OPBs for short. I inspected the five lovely blue eggs in

Male Eastern Bluebird with cricket

Female Eastern Bluebird with mealworms

the nest of one friend's bluebird box. At my brother's house on Wilmington Island, I got caught up in the drama of the nest box wars.

Bluebirds and brown-headed nuthatches were competing for a nesting box. Mr. Bluebird would perch atop the box. If he got hungry and went off in search of insects, Mr. Nuthatch took his place. As soon as the bluebird spied the interloper, he would chase off the nuthatch and re-take his claim. In an attempt at problem solving, I brought over the box from my yard that no bird had bothered to inspect, much less fight for. My sister-in-law reported that the nuthatches were spending a lot of time going in and out of the new box.

In the 1980s, bluebird populations were declining due to loss of suitable habitat for nesting and competition for nest cavities from the more aggressive starlings, house sparrows and tree swallows. Helping the bluebirds proved to be much simpler than helping the red-cockaded woodpecker. Whereas the woodpeckers will only nest in large live pine trees infected with red heart fungus, bluebirds take readily to nesting boxes provided and maintained by humans. Thanks to the efforts of organizations such as the North American Bluebird Society, Boy Scouts (who have built countless bluebird boxes), and private individuals willing to be "birdlords," bluebird populations are once again on the rise.

Providing food for bluebirds can be tricky. Being primarily insect and fruit eaters, they will not – like my painted buntings – be satisfied with a feeder full of white millet. You might tempt them with sunflower chips, chopped peanuts, suet nuggets, raisins or blueberries. However if you really want to win their undying devotion, offer mealworms. This segmented, whitish-tan larvae of the darkling beetle is available from bait shops or your local wild bird store. While refrigerated they are obligingly dormant. When put outside in a slippery dish to prevent them from escaping, they warm up and

> *There's no rational explanation for the way people feel about bluebirds. Why should a small thrush inspire such devotion?*

Bluebird eggs in nest

Eastern Bluebird, female

wriggle tantalizingly, a protein packed treat for bluebirds, wrens, warblers, and other insect eaters. Mealworms can be a lifesaver for Mom and Pop Bluebird when there are four hungry mouths to feed.

Although volumes have been written about every aspect of feeding and housing bluebirds, there are two points I would like to emphasize. If at all possible, pole mount your bluebird box and install some type of baffle on the pole to keep raccoons and snakes from feasting on your bluebird family. Second, be extremely careful about pesticide use while the bluebirds are feeding babies. Mole crickets, while a scourge for homeowners, are a tasty treat for baby bluebirds. Companies like "Gardens Alive" (www.gardensalive.com) offer alternative solutions for getting rid of troublesome pests.

To get more detailed answers to your bluebird questions, visit the web site of the North American Bluebird Society (www.nabluebirdsociety.org) or visit your local bird feeding store.

Cheer up! Be happy! Particularly if you've got the "blues" – birds, that is!

Eastern Bluebird nestlings

FISH HAWKS MAKE GOOD NEIGHBORS

Every time I leave my neighborhood, I inspect "the tree." This is a marvelous, weathered dead trunk, strategically placed behind a small pond. The best part about it is that you never know what you might find there at any given time. One day it may host a flock of white ibis, resting until the tide gets low enough for them to probe for fiddlers in the marsh.

Another day, the belted kingfisher might be perched there to scan for fish. Quite often, "the tree" is the dining spot of choice for the local osprey.

No matter how often I see this striking raptor, I always have to stop for another look. With its dark brown

Osprey on its nest

back, white underparts, hooked beak, and sporty brown eye stripe, the "fish hawk" is unmistakable. All around the world, where there is an ocean, a lake, or a river, there will most likely be an osprey. In flight, their long narrow wings, kinked at the "wrist," are distinctive. Ospreys patrol the waterways in search of their favorite dish – fish, fish and more fish. A desperate osprey might resort to eating a small mammal or bird, but only if there were a shortage of fish.

Ospreys are so skilled at catching fish that people once believed that they

Osprey splash

cast a spell on the fish, or that they released an oily substance from their bodies that would lure the fish to the surface. Most likely, their success is due to the fact that they are specialists, well equipped with technique as well as tools.

Patrolling 30 to 100 feet above the water, the ospreys scan for fish swimming near the surface. They have the ability to hover in place, like helicopters, kingfishers, and kestrels. When a fish is spotted, an osprey half closes its wings, stretches its feet forward with

Osprey on piling wi.h its catch

APRIL

Osprey pair on their nest

talons extended, and plunges into the water head and feet first. Osprey feet are especially suited to the task of gripping fish. The outer toe on each foot can be extended either forward or back. This allows it to grab a fish with two toes on each side. Spiky pads covering the bottom of its feet help it hold its slippery prey.

Emerging with the fish, the osprey shakes off excess water, adjusts the fish to an aerodynamic, head-forward position, and looks for a place to enjoy the feast. Small fish are swallowed whole, head first, while larger ones are torn in chunks and eaten sushi style.

Ospreys seem to have little fear of people, while people have found ospreys to be good neighbors. They make excellent "watchbirds," calling loudly at the approach of intruders and driving off crows and other birds of prey. Unlike other raptors, ospreys do not generally raid the hen house or carry off small pets. They can, however, present a problem if you happen to run a fish hatchery.

Come spring, ospreys conduct their courtship and nesting in grand style. The adult male arrives on the territory first and begins an elaborate sky dance to advertise for a mate. He flies sharply upward above the nest, then hovers and dives, carrying sticks or a fish. During the three-week courtship, he brings fish to his beloved and the two

Osprey landing

of them spend time together in the nest. Nests are generally built in the tops of tall trees or on man-made structures such as utility poles, channel markers, cell phone towers, or specially constructed osprey platforms.

Mrs. Osprey lays two to four eggs, and spends about thirty-eight days incubating them. When she leaves the nest to eat, her mate will take her place on the eggs. Once the eggs hatch, she sticks close to the chicks, protecting them from sun and rain. Mr. Osprey is a devoted husband and father, faithfully bringing fish for Mom and the kids while she is tied to the nest. At three to four weeks of age, the young birds begin wing-flapping exercises on the edge of the nest. First flight comes when they are seven to eight weeks old. Juvenile ospreys look like their parents, except that the dark feathers of their backs are edged in silver.

Osprey populations declined precipitously from the 1950s to the 1970s, primarily because of the use of DDT and other pesticides. The run-off of chemicals into the water supply built up in the fish that were then eaten by ospreys, eagles, pelicans, and other birds. In the birds, the chemicals produced eggshell thinning that resulted in reproductive failures. Finally, after the use of DDT was banned in 1972, the osprey population has made a slow but steady comeback.

Although the fish in Chimney Creek may beg to differ, I, for one, am convinced that ospreys make good neighbors. May they frequent "the tree" for many years to come!

Osprey on patrol

With its dark brown back, white underparts, hooked beak, and sporty brown eye stripe, the "fish hawk" is unmistakable.

Osprey with fish

Look Out for the Lord of the Flies

While the glamour birds — rose-breasted grosbeaks, Baltimore orioles, scarlet tanagers, and painted buntings – elicit a chorus of "oohs" when they stop off in the Low Country, an astonishing number of spring migrants slip in with little or no fanfare. They hang out in the tops of trees, eat insects, and rarely visit feeders. Unless you know what to look and listen for, you may never spot a worm-eating warbler, a red-eyed vireo, or a great crested flycatcher.

"Wheeeep, Wheeep, prrrrreeet, prrrrreeet, wheeep." The loud, harsh, unmusical notes add a distinct cacophony to the spring symphony of birdsong. Staring into the top of an oak, I wonder how an 8 1/2 inch bird can vanish so completely into the foliage. It must have learned at an early age that flycatchers should be heard and not seen. Certainly, with the exception of the showy vermillion flycatcher that makes an occasional cameo appearance on the east coast, none of the other members of this family are likely to wow you with their visual beauty.

If you succeed in locating the source of the "wheeep" in the treetops, you may find the great crested flycatcher attractive in an understated way. It has an olive brown back, pale gray throat and breast, lemon yellow belly, and long, cinnamon tail. Its scientific

Great Crested Flycatcher

Great Crested Flycatcher househunts

name, *myiarchus crinitus*, offers a fitting commentary on its appearance and habits. *Myia* comes from the Greek meaning "a fly" while *archos* is "lord, prince, or ruler." *Crinitus* comes from Latin and means "long-haired." The "long-haired lord of the flies" sports a rounded, bushy crest that gives it a rakish, somewhat punk appearance.

The name is not strictly accurate, since this insect connoisseur does not limit itself to flies. In fact, these birds should get the "Friends of the Earth" award for natural pest control. They consume more than fifty kinds of beetl as well as mosquitoes, wasps, bees, sawflies, stable flies, crickets, grasshoppers, katydids, moths, caterpillars, cicadas, and other insects. They supplement this high protein diet with the occasional sweet treat in the form of fruit and berries.

Flycatchers can be hard to locate because their favorite feeding style involves sitting erect and motionless on a perch where they use their large eyes to scan for flying insects. The best chance to spot them is when they leave the perch in fast, agile pursuit of their prey. Their wide mouths flanked by stiff bristles are perfect for grasping wiggly bugs.

While great crested flycatchers are common summer residents in the Low Country, they don't have big fan clubs or web sites that track their migration. The main reason for this is that they don't visit feeders. Unless you want to offer trays full of crickets and beetles, the best way to get better acquainted with great cresteds is to offer them housing. They are cavity nesters, using abandoned woodpecker holes as well as nest boxes. A box that is six inches wide, six inches deep, and ten inches tall, with a two-inch entrance hole placed six to eight inches above the floor should be ideal. Place the box on a tree, eight to twenty feet above the ground. They may also nest in gourds or ventilation holes in the side of a house.

Great crested flycatchers often return to the same nesting location

> *Staring into the top of an oak, I wonder how an 8 1/2 inch bird can vanish so completely into the foliage. It must have learned at an early age that flycatchers should be heard and not seen.*

Great Crested Flycatcher with Katydid

Great Crested Flycatcher fledgling begs

Modern living has altered the pattern, and the birds now may add bits of cellophane or aluminum foil.

While some young birds learn their calls listening to the adults that raise them, research has shown that some flycatchers are born knowing their calls and can sing them perfectly, even if raised in isolation. This is more evidence that for flycatchers, being heard is more important than being seen.

Occasionally, my colleague who raises orphaned birds will walk into Wild Birds Unlimited carrying a basket of baby birds that "wheeps." Peering

year after year. Males can be fiercely territorial, waging intense battles with other males, clawing one another, and even pulling out feathers. Once the territory is secured, he woos his intended by repeatedly dashing after her near the potential nest site.

Mr. and Mrs. Great Crested work together to build a bulky nest of twigs, grass, rootlets, fur and feathers. Their signature touch is a piece of snakeskin woven into the nest lining. This was once believed to scare off intruders.

Great Crested Flycatcher nesting cavity

Great Crested Flycatcher feeds nestling

into the bowl nest, I see the distinctive large head, broad beak, and bright yellow mouth of a miniature great crested flycatcher. It is amazing to see the tiny wing bars, yellow belly, and even rusty edging on tiny tail feathers.

I offer you this challenge, dear reader. Use your ears or eyes in May to track down the "lord of the flies" nesting in your neighborhood.

BUNTING FEVER

Painted Bunting, male

It was ten before seven on a Saturday morning in early May. The members of the Chapman family were sleeping peacefully in their Kiawah Island home except for Marcus, age nine, an exuberant early riser. His parents and his brother Andrew, thirteen, were wrenched from their dreams by screams – Marcus's screams! Fear gripped them. The house was on fire! Danger threatened! As his pounding feet came closer, they were finally able to make sense of his cries. "Painted bunting!" emerged from the muffled loudness, and everyone jumped up to follow him back to the living room where, indeed, this small brightly-colored songbird was making his premiere appearance at their birdfeeder.

Even people indifferent to birds find themselves captivated by the painted bunting. It's so exotic – so improbable – with its bright blue head, red breast, and greenish-yellow back. The bright colors whisper of faraway lands and tropical places, and rightly so. The painted bunting spends its winters in Central and South America and the Caribbean Islands. Each spring, it makes its way to southeastern North America to nest. It favors shrubby, brushy wax myrtle habitat and rarely ventures further north than southern

> *Even people indifferent to birds find themselves captivated by the painted bunting.*

96

MAY

Painted Bunting nest in Spanish moss

North Carolina.

During migration, from mid-March to mid-May, painted buntings may stop off at any feeder containing white millet, a seed sought after by sparrows but tossed out by the sunflower-loving cardinals, blue jays, and woodpeckers.

Female and first-year-male painted buntings look like a different species altogether. They are a drab, greenish-yellow and easy to overlook. Only their broader, seed-eating beaks indicate that these birds are not warblers. A green bunting singing is almost certainly a young male working extra-hard to attract a mate. It will take him about fourteen months to acquire his showy multi-colored plumage.

On a more serious note, there are fewer painted buntings than there used to be. Studies conducted by researchers with the U.S. Geological Survey's Patuxent Wildlife Research Center have estimated that the East Coast population has been declining about three percent per year since 1966. No one is quite sure why, but there are a number of theories.

Forest fragmentation is cited as one possible problem. There has been a decrease in large tracts of continuous woods. We don't know how much woods is enough. We do know that there are areas where people report that they used to see painted buntings in their yards but don't see them now. What has changed? A drive through the area in question often reveals that

Painted Bunting, female

many new subdivisions have been built. Large trees are left standing, but the shrubby, brushy tangles of wax myrtle where the painted buntings used to build their nests have been cleared.

Fragmentation can open the buntings to another threat – brown-headed cowbirds. Cowbirds were named centuries ago for their habit of following the bison herds on the plains in search of food. Constantly on the move, they couldn't maintain regular nests. Cowbirds prefer semi-open country and forest edges. They tend to avoid dense, unbroken forest. With smaller wooded tracts, there are more

Juvenile male Painted Bunting bathes

edges so that cowbirds have greater access to nests.

"No time to chat, gotta go," the female cowbird exclaims as she artfully deposits her egg in another bird's nest and pushes out one of the other eggs. When the young cowbird hatches, it usually hogs all the food and may even get rid of the other nestlings. I have watched a tiny northern parula feed a baby cowbird twice its size.

If you've never seen a painted bunting, May is a great time. Males will be singing to set up territories and attract their mates. They are regular feeder visitors at Skidaway Island State Park, Harris Neck National Wildlife Refuge, and on any of our barrier islands. Look for stands of wax myrtle and listen for their sweet musical warble. You might not get quite as excited as Marcus Chapman, but a good look at a painted bunting is sure to bring a smile to your face!

Disturbing the Peace

Chuck-will's-widow nests on ground

"Goatsucker." "Nightjar." "Chuck-will's-widow." The names accorded this nocturnal loudmouth of the southern woods are infinitely more colorful than the bird itself. As early as the third century B.C., residents of Greece saw birds of this family swooping low over pastures at night and speculated that they sucked milk from the udders of goats, causing the udders to wither and the goats to go blind. From this superstition comes the family name, *caprimulgidae*, derived from the Latin *caper*, "goat," and *mulgere*, "to milk."

"Nightjar" is an easier designation to understand and appreciate, particularly at 4 a.m. when one is "jarred" awake by the emphatic, ringing syllables often rendered as "whip" or "chuck"-

"will's-widow." This litany is repeated with annoying frequency in early spring, particularly during the full moon, as Mr. Chuck sets up his territory and advertises for a Mrs.

Our family's first experience with nightjars came when we were camping in a tent rather than an RV on the north end of Jekyll Island. Without the buffer of insulation or double-paned windows, the birds hollering in the oak trees overhead might as well have been sharing our sleeping bags. We assumed at first that we were hearing whip-poor-wills, until someone more in the know told us that it was chuck-will's-widows that nested in coastal Georgia. With practice, we could pick out the sharp "chuck" at the beginning of the call.

Thirty-plus years later, as I trekked around the Boston area with the Brookline Bird Club, I finally heard the whip-poor-will in the wild. While I knew it sounded different, it was only after time spent listening to recordings of the two calls that I finally felt confident in telling the species apart by voice.

Telling them apart visually can be

Chuck-will's-widow eggs

even more difficult. First you have to find one. Among the least visually showy of our Neotropical migrants, the nightjars dress in subdued shades of buff, gold, rufous, brown, and black. This bird version of camouflage lets them play "bump-on-a-log" stretched out lengthwise on a tree limb, or snooze the day away disguised as leaf litter on the forest floor.

Occasionally, a keen-eyed observer happens upon a roosting bird. Word spreads like juicy gossip and soon a dozen birders gather to stare with high powered binoculars and spotting scopes discussing the color of the throat: black for the "whip," buffy brown for the "chuck"; the size – 9 3/4 inches for the "whip," 12 for the "chuck"; or the amount of white in the outer tail feathers – more on the "whip" than on the "chuck." In the Low Country, the chuck-will's-widow is the common summer resident. Whip-poor-wills pass through during migration and are regular north-Georgia nesters. A wintering nightjar, reported occasionally from our southern barrier islands, is more likely to be a whip-poor-will.

Whip-poor-will, male

Unlike owls, nightjars have short legs, weak feet, and small beaks. Behind their deceptively petite bill is a huge gaping mouth with which they engulf flying insects as well as the occasional migrating warbler or hummingbird. Large moths and beetles are favorite foods, but nightjars also dine on flying ants, termites, mosquitoes, and small flies. A feasting chuck-will's-widow might stuff its gullet with as many as 2000 small insects.

When it comes to nesting, chuck-will's-widows take the lazy bird's approach. Why put all that time and effort into building? The forest floor will do just fine with perhaps a shallow depression scraped out for the eggs. Generally two eggs are laid – creamy white with brown or gray blotches. If the nest is disturbed, the female may actually move the eggs some distance away. She gets stuck with the role of single mom when it comes to incubating the eggs and feeding the chicks. Whip-poor-will females get a bit more help from their mates. She still does the incubating but he helps out feeding the young birds.

Since nightjars are easier to hear than to see, photographing them is a challenge. I was fortunate to get news of a chuck-will's-widow nesting in a yard on Skidaway Island. When I went to see for myself, "Mrs. Chuckles" posed obligingly and even fluttered backwards to reveal her two creamy eggs.

By late May, the fever of courtship has passed and the neighborhood is oddly quiet at dusk and dawn. I can only hope that somewhere, beneath a tangle of branches, little chuck-will's-widows are hatching and growing. With luck, they'll survive to disturb my peace again next year.

> *"Goatsucker" or "nightjar," the names accorded this nocturnal loudmouth of the southern woods, are infinitely more colorful than the bird itself.*

GET THEE TO A ROOKERY

If you've considered watching birds but you simply don't have the patience to stare into the tops of trees looking for small, flitting objects, take heart. On the coast in the Low Country we are blessed with an amazing variety of long-legged wading birds – herons, egrets, ibises, and even a stork! These birds are large and easy to see, even without binoculars. They stand still or walk slowly while feeding. Even when they fly, they do so in a languid, unhurried, typically southern manner. Best of all, in the spring, the long-legged wading birds opt for together-

American Bittern

ness. They gather by the tens, hundreds, and even thousands in a colonial nesting spectacle known as a "rookery." While the birds are busy bringing in sticks and sitting on nests, you should have ample time to observe and compare many different species.

The North American long-legged wading birds are grouped into four families. One family consists of herons, egrets and bitterns. Three species of ibis and the roseate spoonbill are grouped into another family. Family three contains only the wood stork, while the greater flamingo is the lone member of the fourth family.

The herons, egrets and bitterns all have long, straight, pointed beaks that are used to stab or grasp their prey. Most nest in colonies, although green

Green Heron

herons and bitterns may opt for the privacy of single family living rather than the communal bustle of a rookery.

You can begin the task of identifying these birds by paying attention to certain key characteristics: color of the feathers; length and color of the legs; color and shape of the beak; flight style and what and how the bird is eating.

The great blue heron, little blue heron, and tricolored heron are all bluish-gray. The largest of the group, the great blue heron, stands 46 inches tall with a 71-inch wingspan. It has a heavy, yellow bill and stylish black crown plume. Standing erect and motionless, it watches for the fish, frogs, insects, snakes, or rodents that it will spear for dinner. The great blue, like all the herons and egrets, flies with its head hunched back against its shoulders.

The tricolored heron is slightly larger and longer-necked than the little blue heron. It is best identified by its prominent white underparts. The little blue heron is solid blue-gray except during breeding season when its neck feathers get long, fluffy and

Great Blue Heron

pink. Both species tend to be solitary feeders, staking out and defending a small fishing territory.

Sorting out white egrets can be tricky. The three common ones, from large to small, are great egret, snowy egret and cattle egret. The long black legs of the stately – at 39 inches – great egret allow it to feed in deeper water. Like the great blue heron, it prefers to stand still and wait for its prey to approach. With a rapid thrust of its spear-like yellow beak, it impales an unsuspecting fish.

The snowy egret has black legs, a slender black bill, and startlingly yellow feet. It looks as if it has walked through a bucket of yellow paint. Relatively small at 24 inches, it prefers feeding in shallow water along the banks of creeks, rivers, and ponds, actively darting and lunging for fish.

The cattle egret received its name from its habit of foraging in dry fields for insects kicked up by grazing animals. During breeding season its normally

Black-crowned Night-Heron

black legs and yellow bill both turn reddish, and it acquires mustard-yellow plumes on crown, back and chest.

Just to confuse novice birdwatchers, the juvenile little blue heron is also white. It is the same size as a snowy egret but has greenish legs and a flesh-colored beak with a dark tip.

At 18 inches, the tiny green heron has a combination of dark green and rufous feathers. An unconscious comedian, the green heron can change its profile dramatically. One moment it

Rookery with nesting Wood Storks and Great Egrets

Cattle Egret, breeding plumage

the nickname "thunder boomer."

At 13 inches, the petite least bittern does nest in Georgia but does not spend the winters here. Its tawny neck and two-toned brown and cream wings distinguish it from the slightly larger green heron. If you drive through a fresh water wetland in the spring, listen carefully for the soft "coo, coo, coo" that lets you know this tiny wader is nearby. It spends much of its time climbing about in the cattails and reeds rather than wading in the shallows like the herons.

The two species of night-heron do most of their active feeding at night, at dawn and at dusk. They are easy to see during the day as they hang out somewhat lethargically in loose groups near ponds or marshes. The adult yellow-crowned night-heron boasts a bold head pattern with white cheek patch, and usually assumes a more vertical posture. The black-crowned night-heron sits hunched horizontally on the branch, showing off a sleek black cap

hunches motionless, alert for the movement of passing prey. Its neck shoots out like a jack-in-the-box to grasp an unfortunate fish. Green herons can be noisy, squawking "skeow, skeow," while erecting a punk-rock head crest.

The two species of bittern take exception to the label "easy to see." The larger of the two, the American bittern is particularly adept at extending its streaked brown neck skyward and freezing motionless among the reeds and cattails of the freshwater marsh that is its preferred habitat. Since this bittern is a winter visitor in the Low Country, it quietly heads north just about the time the other wading birds are fighting for spots in the rookery. Only rarely are we treated to the American bittern's "oonk-a-lunk" call, most often heard at dusk in the spring as it seeks to establish a nesting territory. This strange noise, made by pumping air down its throat, has earned the bird

Little Blue Heron

and startling red eye. The juveniles of both species are brownish with white spotting on the wings. They are difficult to tell apart, even for the experts.

Ibises have unique bills that enable them to feed quite differently from the herons. Ibises often feed in noisy flocks, probing in soft mud or dirt with their long, down-curved bills. As an ibis comes in contact with its prey, the sensitive bill snaps shut to capture the fiddler crab, marine worm, or other tasty invertebrate. The curved, bright red bill and red legs of the adult white ibis are distinctive field marks. Black wing tips are visible when it flies. The juvenile white ibis is mottled brown and white. In poor light the glossy ibis just looks dark. In the sun its feathers shimmer shiny green and crimson, particularly in breeding plumage. It has a brownish bill and dull reddish legs. Both species of ibis often fly in V-formations like geese, with stiff, rapid wing beats and necks extended.

Yellow-crowned Night-Heron

Spoonbills have broad, spatulate bills that they sweep from side to side searching for small fish, shrimp, crabs and aquatic insects. The wonderfully

Great Egret up close

Tricolored Heron

In the Low Country, we are blessed with an amazing variety of long-legged wading birds — herons, egrets, ibises, and even a stork.

White Ibis

exotic roseate spoonbill breeds in Florida in the winter and is showing up more frequently in Georgia and South Carolina, perhaps driven north by development and wetland changes. Mature birds are bright pink. Juveniles are white with a pinkish wash. Imagine scanning a tree full of herons and egrets: "white, white, blue-gray, brown, blue-gray, pink!" That's one reason I like watching birds. There's always a surprise if you keep your eyes and ears open.

The wood stork has a black, leathery-looking head and a heavy, down-curved beak. On land, it is an awkward, homely creature. In flight, with neck fully extended and feet trailing, it soars on the thermals displaying wonderfully patterned black and white wings. Wood storks do not spear their food like herons or egrets. Instead, they wade in shallow water, head down and sensitive bill open. The bill quickly snaps shut when it detects the movement of prey.

Now if only we could get these long-legged birds to line up according to size for a Rockette-style dance number, telling them apart would be a piece of cake. As they kicked and twirled we could compare their feathers, legs and beaks. Between March and July, active rookeries can be found at Harris Neck National Wildlife Refuge, on Skidaway Island, in the ponds near the Savannah airport, at Pinckney Island National Wildlife Refuge, and at the Alligator Farm in St. Augustine, Florida. Certainly, to study these long-legged wading birds in the spring, I would admonish the eager birdwatcher to "Get thee to a rookery."

SUMMER

SUMMER - AN OVERVIEW

Summer in the Low Country is better for birds than for bird watchers. With summer temperatures soaring into the 90s, and plenty of humidity, the savvy bird watcher ventures out early or late, equipped with hat, sunscreen, insect repellent, and plenty of water. The birds are thrilled to have all those bugs to eat, but they can be less than pleasant for humans.

During the summer, you'll find lots of birds feeding babies. These soon turn into awkward teen-agers that can be very entertaining to watch as they try to master all the techniques of surviving on their own.

Eastern Bluebird on nest box

Eastern bluebirds are the "energizer bunnies" of the small songbirds, nesting once, twice and even three times in a season. Some will be feeding babies well into August.

Chimney swifts are late nesters, with many of them hatching during June and July.

Wading bird activity in the rookeries continues well into July as well, with white ibis being notoriously late nesters.

There are certain birds or happenings that warrant braving the summer heat. Beginning in mid-July, Mississippi and swallow-tailed kites begin gathering in post-breeding flocks to feed on insects over freshwater impoundments and newly mown hayfields, mostly in the counties west of I-95. As the day warms up, the birds take advantage of hot air thermals to soar and dive in search of dragonflies, beetles and June bugs. This aerial display is worth the price of admission.

Summer is a good time to find purple gallinules and least bitterns in the freshwater wetlands. If you're lucky, you may see small families of common gallinules and purple gallinules walking about on the water lilies.

On the beaches, most of the shorebirds are gone during June and July, raising their families on the Arctic tundra or in the boreal forests of Canada. Exceptions are American oystercatcher, willet, killdeer and Wilson's plover, all of which remain in the Low Country to nest. Beach activity during this time features laughing gulls, royal terns, sandwich terns, least terns, black skimmers and brown pelicans. There is lots of noisy activity involving fish, both courting mates and feeding young birds.

In August, swallows begin gathering in pre-migratory flocks, hummingbird activity picks up at the feeders, and the first songbirds begin their southward migration. Also in August, shorebirds begin returning from their brief Arctic sojourn.

August also is a good time to find small groups of migrating black terns. By late August, look for Caspian terns to show up on the beach, along with common, Forster's, royal, sandwich, least, and black terns.

CAVITY NESTERS – WILL USE BIRD HOUSES
Carolina Chickadee
Tufted Titmouse
Brown-headed Nuthatch
Carolina Wren
Eastern Bluebird
Prothonotary Warbler
Downy Woodpecker
Red-bellied Woodpecker
Red-headed Woodpecker
Northern Flicker
Pileated Woodpecker
House Sparrow
Eastern Screech-Owl
Great Crested Flycatcher

BUILD NESTS IN SHRUBBERY OR ON BRANCHES
Northern Cardinal
Northern Mockingbird
Brown Thrasher
American Robin
Ruby-throated Hummingbird –
    on branch using lichen
Northern Parula – in Spanish moss
Yellow-throated Warbler –
    in Spanish moss
Blue-gray Gnatcatcher –
    on branch with lichen
Pine Warbler

Carolina Chickadee in birdhouse

Blue Jay
American Crow
Fish Crow
House Finch – sometimes in
    bird house

BUILD NESTS IN SHRUBBERY OR ON BRANCHES (cont'd)

Yellow-billed Cuckoo
Eastern Kingbird
Eastern Wood-Pewee
Summer Tanager
Orchard Oriole
Painted Bunting
Indigo Bunting
Blue Grosbeak
Eastern Towhee – or on ground
Acadian Flycatcher
Hooded Warbler
Swainson's Warbler

Eastern Wood-Pewee

Barn Swallow feeds nestlings

OTHER SUMMER NESTERS

Mississippi Kite – high in tall tree
Swallow-tailed Kite – high in tree near river
Chimney Swift – inside chimneys
Barn Swallow
Northern Rough-winged Swallow
Cliff Swallow
Seaside Sparrow
Clapper Rail
Marsh Wren

FRESHWATER WETLAND NESTERS

Anhinga
Common Gallinule
Purple Gallinule – rare; needs surface vegetation
Boat-tailed Grackle
Red-winged Blackbird
Common Yellowthroat
King Rail
White Ibis
Wood Stork
Tricolored Heron
Great Blue Heron
Little Blue Heron

FRESHWATER WETLAND NESTERS (cont'd)
Great Egret
Snowy Egret
Cattle Egret
Yellow-crowned Night-Heron
Black-crowned Night-Heron
Green Heron
Least Bittern

BEACH NESTERS
Royal Tern
Sandwich Tern
Least Tern – also on flat gravel rooftops
Laughing Gull
Brown Pelican
Black Skimmer
American Oystercatcher
Wilson's Plover
Gull-billed Tern – uncommon

Least Bittern nestlings

GRASS NESTERS
Killdeer – also gravel rooftops, parking lots
Willet*

*There are two sub-species of willet. The eastern sub-species nests in the Low Country and moves south in the winter, to be replaced by the western sub-species which is slightly larger and grayer.

Summer title page features a Purple Gallinule, King Rail and a female Ruby-throated Hummingbird at a Mexican sunflower, pictured top to bottom.

Willet shows its wing stripe

ALL THOSE BEGGING BABIES

*Richard & Becky sitting in a tree,
K - I - S - S - I - N - G.
First comes love, then comes marriage,
Then comes Becky with a baby carriage.*

It's summer in the world of birds. This is the time when the thrill of courtship and mating inevitably gives way to the demanding responsibilities of parenthood. The process of rearing the young, which can take some eighteen years for modern day Americans (cradle to grave insists my Dad), is accomplished by the medium-sized songbirds in a mere eight weeks.

For a bluebird parent, the average cycle looks like this: five days to lay the eggs, two weeks to incubate them, three weeks to tend the nestlings until they *fledge* (leave the nest), then two-plus more weeks of feeding the little critters until they can make it on their own. If all goes according to schedule, week six should bring a plethora of begging babies. The adult-sized juvenile birds trail their parents with gaping mouths. They lower their heads and flutter their wings in an engaging display of pathetic helplessness.

One year my parents added a suet feeder to the arsenal adorning their

Brown Thrasher fledgling

back deck. They were amazed by the constant parade of birds taking advantage of this high-energy fast food. Woodpeckers, brown thrashers, mockingbirds, wrens, titmice, chickadees, and even warblers attacked the rendered beef fat cakes. An unanticipated bonus was that the parents began bringing the fledglings to the feeder to teach them to feed themselves. I was entranced to see a young woodpecker flop awkwardly atop the feeder cage, wings spread like a butterfly. Haltingly he got his footing and found his way through the wire cage to the tasty treat within. That he could now secure food on his own did not, however, prevent him from begging.

Red-bellied Woodpecker nestling

Orphaned Carolina Chickadee nestlings

While there are no car pools to drive or college tuitions to save for, the process of raising a baby bird is certainly no piece of cake. I walked into work at Wild Birds Unlimited one Friday morning to find my co-worker Nicole and a couple of our long-time customers hunched over a box of squawking baby bluebirds. The customers had been monitoring their bluebird box and got worried when Mama & Papa didn't show up to feed the four hungry chicks. They brought the birds to the shop for advice. Nicole spent the rest of that day feeding those birds every half-hour with mealworms and a specially concocted smelly brown formula containing dried cat food, baby food, powdered egg white, and avian vitamins. In addition to feeding, there was nest tissue to change. This routine continued non-stop from dawn to dusk.

I confess that while I have spent a lot of time in the field watching birds, tending babies or injured birds just isn't my thing. Thanks to the efforts of licensed bird rehabilitator Pat Wolters, I've gotten an education. Pat has shared knowledge she acquired during 13 years as a volunteer at Tri-State Bird Rescue and Research in Delaware.

Here are a few of Pat's guidelines for dealing with baby birds:

1. If a bird has been rescued from a cat, the bird will need to see a vet immediately and be given antibiotics since cats' mouths are full of bacteria.

2. If possible, return a fallen nestling to its nest. It is a myth that parents will reject the baby bird if a human has touched it.

3. A fully feathered bird hopping about on the ground is a fledgling and is supposed to be out of the nest. Watch carefully before rushing to the rescue as there is often a parent nearby tending the teen-ager. If it is in danger from a

Northern Mockingbird nestling begs

predator, you may be able to place the bird up high in a basket that the parents can access.

4. If rescue is called for, make a temporary nest for the bird by lining a plastic container with folded paper towels. This can be covered with facial tissues that are easily replaced. Place the "nest"

Northern Mockingbird fledgling

in a ventilated box with a heating pad set on low for warmth. Offer water with a small paintbrush rather than an eyedropper. For emergency rations, combine canned dog food, crumbled up egg yolk, and applesauce, and blend well. This can be offered with the paintbrush or a one cc syringe sans needle. Clip the tip of the syringe to enlarge if necessary.

5. Call a nearby vet or bird clinic for a referral to a skilled bird rehabilitator.

6. Consider making a monetary contribution to whomever will be caring for the bird. Most rehabbers do this work out of love and don't get paid for it.

The process of rearing their young is accomplished by the medium-sized songbirds in a mere eight weeks.

Now, as I watch the male red-bellied woodpecker break off a piece of suet and carry it to the noisy juveniles clinging to the tree trunk, I can really appreciate what it takes to care for all those begging babies!

Carolina Wren family eats mealworms

ALL HAIL THE BROWN THRASHER

I've always been fond of brown thrashers. They aren't flashy dressers like cardinals, bluebirds, or painted buntings. Their rusty brown plumage is modest, perfect for keeping a low profile and blending into the leaf litter. Their long tails, sharp down-curved bills, and startling yellow eyes do lend the Georgia state bird an air of understated elegance.

Brown Thrasher on birdbath

During most of the year brown thrashers spend their time skulking in the underbrush or thrashing in the leaf litter in search of insects. While they also enjoy berries and acorns, they don't turn into berry bullies like their aggressive cousins, the northern mockingbirds. They do occasionally visit bird feeders, preferring suet, raisins, or peanuts.

Only in the spring does Mr. Brown take to the treetops, courting his lady fair with a tireless outpouring of burry couplets. Once he has won her heart, he doesn't rush off in search of other conquests but stays around to build the nest, sit on the eggs, and help with the kids.

The brown thrasher also enjoys a reputation as being a friend of the farmer. Besides dining on potentially harmful grasshoppers, caterpillars, beetles, and worms, brown thrashers can be heard to offer a stream of advice on when to "drop it, drop it, cover it, cover it, pull it up, pull it up."

Brown thrashers may squabble fiercely among themselves over territories or mates, but if one bird sounds the alarm with a loud "tchuck, tchuck," all quarrels are forgotten as they quickly band together to chase off the common enemy.

John James Audubon, in his *Birds of America*, speaks admiringly of the rust-colored mimic that he refers to as the "ferruginous mockingbird." He praises the brown thrasher for its vocal abilities.

No sooner has the bird reached its destined abode than whenever a fair morning occurs, it mounts the topmost twig of a detached tree, and pours forth

Brown Thrasher sings to woo mate

Brown Thrasher fledgling

its loud, richly varied, and highly melodious song.

Professor Donald Kroodsma, author of *The Singing Life of Birds*, devoted an entire chapter to the brown thrasher. As I read, I realized that my listening skills were rudimentary. I hear a series of burry couplets coming from the top of tree, think to myself "brown thrasher," and stop listening. Professor Kroodsma tells of rising well before dawn to await the day's first thrasher serenade. For nearly two hours he listened and listened, using a parabolic microphone and a tape recorder to capture 4654 distinct couplets.

Back in the lab, using a high tech "continuous spectrum analyzer," he calculated that a brown thrasher has more than 2000 different songs. Why so many? Presumably they do it to impress the ladies. Female brown thrashers grant their favors to the winner of the neighborhood vocal competition.

Brown thrashers don't just sing. They also fight. Discussing the brown thrasher's fierceness, Audubon writes, *The Brown or Ferruginous Thrush is the strongest of the genus in the United States, neither the Mockingbird nor the Robin being able to cope with it. Like the former, it will chase the cat or the dog, and greatly teas the raccoon or the fox. I follows the Astur Cooperii and the Goshawk, bidding them defiance, and*

During most of the year, brown thrashers spend their time skulking in the underbrush or thrashing in the leaf litter in search of insects.

Brown Thrasher blends into the leaf litter

Brown Thrasher sings on wire

few snakes come off with success when they attack its nest.

I was glancing idly about the yard one year in mid-June, when I noticed a brown thrasher scratching about in the dirt in front of the birdbath. I expected to see it grab a juicy insect. Instead, it gathered two twigs and a dry leaf in its bill and flew off to the other side of the driveway.

"Ah, hah!" I thought to myself. "Nesting... Round Two."

I followed the bird in the direction it had flown and gazed up into the tangle of oak and red bay leaves. There, about five feet above my head was a large, bulky nest made mostly of twigs. It's one thing to read these details in a book, quite another to see them in real life. As I watched, first one, then a second brown thrasher flew in carrying small sticks and dry leaves. My observations confirmed what the books report. Both Ma and Pa Thrasher work together to build the nest, probably their second one this season.

The brown thrasher's road to renown as Georgia's state bird was not without drama. In 1928, the school children of Georgia, at the instigation of the Fifth District of the State Federation of Women's Clubs, campaigned for the brown thrasher to be named Georgia's avian symbol. Groups such as the Atlanta Bird Club came to their aid. No action was taken until April 6, 1935, when Governor Eugene Talmadge declared the brown thrasher to be Georgia's state bird.

That should have been that, but the state Attorney General issued an official opinion that the designation of state symbols should be a legislative power. Thus, 35 years later, on March 20, 1970, Joint Resolution 128 was passed. *Toxostoma rufum*, the "reddish bow mouth" with the down-curved bill, yellow eyes, and as many tunes to croon as Johnny Mercer, assumed its position as Georgia's official, feathered ambassador.

Brown Thrasher nest built of sticks

Mud Hens & Swamp Chickens

When it comes to identifying birds, the old adage that a picture is worth a thousand words holds true with a vengeance. In my role as "bird expert," I have puzzled over a multitude of verbal descriptions of birds that leave me shaking my head and longing for the simple eloquence of a photograph.

I was nearly stumped recently by a reader's account of a bird she had seen while on a June visit to the Savannah National Wildlife Refuge. The bird in question was "blue like a parrot with a little red beak." I imagined some exotic escapee perched in a tree while its owner mourned its loss.

"Where did you see this bird?" I queried.

"Poking around in the marsh grass and the water lilies," came the reply.

"A parrot in the marsh?" Dubious, I tried to come up with some better

Purple Gallinule, juvenile

questions. "Was it bigger than a robin? What shape was the beak?"

I might still be pondering if my mother, listening from the kitchen, hadn't chimed in with "purple gallinule."

I have never thought of the chicken-like gallinule – derived from the Latin for *little hen* – as resembling a parrot. With its iridescent bluish-purple head, greenish back, long yellow legs, and bright red bill tipped in yellow, it does evoke faraway places and tropical

Purple Gallinule on water lilies

American Coot eating vegetation

times. Certainly it is well known throughout the Caribbean islands and much of South America where it spends the winter. Here in the Low Country we start scanning the freshwater marshes for purple gallinules in early April – about the same time that colorful painted buntings begin visiting area feeders to snack on white millet.

Throughout most of the year, the marshes are home to the purple gallinule's less exotic cousins, the common gallinule and the American coot. All three species are members of the rail family. All have been likened to chickens, with nicknames such as "mud hen," "rice hen," or "blue peter." Their manner of keeping their heads still while moving their bodies allows them to see better but makes them look like aquatic pigeons.

The coot and the common gallinule are drab compared to their tropical cousin. Coots are black with a white bill and greenish legs. Common gallinules are black and brown with an orange bill tipped in yellow that reminds me of Halloween candy corn. Coots and both gallinules have a habit of flicking their short tails to display their snowy white "undergarments," with the coot having the least white and the purple gallinule the most.

Often these birds are mistaken for ducks. However, a close look at their feet will reveal amazingly long toes with no connective webbing between the toes. These feet allow them to wander across the lily pads and aquatic vegetation, practically walking on water. The coot is unique in having broad, lobed toes that make it a better swimmer than the gallinules.

All three species are confirmed omnivores with versatile dining habits that aid their survival. Equally happy while swimming, walking or clambering about in the reeds, they dine on plant seeds and stems, berries and fruit, as well as on insects, frogs, snails, spiders, worms and fish.

Shortly after the purple gallinules arrive here in the spring, the coots say sayonara and head for more northerly ponds and marshes to raise their offspring. Locally, common gallinules and purple gallinules settle in to the task of building platform nests concealed by dense marsh grass.

A special treat throughout the summer is the sight of small, blackish puffballs with comically large feet trailing their head-bobbing parents. The young can swim almost immediately after hatching, but are fed for three to six

Common Gallinule shows off long toes

Common Gallinule with two chicks

weeks by both mother and father. Juveniles often hang around to help their parents with subsequent broods.

What I enjoy most about these birds is listening to them. They are remarkably vocal – chattering among each other with an extensive repertoire of nasal clucks, whistles, and grunts. To my ears, the coot always seems to whine, complaining to anyone who will listen that life just isn't fair. The common gallinule plays the nag. As the petulant notes drift out from the tall clumps of marsh grass, I can just imagine the wayward chicks being admonished to clean their nests or eat their vegetables.

To enjoy the sights and sounds of these natural entertainers, I suggest an early morning or late afternoon summer visit to a fresh-water wetland. Who knows? You might catch a glimpse of a "mud hen," a "swamp chicken," or a bird that is "blue like a parrot with a little red beak."

HOW MUCH WOOD COULD A WOODPECKER PECK?

"Rat-tat-tat-tat-tat! Rat-tat-tat-tat-tat!" The sound comes explosively at dawn, right above my head, like a machine gun. It's those woodpeckers again! Don't they know there are no ants in a metal chimney? I try to settle back to sleep but the drumming continues.

Oh, right. Now I remember. This is not the slightly uneven pecking which signals the probing hunt for tasty morsels in a tree trunk. It's the mating game, where boy woodpecker attempts to impress girl woodpecker and warn off other boy woodpeckers by making the most noise. It's a fascinating courtship ritual, except when the prime drumming surface happens to be on my roof. Oh well, I really do like woodpeckers, even when they are masquerading as alarm clocks.

The woodpecker family has 22 North American species, all but five of which are mostly red, white and black.

Their short legs, with two backward reaching toes, help them grasp branches and tree trunks. Extra-stiff tail feathers serve as supports for their vertical clinging. Thick chisel-like beaks are perfect for excavating for bugs or drilling out nest cavities, and their long, forked, sticky tongues don't give the insects much of a chance.

Eight of the 22 species spend time in the Low Country. They vary in size

Downy Woodpecker, female

Pileated Woodpecker, female

from the petite (6 3/4") downy woodpecker to the statuesque (16 1/2") pileated woodpecker. Of the eight species, all but one, the Northern flicker, adhere to the red, white and black color scheme.

Three of the eight species – red-headed, red-bellied and downy – are regular feeder visitors, coming for sunflower seed, peanuts and suet. The showy red-headed woodpecker always looks like it is dressed for a fancy dinner party with completely red head, black upper wings, and striking white belly, rump, and wing feathers. It has a reputation for being a bully and chasing other birds off the feeders.

The highly vocal red-bellied woodpecker is a candidate for "Most Poorly Named Bird." The male has a brilliant red cap extending from the top of his beak to the nape of his neck. The red on the female extends only from the back of the head to the nape of the neck, and juvenile red-bellied woodpeckers have only a hint of red on their heads. If you see the male bird during

Red-headed Woodpecker

Red-bellied Woodpecker, male

wonderful pattern of black and white stripes and spots. A small red accent at the back of the head distinguishes the male of each species. The smaller downy is feeder-friendly and seems to enjoy a suburban environment, while the hairy favors mature forest.

A winter visitor to Georgia, the yellow-bellied sapsucker leaves a distinctive calling card: neatly spaced row of holes in tree trunks from which it extracts sap. It also dines on berries and the insects that are attracted to the oozing sap. Other creatures – warblers, hummingbirds, squirrels and more – also feast at sapsucker holes.

The elusive red-cockaded woodpecker has pecked its way onto the endangered species list by virtue of its preference for mature pine forest, preferably longleaf. As these forests have been logged and replaced by the faster growing slash and loblolly pine, the populations of this once fairly common woodpecker have shrunk.

breeding season you may note a wash of pinkish red on its belly. Woodpeckers, however, spend much of their time with their bellies hidden against tree trunks.

Downy and hairy woodpeckers are almost identical except for size, bill length, and call. Their backs have a

The predominantly brown northern flicker, formerly called "yellow-shafted,"

Pileated Woodpecker, young male

…as a red "V" on the back of its neck and
…ashes beautiful yellow underwings when
… flies. Flickers often spend time on the
…round, as they are extremely fond of ants.

The pileated woodpecker, with its
…npressive size, bushy red crest and
…aniacal, laughing call brings to mind
…he cartoon "Woody Woodpecker" of
…ld. Pileated woodpeckers are very
…ond of ants, particularly carpenter
…nts. They also dine on beetle larvae,
…ermites, wild fruits, berries, and nuts.

One day, my mother heard what
…ounded like someone pounding on
…he house with a baseball bat. To her
…ismay, she found a pileated excavating
… trench on a board of the house.

It is hard to truly appreciate wildlife
… it is damaging your property. If
…ou're having woodpecker problems,
…ere are four questions to consider.

- Are there insects in the wood? The woodpecker may be alerting you to an ant or termite problem.
- Can you prevent the bird from getting to the problem area? Covering the area temporarily may help.
- Can you repel the bird with visual, sound or chemical repellents? Try rock music or foil streamers.
- Can you remove the birds safely? Contact a company that specializes in animal removal.

I gained an even greater appreciation
…r woodpeckers while traveling in
…ustralia. Australia boasts an amazing
…riety of parrots, electric blue fairy
…ens, and fabulous laughing kookabur-
…s, but there are no woodpeckers. They
…em to get along without them, but I
…d woodpeckers a unique and fasci-
…ting addition to the Low Country
…d kingdom.

Northern Flicker, male

*Rat-tat-tat-tat-tat!
It's the mating game.
Boy woodpecker
attempts to impress
girl woodpecker and
warn off other boy
woodpeckers by making
the most noise.*

Yellow-bellied Sapsucker, male

It's a Stick! It's a Snake! It's a BIRD??

You're out for your usual two laps around the lake when out of the corner of your eye you see movement in the water. Something that looks like a stick extends about 18 inches above the surface, pointed at the sky. You pause, curious, as this object begins to move sinuously through the water like a vertical snake.

As you watch, the upper, pointed end of the "stick" vanishes below the water, and then emerges grasping a wriggling fish. In a neat juggling act, it tosses the fish several times until it is lined up head facing down. The "stick" beak opens and engulfs the fish, a wriggling bulge betraying its progress down what has been revealed to be a neck.

The sinewy neck now approaches a low hanging tree limb where it drags its body out of the water, grasps the branch with webbed feet, and teeters back and forth. Once secure, it spreads its wings revealing its true avian nature.

Congratulations! You have just witnessed the behavior that gives the

Anhinga as "snakebird"

anhinga its nickname – the "snakebird".

The anhinga, like its close relative the cormorant, perches dramatically with outstretched wings for a highly practical reason. Biologists once thought that these birds did not have enough oil on their feathers. They since have

Female Anhinga dries her wings

Female Anhinga has a tan neck

...arned that the degree of waterproofing ...feathers is related to their microscopic ...ructure. Anhinga and cormorant ...athers are structured for less buoyancy. ...his is great for effortless underwater ...imming, but creates major problems ...en it comes time to fly. After 20 or ...minutes of fishing, the birds must ...ng themselves out to dry.

If you are in a saltwater habitat and ...e a bird with outspread wings, it is ...most certainly a cormorant. The ...hinga generally sticks to sub-tropical ...d tropical freshwater swamps and ...tlands where, to make things compli-...ed, the cormorant can also be found.

If you are struggling to tell the two ...art, look first at the beak. The anhinga ...s a long, straight, spear-like beak, ...rfectly suited for impaling fish. It ...s another of its names, the darter, ...m the way it feeds by prowling ...derwater, peering from side to side. ...nen it spies its prey, the snake-like ...:k "darts" forward and the sharp beak spears the fish.

Cormorant beaks are shorter with a distinct downward hook at the tip. Cormorants have yellowish skin around the eyes and below the beak.

When the anhinga spreads its wings to dry or extends them in flight, look for the white pattern that spreads like a cape on the forewings. The cormorant's wings are all black.

After initial awkwardness on take-off, anhingas are elegant flyers. With long slender neck and tail extended, they flap and soar, looking like a flying cross while gliding effortlessly on the mid-day thermals. Cormorants don't have the luxury of soaring. Like ducks and geese, they just have to keep on flapping. Cormorants also migrate in large V-shaped formations.

You can tell male and female anhingas apart by their neck color. The male anhinga has an all black neck while the female has a tan neck with feathers so fine and soft they resemble fur.

When spring arrives, male anhingas dress up for the ladies. The skin around

Male Anhinga spreads his wings

Double-crested Cormorant

with other herons, egrets, and ibises. Both parents incubate the eggs for almost a month. The chicks, when they hatch, are a creamy white. As they grow, they develop yellowish necks and dark wings.

We are fortunate to have nesting anhingas at three of our nearby wildlife refuges – Savannah, Pinckney Island and Harris Neck, as well at many of the area freshwater ponds and lagoons. A visit to any of these sites should give you the opportunity to get better acquainted with the marvelous "snakebird."

Anhingas in flight

their eyes turns a bright turquoise. After setting up a nest of loose sticks, the male begins his display by raising his neck feathers like a punk rock star. He spreads and raises one wing, then the other to show off their silvery patches, following this with a deep bow. If the female is interested, she may bow in return, and the two birds may twine their necks together.

The birds nest in loose colonies, often

CHIMNEY SWIFTS TAKE LIFE ON THE WING

I went to church in downtown Savannah one Sunday morning and heard a noisy, high-pitched chittering that drew my eyes skyward. Overhead, half a dozen stubby black birds with crescent-shaped wings were zooming about in a dizzying aerial display.

"Ah." I smiled to myself. "Chimney swifts!"

These tiny, fast-moving "cigars with wings" were once thought to be related to swallows, and were dubbed "swift swallows," reaching speeds of close to 100 miles an hour. Now they are in a class by themselves with their closest relative considered to be the hummingbird. Both swifts and hummingbirds have a similar wing configuration with a very short *humerus* (the inner wing bone) and elongated outer wing. This enables them to do the fast flapping

Chimney Swift - a "cigar with wings"

A basket full of orphaned Chimney Swift babies

essential to their survival.

Swifts spend almost all their time in the air. They eat, drink, gather nest material, court, sometimes mate, and reputedly even occasionally sleep on the wing. Their long, saber-like wings are either fully extended in flight or folded back at rest. They are never bent at the "elbow."

Chimney swifts haven't yet developed the devoted following enjoyed by the larger, luminously iridescent purple martins, but both species arrive in North America each spring with exactly the same mission: to eat bugs and reproduce. While both martins and swifts are voracious insect eaters, it seems that martins have gotten all the good press, perhaps because they are more user-friendly. During all the years I have worked at Wild Birds Unlimited, not once has anyone walked into the shop asking how they could attract chimney swifts.

The difference in popularity may all come down to their feet. Swifts are members of the family *apodidae* which comes from the Greek *a*, "without," *pus*, "foot." This name is misleading. Swifts definitely have feet; they just don't use them for standing or perching. Their four forward-facing toes are equipped with sharp, pointy claws and function like grappling hooks, allowing the birds to cling to rough vertical surfaces.

While purple martins nest colonially in houses and gourds, and can perch out in the open where humans can see them, swifts take the single-family approach, locating a solitary nest inside a hollow tree or chimney. They build a shallow, half-saucer-shaped nest out of twigs and feathers, and secure it to a vertical surface with their sticky saliva. The nest is usually located well down inside the structure to protect the babies from direct sun and rain. The female will lay three to six eggs that both parents tend for the 19-21 days it takes the babies to hatch. Hungry nestlings make a real racket, enabling the parents to find them in the dark. Fledging time, which comes after about 28 days, is the most perilous time for young swifts. If they survive that, they are likely to enjoy relatively long lives – up to as many as twenty years.

> *These tiny, fast-moving "cigars with wings" were once thought to be related to swallows, and were dubbed "swift swallows," reaching speeds of close to 100 miles an hour.*

Chimney Swift nestlings in an improvised nest

126

Chimney Swifts cling rather than perch

During early summer rainstorms, it is not uncommon for chimney swift nests to fall down the chimney. After such storms, bird rehabilitators are besieged with calls. One creative individual used a washcloth to create a soft nest for the babies on the floor of her fireplace. She watched in amazement as the parent birds came all the way down the chimney to feed their babies. She kept the fireplace screen closed so the birds wouldn't escape into the house, but she could tell by the noise when the babies were being fed. Eventually, the young swifts followed their parents up the chimney and out to freedom.

In previous centuries, chimney swifts adapted to the decrease in hollow tree cavities, mostly because as people cut down trees, they built houses with chimneys. Now, however, with older structures being torn down, new homes being built with metal flue pipes, and more homeowners capping their chimneys, the swifts are facing a housing shortage. In Texas, the Driftwood Wildlife Association has started the North American Chimney Swift Nest Site Research Project. They have prepared a handout which is available online at http://www.chimneyswifts.org. They advise cleaning a chimney once a year in early March to prevent creosote build up, which can lead to fires. This will also give the swifts a better surface on which to anchor their nests. Fireplace dampers should be closed during nesting season to prevent birds from accidentally flying into the house. If the fireplace is old and lacks a damper, a large piece of foam rubber – not fiberglass insulation – can be wedged up from the fireplace to serve the same purpose.

The brochure also provides plans for constructing a chimney swift nesting tower. If your backyard habitat has too many trees to attract martins and you want active, insect-eating birds around, chimney swifts may be just the ticket.

After nesting is completed, usually in August, chimney swifts abandon their solitary ways and gather communally in pre-migration roosts. The sight of hundreds of birds entering an old chimney at dusk, or emerging at dawn is quite a spectacle.

By mid-October, most of the swifts will be well on their way to the tropical lowland forests of Amazonian Peru, leaving our urban skies oddly empty. So make sure, when you're cruising around city streets in the summer, to look up and listen. The chirping, twittering, swooping, zooming, chimney swift symphony is playing for a limited time only. Don't miss it!

THE MARVELOUS TALE OF THE CLAPPER RAIL

Imagine the coast of Georgia and South Carolina – a mere 200 miles from top to bottom – lined with barrier islands and buffered by salt marsh. In fact, the Low Country boasts a full 30 percent of all the salt marsh on the East Coast. Living near the marsh, I have been able to get well acquainted with a bird more often heard than seen, the clapper rail, or "marsh hen."

If I could nominate a bird to be the "voice of the salt marsh," it would be the clapper rail. I love to hear its descending, grunting cackle. First one bird will call, followed almost immediately by another, and then another, until the rail chorus echoes along the length of the marsh.

It can be frustrating to hear the rails and not see them. However, knowing their habits makes a difference. Their activities are governed by the rise and fall of the tide. At low tide, when the mud flats are exposed, the clapper rail wanders the marsh in search of food. With its long, heavy, yellow-orange bill it pokes and probes for small crabs, mollusks, worms, and insects.

Another favorite low tide activity is bathing. The rail ventures hesitantly down to the edge of the water to immerse itself with a series of dips and splashes – rocking forward to plunge its head underwater, then surfacing to

> *At low tide, when the mud flats are exposed, the clapper rail or "marsh hen" wanders the marsh in search of fiddler crabs, mollusks, worms, and insects.*

Clapper Rail bathing

vigorously shake its entire body. Any sudden movement or sound will send it scurrying back to the safety of the marsh grass, to emerge, when the coast is clear, to complete its almost ritual ablutions.

Once bathing is complete, the clapper rail proceeds to grooming and preening. This is carried out with great thoroughness, often while perched atop a platform of dead marsh grass (scientifically termed *detritus*). Its drab, buffy brown colors serve as excellent camouflage against the backdrop of mud or dead reeds.

High tides, particularly in spring and fall, present special challenges for clapper rails. In the spring, the rails build their nests out of dead marsh grass, instinctively locating them in the taller grass above the high tide line. They join together a few strands of green marsh grass over the top, making a loose canopy that attempts to conceal the nest. A full or new moon high tide can wash away the nest or float it to the surface where

Clapper Rail preens

it is vulnerable to predators.

One spring, I looked out over a tide-covered marsh and saw a huddled lump on a raft of floating detritus. Through my binoculars, the lump became a clapper rail. I watched it prod at something beneath its body. As I stared, now with my spotting scope, a boat-tailed grackle approached the rail and began to peck at it. The rail stood and used her heavy bill to fend off the attacker. On the spot where she had been sitting was a mass of downy fluff balls. I counted five black chicks before she returned to settle on top of them, prodding until all were safely concealed under her feathers.

Fall high tides bring a different danger. The legal hunting season for clapper rails runs from early September to mid-November, with a 15 per day limit per person. Again, the extra high tides are the favored hunting times. Hunters head for the small remaining patches of exposed marsh where they are able to close in on the marsh hens and flush them at close range. The

Clapper Rail pair in the marsh

clapper rail's flight pattern is slow, relatively weak, and direct, making it an easy target.

When John James Audubon was studying birds in the 1840s, collecting clapper rail eggs was common practice. He bragged of having picked up 72 dozen (864) eggs in a single day. Audubon also described encountering two clapper rails at every eight to ten steps while traversing the salt marsh. Both egg collecting and hunting contributed to a noticeable decline in the clapper rail population. Fortunately for the rails, egging has been banned, and hunting is now closely regulated.

The six species of North American rail – clapper, king, sora, Virginia, yellow, and black – enjoy a special mystique among bird watchers, perhaps due to their ability to call tantalizingly from the middle of a boggy marsh. They can vanish, "thin as a rail," between the stalks of marsh grass. Black and yellow rails are two of the most secretive and

Clapper Rail dines on fiddler crab

highly sought after birds in North America. King and Virginia rails, as well as the diminutive sora, can be regularly found in the Low Country, primarily in freshwater marshes.

Clapper rails are sometimes found in brackish marsh but are most faithful to salt. I welcome their continued presence and marvel anew each time I am lucky enough to hear their cackles or glimpse them going unconcernedly about their daily rail routines.

"Marsh Hen" hunting

A Visit to the Breakfast Club

If you drive down Tybee Island's main drag, Butler Avenue, on a Saturday or Sunday morning in June, July or August, you're likely to encounter a long line of people snaking along the sidewalk at the corner of 15th Street. Stopping to inquire, you discover that these are hungry folks, waiting to be seated at one of Tybee's most popular eateries – The Breakfast Club. Residents and tourists alike are salivating over visions of seafood omelets, shrimp and grits, or tasty fish sandwiches.

If, however, you happen to find your way to Catalina Drive on nearby Spanish Hammock, you may encounter quite a different gang of eager diners. On certain mid-summer mornings, the branches of several dead trees are crowded with an astonishing assortment of long-legged birds, waiting patiently for the tide to ebb. Although

Diners wait at The Breakfast Club

these patrons, too, are dreaming of shrimp and fish, they don't need to don shirt and shoes for service. There's no waitress serving coffee, and best of all, the food is free for the taking.

While The Breakfast Club remains firmly fixed at its 15th Street location, the bird buffet is a moveable feast. Word spreads fast as to where to find that day's best eating. One morning, the small, wet area just north of the Chimney Creek Bridge holds fifteen snowy egrets, three tricolored herons, four green herons, six boat-tailed grackles, and a clapper rail.

The next day, most of the action has moved to a small wetland area across the road and closer to Highway 80. While snowy egrets fly back and forth dragging their yellow feet across the water's surface, eight wood storks stride through the tide pool swishing their ponderous beaks back and forth. Great egrets stand motionless at the water's edge, occasionally lunging with snake-like necks to grasp tasty tidbits with their yellow bills. Male and female boat-tailed grackles lurk in the marsh grass at the edge of the water, picking

Birds wait for "Club" to open

at something in the mud.

Occasionally, a celebrity is spotted mingling with the locals. Word buzzes along the line on 15th Street. Someone thinks they may have glimpsed Sandra Bulloch.

Back at the tidal pool, I spy something pink. Quickly I grab my cell phone to spread the word that a roseate spoonbill has joined the club.

Snowy Egret with minnow

Roseate Spoonbill

Why are they all here? What's the big attraction? Just what is it that they're eating? Searching for answers, I grab John and Mildred Teal's classic *Life and Death of a Salt Marsh*, first published in 1969. In the chapter about marsh animals I find part of the answer: minnows.

Although I've watched schools of minnows dart about the creek for years and years, it never occurred to me to wonder about their role in the scheme of things. Saltmarsh minnows come in a variety of flavors. There are mummichogs, killifish, sheepshead minnows, and Atlantic silversides, just to name a few. These tiny fish enter the creeks and tidal pools on a flooding tide with empty stomachs. Their ideal breakfast consists of hearty helpings of detritus, algae, amphipods, insects, and (joy of joys!) mosquito larvae.

Mummichogs, commonly called

The Birds' Breakfast Club

Snowy Egret drags its feet

Snowy egrets fly back and forth dragging their yellow feet across the water's surface, while wood storks stride through the tide pool swishing their ponderous beaks back and forth, and great egrets stand motionless at the water's edge.

Wood Stork feeding

"mummies" or "mud minnows" get their name from a Native American word which means "going in crowds." They have an unusual resistance to low oxygen conditions and spend most of the winter buried under six to eight inches of mud. They emerge in the spring, ready to eat and mate.

Spawning generally takes place at night during a high water spring tide. Female mud minnows lay from ten to three hundred eggs that usually hatch two weeks later when high water again reaches them. Six to eight weeks later, in June and July, just when the rookeries are full of young birds, the tidal pools are conveniently full of wriggling baby minnows. As the tide goes out, large numbers of fish are concentrated in a smaller amount of water, creating wading bird bonanza.

It appears that mummichogs are to wading birds what insects are to songbirds, and horseshoe crab eggs are to shore birds – delectable staples of the bird buffet, as well as essential strands in the delicate and complex Low Country web of life.

Why Do Hummingbirds Hum?

"Why do hummingbirds hum? Because they can't remember the words." The old joke came unbidden as I began to reflect on these tiny, winged wonders.

I must confess that for most of the spring and early summer, I am guilty of hummingbird envy. When friends report on the fifteen to twenty hummingbirds that zoom around their yards, slurping up the nectar from multiple feeders, I gaze mournfully at the wasps buzzing about my two bare feeders. In April, I had three or four hummingbirds stop by, but since then there has been no activity. For almost three months I have changed my sugar water (correct ratio: one part sugar to four parts water) every three to five days, and tried not to lose hope.

Finally, in late July, while I sat working at my computer, a hummingbird magically appeared. Since then, I have seen several birds on an almost

Ruby-throated Hummingbird, male

daily basis. The birds I see have greenish backs, white bellies, and no ruby throats. Since, of the more than 300 species of hummingbird in the Americas, only the ruby-throated nests in the Low Country, these are most likely female or juvenile male ruby-throateds. The juvenile male often has some streaking or a few red feathers on his throat.

If you are lucky enough to have hummingbirds nesting near you, you may be treated to their courtship displays. It is primarily the male who courts. He flies back and forth in a broad, U-shaped pendulum arc. His wingbeats, normally 50-80 per minute, can increase to a blurring 200 per minute as he makes his dives. He may also fly back and forth in front of a perched female. If the female is impressed with his performance, they mate. The female carries out the remainder of the process alone. She builds the nest out of plant fibers and lichens, held together with spider silk and lays (as a rule) two white eggs. Alone, she incubates them for eleven to sixteen days, and then feeds the young by herself for twenty days before they

Ruby-throated Hummingbird, female

Ruby-throated Hummingbird, female, at Bottlebrush

fledge. While she is busy gathering nectar and small insects that she regurgitates to feed the babies, the male hummingbird continues to display on his territory, hoping to attract another female. Does he have the life or what?

In late summer when the hummingbirds have finished nesting, preparations begin for the long flight south. Those that have nested in the northern United States or southern Canada will travel 1000 miles to the southern United States, and then another 500 to 1000 miles to reach their winter homes in Central or South America or the Caribbean Islands. Many of these birds stop off in the Low Country to chow down and bulk up. After adding an extra 35-70 percent to their body mass, fall hummingbirds look positively portly compared to their breeding season counterparts!

Although the ruby-throated hummingbird is the only one to nest in the Low Country, it is not the only one to visit here. One year, on August 18th, an adult male rufous hummingbird had already found his way to a feeder in southwest Georgia. Twelve different hummingbird species have now been reported wintering in Georgia and South Carolina, including green violet-ear, green-breasted mango, broad-billed, buff-bellied, magnificent, black-chinned, Anna's, calliope, broad-tailed, rufous, Allen's and ruby-throated. All except the ruby-throated nest in the western United States and Mexico, and for some unknown reason come east for the winter.

Many people are concerned that if they leave their feeders up in the fall,

> *Of the more than 300 species of hummingbird in the Americas, only the ruby-throated nests in the Low Country.*

the hummingbirds won't know when to leave. Hummingbird experts Bob and Martha Sargent assure us that it is not the presence or absence of feeders which determines migration, but the shortening of the days and the decrease in the amount of light.

Amazingly, hummingbirds can cope with even extremely cold temperatures. They slow their heartbeat and breathing, lower their body temperature, and enter a state of torpor, seeming practically comatose.

So, I can only hope that each of you gets your daily dose of humming-

Rufous Hummingbird, female

birds. For me, a hummingbird a day keeps depression at bay. Happy humming!

Let's Go Spy a Kite

Bird sightings have always been a worthy topic of conversation in my family. What was seen where by whom gets airtime – even long distance airtime. In some families the conversation default is set to the weather. In ours, it's set for birds.

My brother stopped to report by cell phone on the bald eagle perched atop a telephone pole. My mom called me to report the pileated woodpecker excavating in her house. I called her to report the summer tanager in my birdbath.

When I lived in Massachusetts, my parents began to report by phone each spring, "the kites are back."

"Kites?" the uninitiated may puzzle. Do they mean colorful shapes on strings flapping in the breeze? When did they leave? Why would they come back?

The kites in question are, of course, birds. The steely gray Mississippi kites and their showy cousins, the swallow-tailed kites, make their way up from Central and South America to nest in loose colonies. A type of raptor, the kites get their name from the way they swoop and dive, "kiting" for insects on the wing. Or perhaps the toy kite was

Mississippi Kite, juvenile

AUGUST

named for the bird? Who knows? One year the call came from my sister-in-law.

"I'm at my parents' house, and there are these birds. There must be five of them flying around and they're big – like baby eagles. They have whitish heads, gray backs, and pointy wings. And they make this noise. It's hard to describe. Something like 'whee-wheeeeeee.'"

That clinched it.

"Congratulations!" I said. "You've found the kites!"

While the Mississippi kite can be tricky to identify, the swallow-tailed kite is unmistakable. With its white head and underparts, black outer wing feathers, and long, deeply forked black tail, this bird makes a strikingly dramatic avian statement. Its aerial acrobatics can captivate even someone who claims to be "ho-hum" about birds.

Both kites list coastal Georgia and South Carolina as "destinations of choice." Swallow-tailed kites prefer to build their comparatively skimpy stick nests at the top of 60 to 100 foot trees. Here in the Low Country, the tree of choice is the loblolly pine – generally located in bottomland forest adjacent to a river such as the Altamaha, Ogeechee, Savannah, or Satilla. They line the nest with Spanish moss and lay one to three creamy white eggs. Kites are sociable creatures and often nest in clusters.

The Mississippi kites are more acclimated to people and civilization. A nice suburban neighborhood with a good selection of tall pine trees suits

> *The steely gray Mississippi kites and their showy cousins, the swallow-tailed kites, make their way up from Central and South America to nest in loose colonies in the Low Country.*

Swallow-tailed Kite capturing dinner

Mississippi Kite, adult

them just fine. They might return to an old nest – a rather flimsy platform of dead twigs lined with green leaves – or they might build a new one. Being liberated parents, both male and female incubate the one to two white eggs for nearly a month. Then they share the duties of bringing food to the young. In late summer, I have often followed the whistled "wheeee-whee" call to its source – a streaked brown and tan juvenile Mississippi kite perched high in a tree begging to be fed.

Unlike other birds of prey, kites have relatively weak beaks and feet. They specialize in catching insects such as dragonflies, wasps, beetles, and grasshoppers. They will also eat frogs, lizards and small birds. Both swallow-tailed and Mississippi kites eat on the wing. While nightjars open their cavernous mouths to engulf insects, kites grasp them in their talons and somehow manage to stay aloft while doing inverted in-flight sit-ups, ducking their heads underneath their bellies to get the food to their beaks.

Until recently, very little was known about where the swallow-tailed kites went when they left the southeast in the fall. In 1996, Ken Meyer of the Avian Research & Conservation Institute in Gainesville, FL, attached radio transmitters to seven kites and tracked them, using satellite technology, to wintering grounds in southwestern Brazil. He found that the birds traveled a narrow corridor from Florida to Cuba, over to the Yucatan Peninsula, down the Pacific side of Central America into Colombia where they crossed the Andes and continued down the west side of the Amazon basin to end up at a grassy savanna habitat in Brazil - a leisurely journey of about 4500 miles.

If you don't have kites in your neighborhood, don't despair. Visit the Savannah National Wildlife Refuge, or an area hayfield in late July or early August. With nesting complete, the birds gather in mixed flocks prior to heading south. They soar on the mid-day thermals and feed on the abundant summer insects. You might see one or 50 or even 500. Now that is a quite a kite sight.

Swallow-tailed Kite

AUGUST

Making a Living at Low Tide

If you spend much time on the coast in the Low Country, you can't help but notice the tides. Ask any boat captain or fisherman about going out in the creeks and marshes, and they're sure to respond, "let me check the tides."

People living in the mountains of Colorado, the plains of Kansas, or even in Atlanta, aren't treated to a daily graphic display of the way that the gravitational pulls of the moon and sun affect the oceans of the earth.

Living on Chimney Creek, I see more of the tides than most people. At high tide, I see an expanse of water stretching sixty yards to the opposite shore. Six hours later, all that water has vanished, leaving the creek bottom exposed as a vast, rippled mud flat. Only a narrow channel of deep water remains, close to the shore.

One of our favorite summer activities is to swim across to the sand bar at low tide and poke around exploring all the pools for whelks, hermit crabs, minnows, and shells. Then, when the tide turns, we launch ourselves from the point and let the rush of incoming water carry us back to the dock.

For us, low tide is playtime. However, for many of the neighborhood's non-human residents, low tide is when they find the food they need to keep on living. At low tide the fiddler crabs emerge from their burrows. This army of the salt marsh is enormous – estimated at more than 500,000 crabs per acre of marsh. As

> *At high tide on Chimney Creek, I see an expanse of water stretching sixty yards to the opposite shore. Six hours later, all that water has vanished, leaving the creek bottom exposed as a vast, rippled mud flat.*

Whimbrels and Willets in the marsh

Many bird species feed on the river bank at low tide

the tide ebbs to expose muddy banks, these tiny creatures remove the plugs sealing their burrows and begin the process of scraping tiny morsels of food from the mud around them.

Female fiddler crabs have two small claws that are used for eating. Male fiddler crabs have one large, fiddle-shaped claw and one small claw. Males use this large claw to attract female crabs, or wield it like a weapon to fight with other males.

Fiddler crabs are viewed as tasty treats by a variety of marsh diners, including raccoons, birds, and even fish. The down-curved beaks of clapper rails, whimbrels, and white ibis are just the ticket for reaching into a hole in the mud to grab a tasty crab or marine worm. Clapper rails tend to forage independently, while ibises and whimbrels go in for togetherness, generally

Fiddler Crabs

feeding in flocks of five, ten, twenty, fifty or more.

Yellow-crowned night-herons also put crustaceans at the top of their list of favorite foods. They'll go for any type of crab, including blue crabs, ghost crabs, and fiddler crabs. They also eat insects, snails, fish, lizards,

Raccoon and Egret prints in the mud

AUGUST

marine worms and even mice.

Other long-legged wading birds also schedule their meals by the tides. High tide is the time to rest or roost. Low tide offers easy walking, shallower water, and tidal pools that trap food. At a recent low tide, I counted three great blue herons, half a dozen great egrets, two snowy egrets, a tricolored

Yellow-crowned Night-Heron hunts

Wood Stork looking for food

heron, two green herons, three wood storks, and even a rare reddish egret feeding on and around the sandbar. This crew eats mainly fish, but they wouldn't turn down a shrimp, squid, frog, crayfish, snail, worm, or lizard.

Another crowd of sand bar visitors are the gulls and terns. Laughing, herring, and ring-billed gulls all find that the exposed creek bottom offers a delectable selection of crustaceans, mollusks, and marine worms. Least, royal and Forster's terns use the bar as place to rest from the rigors of plunge diving for fish.

Occasionally, I'll be treated to the elegant feeding ballet of the black skimmers. Several birds, flying with effortless synchrony, will cut through the water with their elongated lower beaks or *mandibles*. At low tide, the water is shallower and the fish are close to the surface.

Still another family of birds that takes advantage of low tide to feed, particularly during spring and fall migration, are the shorebirds. One of my favorites is the American oystercatcher. While these chunky black and white birds with the bright orange chisel of a bill do most of their low tide feeding on the oyster beds, they visit the sandbar for a change of cuisine. Here they might just

Low tide living on the exposed sandbar

nd a tasty marine worm, a sand crab, or even a sea urchin.

Other shorebirds who patronize the sand bar's insect, crustacean and marine worm buffet include willets, whimbrels, semipalmated and black-bellied plovers, least, semipalmated, and spotted sandpipers, dunlin, dowitchers, greater and lesser yellowlegs, and rarely, the elegant American avocet.

Oh, and I almost forgot two of the larger low-tide loungers. When the fishing is good, brown pelicans and double-crested cormorants are a common sandbar sight.

In fact, if the wildlife on Chimney Creek went in for musical drama, we might get a stirring rendition of that old favorite "Low tide, and the living is easy. Fish are jumping, and the crab count is high."

To Everything, Tern, Tern, Tern...

One thing I love about watching birds is that there is always more to learn. Each year I can choose a "birding improvement project." One fall I made numerous pilgrimages to the top of Mt. Wachusett in Massachusetts to watch for migrating hawks. Another year I wandered between the plots of a community garden determined to master the "little brown jobbies" (i.e. sparrows) that confound even experienced birders.

Least Tern

Since returning to Georgia, I have discovered that the beach in late summer is a great place to study terns.

As a group, terns share a number of traits. Standard attire is black, white and gray. Most appear slender and sleek with pointed swept-back wings, and forked tails. Their heads usually look elongated and are sometimes crested. Flight is snappy and aerodynamic. "Sea swallows," as they are sometimes called, feed by plunging head first into the water, or by swooping low over the surface to grab bits of food.

Learning to tell one tern from another takes patience and practice. It helps if the birds in question can be

Royal Tern with a fish

Sandwich Terns courting

convinced to stand side by side on the beach for an extended period of time. Fortunately, with terns, this is much more likely than with warblers or sparrows. On a late summer visit to a barrier island beach, one may find as many as eight species of terns resting in mixed flocks on the beach, just begging to be identified.

Royal Tern juvenile

Size is the first thing to consider. Our regular Low Country terns come in small, medium, and large. Least and black terns are the smallest – measuring between nine and ten inches. Royal and Caspian terns are the largest – at 20 to 21 inches. The 12 inch common, 13 inch Forster's, 14 inch gull-billed, and 15 inch sandwich terns all rank as medium.

The Caspian tern enjoys the designation of "largest tern in the world." It is bulky and imposing, larger than a ring-billed gull, with an expression not unlike that of a snapping turtle. The dark, triangular tips of the undersides of the wings are apparent as it flies with steady muscular wing beats. Caspian terns never show a completely white forehead, although in the winter they may shift from solid, glossy black

Forster's, Sandwich & Royal Terns, non-breed.

Caspian & Royal Terns, post-breeding

dips its bill in the mustard.

The tiny least tern dresses to impress with a sleek black cap, white forehead, yellow bill, and yellow legs. During courtship, the male flies upward with a small fish in his bill, followed by the female. Then they glide down together. On the ground, he will offer the fish, which she may accept if he catches her fancy. Least terns have suffered for their tendency to nest on

mottled salt and pepper.

Royal terns look the most rakish. They have full black caps for only a brief period during breeding season. The rest of the year, they opt for "punk" with a white forehead and fluttering crest. The royals are loyal to saltwater. They are rarely found more than thirty or forty miles from the ocean. While Caspian terns mostly visit in late summer and early fall, royal terns can be found year-round on Low Country beaches.

The royal tern's summer sidekick – the sandwich tern – is most noted for its long black bill with a yellow tip. While it was actually named for a town in England, I prefer to think that this tern, when making its sandwich, always

Black Tern on patrol

mainland sandy beaches, where they are subject to disturbance by beachgoers, dogs, gulls, or raccoons. Some have adapted by taking refuge on flat gravel rooftops.

Forster's terns regularly winter on our southeastern coast. In winter

Royal Terns and Laughing Gulls, breeding plumage

144

Common Tern, non-breeding plumage

Standard attire for terns is black, white and gray. Most appear slender and sleek with pointed swept-back wings, and forked tails. "Sea swallows" feed by plunging head first into the water, or by swooping low over the surface to grab bits of food.

Gull-billed Tern in flight

plumage, their diagnostic field mark is a white head with dark, pirate-like eye patches. For mating, the Forster's dons a black cap and its bill turns orange with a black tip. During spring and fall migration, young common terns also show up on our beaches. A dark shoulder bar sets them apart from the Forster's terns.

Gull-billed and black terns tend to be birds of the inland marshes, although I occasionally see black terns on the beach or off-shore in late summer. The black tern flight pattern is buoyant and erratic, resembling that of a nighthawk or a butterfly. They swoop and flutter, plucking food from the surface of the water.

The gull-billed tern might more accurately have been named the "gull-winged" or "gull-tailed" tern. It has rounded, rather broad wings and a forkless, straight-cut tail. It is more likely to be seen hawking over the marsh for insects or fiddler crabs than plunge diving for fish at the beach.

By late summer, the tern supply has usually been augmented by this year's crop of juveniles. Like youngsters of all denominations, they specialize in begging. Standard behavior is to crouch down in front of a parent with head lowered and bill raised, squawking piteously.

Yes, indeed. For summer "en-tern-tainment," I highly recommend a trip to the beach.

Fall

FALL - AN OVERVIEW

While fall on the human calendar begins the third week of September, in the world of birds the first signs of fall can be observed in late July. That is when the first shorebirds return to the Low Country from the Arctic, and when the first songbirds begin their southward migration. Some of the earliest migrants are the Louisiana waterthrush and yellow warbler.

Basically, fall is a reverse movement from spring, with some subtle differences. In the fall, the birds are not singing. They aren't rushing to set up territories and attract mates, so their movement is quieter and more leisurely. Also, in the fall, some of the birds that favor the central flyway in spring displace eastward to the coast. It is more common in fall to find warblers such as magnolia, chestnut-sided, bay-breasted and Blackburnian. In many cases, these birds are juveniles or no longer in breeding plumage so identifying them can be challenging.

American Robin in E. Red Cedar

One thing that fall offers is fruit. Trees and bushes offer a wide assortment of nuts, seeds and berries, perfect for a hungry bird. The extent of nature's bounty varies from year to year, as the members of the plant kingdom balance growth and reproduction. Originally, the term *mast* was used to refer to the nuts of forest trees that accumulated on the ground and were used as food for fattening domestic animals. Now scientists refer to a year in which vegetation produces a significant amount of fruit as a *mast year*. During such years, many birds abandon backyard bird feeders to feast on nature's bounty. Berry bushes and trees are good places to look for migrating tanagers, thrushes, vireos, catbirds, robins and warblers.

September and October are great months for raptor migration. Northern harriers are among the first raptors to return for the winter. The falcons – kestrels, merlins and peregrines – tend to migrate right along the coast, while buteos such as broad-winged hawks usually make use of thermals to migrate further inland over mountain ridges.

Shorebirds continue to move during September and October, with many showing up inland in muddy fields or sod farms. Special treats generally found further inland are upland sandpiper, pectoral sandpiper, and buff-breasted sandpiper.

NEOTROPICAL MIGRANTS – HEADING SOUTH

Swallows
Purple Martin
Rough-winged Swallow
Bank Swallow
Barn Swallow
Cave Swallow
Tree Swallow – many remain in winter

Vireos
Yellow-throated Vireo
Red-eyed Vireo
Warbling Vireo – rare
Blue-headed Vireo – some remain in winter
White-eyed Vireo – some resident all year

Warblers – Regular in Fall
Northern Parula
Prairie Warbler
Prothonotary Warbler
Hooded Warbler
Worm-eating Warbler
Swainson's Warbler
Black-throated Blue Warbler
Yellow-breasted Chat
Louisiana Waterthrush
American Redstart
Cape May Warbler
Ovenbird
Yellow Warbler

Warblers – Occasional in Fall
Black-throated Green Warbler
Blackburnian Warbler
Cerulean Warbler
Chestnut-sided Warbler
Blue-winged Warbler
Golden-winged Warbler
Magnolia Warbler
Canada Warbler
Bay-breasted Warbler
Mourning Warbler
Connecticut Warbler
Blackpoll Warbler

Warblers – Remain for Winter
Yellow-rumped Warbler
Pine Warbler
Palm Warbler
Black-and-white Warbler
Yellow-throated Warbler
Orange-crowned Warbler
Common Yellowthroat

Thrushes
Wood Thrush
Veery
Swainson's Thrush
Gray-cheeked Thrush
Bicknell's Thrush
Hermit Thrush – winters

Hooded Warbler

Buntings, Tanagers, Grosbeaks & Orioles

Indigo Bunting
Painted Bunting – occ. in winter
Scarlet Tanager
Summer Tanager – occ. in winter
Orchard Oriole
Blue Grosbeak
Rose-breasted Grosbeak
Baltimore Oriole – occasional in winter

Flycatchers

Great Crested Flycatcher
Acadian Flycatcher
Eastern Kingbird
Eastern Wood-Pewee
Least Flycatcher
Yellow-bellied Flycatcher
Eastern Phoebe – stays for winter

Eastern Kingbird

Miscellaneous Migrants

Chuck-will's-widow
Whip-poor-will – occ. winter
Common Nighthawk
Yellow-billed Cuckoo
Black-billed Cuckoo
Chimney Swift
Bobolink
Ruby-throated Hummingbird

Incoming Migrants (see Winter)

Kinglets
Sparrows
Ducks
Wrens
Sapsuckers
Loons
Grebes

Raptors

Mississippi Kite – leave by early fall
Swallow-tailed Kite – leave by early fall

OTHER RAPTORS

Northern Harrier
Sharp-shinned Hawk
Cooper's Hawk
American Kestrel
Merlin
Peregrine Falcon
Bald Eagle – return to territories

Northern Harrier flies over the marsh

Fall title page features a Baltimore Oriole, Red-bellied Woodpecker on a Magnolia and a Black Skimmer, pictured top to bottom.

MIGRATORY SHOREBIRDS – many remain for winter

Whimbrel
Spotted Sandpiper
Solitary Sandpiper
Sanderling
Ruddy Turnstone
Marbled Godwit
Long-billed Curlew – uncommon
Semipalmated Sandpiper
Least Sandpiper
Western Sandpiper
Red Knot
Dunlin
Long-billed Dowitcher
Short-billed Dowitcher
American Oystercatcher – many migrate in for winter
Greater Yellowlegs
Lesser Yellowlegs
Stilt Sandpiper
White-rumped Sandpiper – uncommon
Baird's Sandpiper – uncommon
Upland Sandpiper – uncommon
Pectoral Sandpiper
Buff-breasted Sandpiper – grassy fields
Wilson's Snipe
American Woodcock
Killdeer – many resident year-round

Wilson's Snipe

ON THE BEACH

Common Tern – migrate through
Black Tern – migrate through late July, August, September
Caspian Tern – common September & October; otherwise uncommon
Royal Tern – year-round
Sandwich Tern – most depart by end of October
Forster's Tern – common fall and winter
Black Skimmer – year-round; large numbers in fall
Herring Gull – common fall, winter, spring; uncommon summer
Ring-billed Gull – common fall, winter, spring; uncommon summer
Laughing Gull – abundant spring, summer, fall; less common mid-winter
Great Black-backed Gull – regular/uncommon fall, winter, spring; uncommon summer
Lesser Black-backed Gull – regular but uncommon late summer through spring
Bonaparte's Gull – uncommon but erratic visitor late summer through spring

Lesser Black-backed Gull

MIGRATION IS THE SPICE OF LIFE

Variety, the saying goes, is the spice of life. Most bird lovers would agree. We certainly enjoy our faithful cardinals, blue jays, chickadees, titmice and red-bellied woodpeckers – content to make the Low Country their full-time home. We are, however, continually on the lookout for what's new and different. We are fortunate that 75 percent of the more than 650 species of birds that commonly reside in North America take part in an activity expressly tailored to provide us with the novelty we seek – migration.

American Redstart, female

Migration, from the Latin *migrare*, means "to change where one lives." Birds take full advantage of the mobility that comes with having wings. Many travel vast distances each spring to mate and raise their families in the United States and Canada. Then, as the days grow shorter and cold weather approaches, they make the arduous return journey to Central and South America in search of longer days, plentiful food, and kinder weather.

Five different groups of birds migrate: land birds, waterfowl, shorebirds, seabirds, and birds of prey.

Migration is a complex phenomenon. There are five different groups of birds that migrate: land birds, waterfowl, shorebirds, seabirds, and birds of prey. There are *long-distance migrants* that travel vast distances between continents; *short-distance migrants* that confine their movements within the continent; and *elevational migrants* that move from mountaintop to lowlands. There are *complete migrants*, where the entire population of a species leaves the breeding range, and partial migrants where some individuals remain on the nesting territory for the winter.

Diurnal migrants migrate during the day. Most birds of prey take advantage of the warm air currents generated by the sun during the day. They conserve energy during migration by taking thermal "elevators" up to a height where they can catch the currents and soar for long distances.

Most songbirds, in contrast, are

American Redstart, male

nocturnal migrants. Since they have to do it all by flapping, songbirds prefer the cooler night-time temperatures, which allow them to dissipate the body heat they generate. The birds begin their flight about half an hour after sunset. Generally, there is less air turbulence at night, as well as fewer predators to contend with.

Looking up in the fall, you may spy the familiar V-formation of waterfowl on the move. Some scientists speculate that each bird in the V creates a circular air current that generates lift and helps its flock mates. The V may also ensure that each bird can clearly see what is ahead of it and avoid colliding with others. Here in the Low Country, fall brings large flocks of double-crested cormorants heading south in the classic V.

One of the challenges involved with all birding is figuring out which bird is doing what. Some species, like painted buntings, summer tanagers, northern parulas, and great crested flycatchers have been here all summer. When fall comes, they hightail it for the tropics. A number of long distance migrants

Black-bellied Plover molting

that nest further north – such as scarlet tanagers, American redstarts, and Cape May warblers – make brief pit stops at feeders, birdbaths, or berry bushes to fuel up for the next leg of their journey south.

Among the short-distance migrants that leave breeding territories up north but don't feel the need to change continents are yellow-bellied sapsuckers, yellow-rumped warblers, ruby-crowned kinglets, and a diverse assortment of sparrows – song, Savannah, swamp, field, white-throated, and chipping. These species view coastal Georgia and South Carolina as ideal winter destinations.

Double-crested Cormorants migrate in V-formation

Cape May Warbler on Lantana

In late September, every field or wetland sports its eastern phoebe. For reasons unknown to me, phoebes prefer to nest further inland or in the mountains, not on the Coastal Plain. When this gray and white flycatcher with the distinctive habit of bobbing its tail makes its fall appearance, it's a sure sign that the seasons are changing. While some phoebes travel all the way to southeast Mexico for the winter, a large part of the population remains in the southeastern United States.

Phoebes endear themselves to novice birders by announcing their identity with repetitive fervor – "fee-bee, fee-bee." They also enjoy an unusual historic distinction. In 1840, John James Audubon began a practice that has become an integral part of the scientific study of migration. While living at his father's plantation near Valley Forge, Pennsylvania, he noticed a pair of phoebes nesting. He tied a light silver thread about the legs of each young bird before it left the nest, and was gratified when two of his "banded" birds returned to the same site the following year.

If you visit a Low Country barrier island in the fall, you may be treated to the sight of large mixed flocks of shorebirds just back from their Arctic nesting sojourns. Red knots, sanderlings, black-bellied plovers, marbled godwits, American oystercatchers, and even the

Swainson's Thrush

occasional long-billed curlew can be found resting on beaches or taking advantage of the smorgasbord of tasty invertebrates available on the mud flat at low tide. They hope for safety in numbers, as merlins and peregrine falcons also migrate along the coast, looking to snack on an unwary gull, tern, or shorebird.

Change is in the air. The first blue-winged teal are back in the wetlands. Piping plovers are back on the beaches. The first sparrows have returned to the salt marsh. Already Low Country bird watchers are anticipating the return of the ever-popular American goldfinches. Migration, for a birder, is indeed the spice of life!

Long-billed Curlew & other shorebirds

BEAUTYBERRY AND THE BIRDS

Gray Catbird on American Beautyberry

Slowly but surely, it's happening. After participating in the Georgia Master Naturalist Program, I'm beginning to pay attention not only to my beloved birds, but also to all those green leafy things that lurk in the background.

I know what to focus on when I look at birds. There's bill shape, tail length, feather color, and the presence or absence of wing bars. With plants, it's a whole different ball game. I have to notice whether leaves are opposite or alternate, simple or compound, pinnate or palmate. What does the flower look like? What about the fruit?

Ah, fruit! Now we're getting somewhere. Birds eat fruit. So, if I learn how to recognize plants and their fruit, I should be able to find more birds!

In the spring, I find birds by listening for their songs. They have territories to stake out and mates to attract and that noisy business. In the fall, it's all about food and putting on enough fat to either migrate or make it through the winter. So fall is when it really comes in handy to know those plants and trees.

Pokeberries are quite popular, as are the red fruits of the magnolia seedpod. The fruits of the spicebush, sassafras, black tupelo and flowering dogwood are high in lipids – think fat – and are particular favorites with long distance migrants like the Swainson's thrush and the veery.

Northern Mockingbird guards berries

SEPTEMBER

154

Robins and eastern bluebirds feed heavily on the berries of the eastern red cedar, while tree swallows and yellow-rumped (formerly myrtle) warblers rely on the tiny blue-black berries of the wax myrtle.

But the one plant that practically screams "eat me" in early fall is the American beautyberry. Its leafy arching stems are loaded down with clusters of nearly-neon magenta berries. This native deciduous shrub is not very picky about where it grows. It will flourish in moist or dry areas, sun or shade, and where there are beautyberries, there are usually birds.

The most visible consumer is that famous berry bush bully, the northern mockingbird. These gray and white sentries use their "mocking" songs in the fall to announce to any interloper that, "these berries are mine, all mine." Fortunately for the other birds, the mockingbirds can't stake out all the beautyberries at once. The brown thrashers, catbirds, cardinals, and towhees usually get their share.

During fall migration, there's no telling who might be stopping by for a berry snack. Red-eyed vireos are regular customers, as are Baltimore orioles, and black-throated blue warblers.

Assorted members of the thrush family can also be found lurking in the berry bushes. While bluebirds and robins are colorful and get the most publicity, the other, less showy thrushes – wood, Swainson's, gray-cheeked and veery – quietly consume their share. These brown-backed birds with their spotted chests have mastered the art of disappearing into the woodwork. However, as if in compensation for their plain appearance, they are blessed with beautifully flute-like and ethereal songs.

In the fall, it's rare to hear the trilling "ee-o-laaay" of the wood thrush or the descending harmonies of the veery. These skulkers may, however, betray their presence with a sharp "veer," or "whip," or "chuck."

Hermit thrushes, dull brown with rusty tail, begin arriving in late September. Many of them spend the winter here, rather than migrating to the tropics. They can be enticed to feeders with mealworms, grapes, or berries. (Freeze some now to put out later!)

If you were wondering, beautyberries are safe for human consumption. Reportedly, they are not particularly flavorful right off the vine, but they do make a fine jelly. For the cooks among you, Dick Deuerling and Peggy Lantz offer a recipe in their book *Florida's Incredible Wild Edibles*.

In the winter, the beautyberry lose

> *The one plant that practically screams "eat me" in the early fall is the American beautyberry.*

Black-throated Blue Warbler

all its leaves and looks like a dead stick. So far, I have presented two friends with their very own sticks. My friends were dubious at first, but both sticks grew leaves in the spring, and now are busy enticing a variety of birds and mammals to partake of their purple fruit. It's not just the animals that benefit. The more fruit that is eaten, the more seeds get spread, resulting, happily, in more beautyberries.

Beauty Berry Jelly
1 1/2 qts. of beautyberries, washed
2 qts. water
Boil 20 min. and strain to make infusion. Use 3 cups of the infusion, bring to boil, add 1 envelope Sure-Jell and 4 cups sugar. Bring to second boil; boil 2 min. Remove from heat and let stand until foam forms. Skim off foam, pour into sterilized jars, cap. (from *Florida's Incredible Wild Edibles,* by Deuerling & Lantz; Great Outdoors Publishing)

THE SHRIEK OF THE SHRIKE

As an avid birdwatcher, I have developed the habit of scanning power lines and fence posts for the shapes of perching birds. Usual suspects include mourning doves, kingfishers, mockingbirds, grackles, and the occasional kestrel. I am always on the lookout, however, for a gray and white shape – almost, but not quite, a mockingbird. A closer study with binoculars reveals a head just a bit too large for the body, a heavy dark beak, and a distinct bandit-style black mask. Yes! It's *lanius ludovicianus,* better known to his friends as the loggerhead shrike. To his enemies, he's "the butcherbird." *Lanius* is Latin for "butcher." It is common knowledge that hawks and owls are murderous carnivores. Songbirds – with their diet of berries, seeds, nuts and some bugs – are regarded as kinder, gentler creatures – all songbirds, that is, except for shrikes. Neither the loggerhead shrike nor his cousin the northern shrike would ever make it as vegetarians. Their taste runs to large insects, rodents, and small birds. Like raptors, they have excellent eyesight and can spot the movement of a mouse some 50 yards distant.

However, unlike raptors, shrikes have weak feet. They have developed the ingenious, but rather repulsive, habit of impaling their prey on sharp thorns or barbed wire, just like a butcher hanging his meat. This serves

Loggerhead Shrike shrieking

Loggerhead Shrike, juvenile

The northern shrike spends its summers far to the north in Canada, ranging south to the western United States and parts of the northeast and midwest only during the winter. Since shrikes hunt from a perch, they favor semi-open country equipped with handy lookouts such as fence posts, wires, tree limbs, and large shrubs.

In flight, shrikes can be distinguished from mockingbirds by their strong, vigorous wing beats and more direct flight path. Mockingbirds have a more leisurely flight with slower wing beats. Unlike the shrike, almost half of a mockingbird's diet is wild berries, one quarter is cultivated fruits, and only one quarter is insects. Thus mockingbirds can afford to take their time. Most of their food isn't going anywhere.

them well in more ways than one. It secures the food while they eat it and it lets them save for later. Shrikes have discovered that a well-stocked larder can tide them through times when food is scarce. They have amazing memories for where they have stored their prey. In Texas, some loggerhead shrikes have been observed returning to mummified frogs hung up as many as eight months earlier.

For male shrikes, a full pantry is an advantage when it comes to attracting a mate. He carries out his wing fluttering, tail spreading displays in front of his larder, showcasing his hunting prowess. He may even woo her with tasty tidbits. Since she depends on him to feed her while she's on the nest, his stash may well be just the ticket to her affections.

Although *ludovicianus* means "of Louisiana," loggerhead shrikes do not confine themselves to that one state. In fact, they are found throughout most of the United States, except the northeast. Here in the Low Country, we have our year-round resident population, often augmented in the winter by northern nesters escaping the cold.

Both mockingbirds and shrikes can be quite territorial, guarding a breeding territory during the summer as well as establishing dominion over a hunting territory or food source during the winter. Mockingbirds, in particular, can be quite bold about dive-bombing birds, snakes, cats, dogs, or even humans who get too close to their nests.

N. Mockingbird, longer tail and no m...

Loggerhead Shrike perched on a fence

Being a songbird, shrikes do actually sing. Both male and female express themselves during courtship with a distinctive assortment of marsh gurgles, squeaks, and shrill couplets. When alarmed, shrikes utter a series of sharp shrieks. The name "shrike" is derived from the Anglo-Saxon *scric* meaning "a shrieker."

Charlotte Hilton Green, a naturalist and columnist for the *Raleigh (NC) News and Observer* from 1932 until 1974, wrote in her book *Birds of the South*, that the loggerhead shrike had been placed on the U.S. Dept. of Agriculture "Bird List of Honor" as a consumer of noxious insects and rodents. Certainly, most grasshoppers, mice, and small birds have learned to beware of the shriek of the shrike.

> *Upon close study, the loggerhead shrike has a head just a bit too large for its body, a heavy dark beak, and a distinct bandit-style black mask.*

ARE YOU A LOVER OF PLOVERS?

Does Rover (*Roh-ver*) chase plovers (*ploh-vers*), or are you a lover (*luvver*) of plovers (*luvvers*)? When referring to the world's second largest family of shorebirds, the *Encarta World English Dictionary* indicates that the correct pronunciation is the one that rhymes with lover (*luvver*). A plover (*pluvver*) is defined as "a wading bird that lives on the shoreline and has a short bill and tail and long pointed wings."

What I love about plovers is that we generally find only six species here in the Low Country. To become a plover expert, you only have to study four pages in *Peterson's Field Guide to Birds*, compared with 22 pages for warblers or 24 pages for ducks. Another plus for plovers is that they hang out in flat, open habitat where they stand still, allowing themselves to be thoroughly studied and identified. No plover in my experience has ever vanished into a thicket or disappeared behind the leaves of an oak tree.

In shape, plovers are rather like doves (*duvvs*). They have rounded heads, thick necks, large eyes, and

Wilson's Plover

Semipalmated Plover

short, pigeon-like bills. Their large eyes serve them well, as they locate most of their food visually, rather than by poking or probing. You can usually spot a plover by watching its behavior, even if you are unable to distinguish its field marks. While sandpipers and sanderlings run about the beach like mechanical wind-up toys, plovers run a few steps, stop, scan the area, and then tilt forward to snatch a bit of food from the surface. They also have developed "foot-patting" strategy. Birds have been observed patting one foot on the sand or mud in hopes of causing small organisms to come to the surface.

The plover that has gotten the most airtime in the last 15 years has been the tiny piping plover. This marshmallow puffball of a bird was placed on the federal endangered/threatened list in 1986. They breed only in three areas in North America; 63 percent on the northern Great Plains and prairies of the US and Canada; another 36 per-

Semipalmated and Piping Plovers

ent on the Atlantic coast; and less than 1 percent around the Great Lakes.

What has made life difficult for piping plovers is their fondness for nesting on open sandy beaches or lakeshores. Their ability to look like another rock or lump of sand protects them from some predators, but not from people and their various recreational activities. While a majority of these birds winter on the Gulf Coast of Texas and Louisiana, the Low Country does play host to a small population. In August 2003, Brandon Noel observed 10 piping plovers on Little St. Simon's Island. He noted 15 birds with bands. Most were identified as coming from the endangered Great Lakes population, but one wore a red/green combination that marked it as having come from Prince Edward Island in Canada.

Killdeer with beetle

Black-bellied Plover, non-breeding plumage

The semipalmated plover is about the same size as the piping plover, but its back is the dark brown of a mud flat. It sports a single dark breast band. The name refers to the fact that it has partial webbing between its toes.

Although unrestricted shooting seriously depleted plover populations in the late 19th century, the semipalmated plover has recovered well and is currently widespread and common. It nests in the far north of Canada and Alaska on gravel bars along rivers or ponds.

Wilson's plovers forego the Arctic journey and stay to nest here in Georgia and South Carolina. They seem to prefer barrier island beaches and dredge spoil sites. Wilson's is one to two inches larger than the piping and semipalmated plovers, has a broader dark breast band, and – for a plover – a long, thick, black bill.

The killdeer is nine to eleven inches long and wears not one, but two dark breast bands. It gets it name from its plaintive call – "kil-deeah, kil-deeah." Killdeer eat mainly insects and frequent a wide range of semi-urban habitats including plowed fields and grassy lawns. They are noted for performing an excellent "broken-wing" distraction

American Golden-Plover

Black-bellied Plover in flight

You can often spot a plover by watching its behavior — "start and stop, walk and pluck" — even if you are unable to distinguish its field marks.

Killdeer fledgling in the brush

display to divert predators from their nests.

The black-bellied plover has a black belly only during breeding season. In the winter, look for a drab, grayish bird, about twelve inches long with the typical stocky plover shape, hunched posture, and short, pigeon-like bill. When they fly, look for black "armpits." These birds nest in the high Arctic and winter on the coasts of six continents.

The American golden-plover is a rare transient in the Low Country. It resembles the black-bellied plover but is slightly smaller and more likely to be found in marshy meadows, open fields, or pastures, rather than on a sandy beach.

Now if you're planning to travel the world, you may need to brush up on the other 60 species of plover (*pluvver*). For the Low Country, however, these six ought to cover (*cuvver*) your bases. Just don't look over (*oh-ver*) a four-leafed clover (*cloh-ver*), and do leave Rover (*Roh-ver*) at home.

May There Always Be Pelicans!

OCTOBER

Brown Pelican in flight

There they come – the wide-bodied jumbo jets of the coastal bird world! With their creamy bellies a mere six inches from the ocean's surface, the brown pelicans flap single-file in an elegant display of synchronized flying that any Blue Angel might envy. Awkward and even downright comical on land, pelicans soar with effortless majesty. How a heavy-bodied bird with a huge, expandable fishing net for a lower beak manages to look regal in the air is beyond me!

Brown pelicans are found throughout the year in the Low Country. During the spring and summer they busy themselves with nesting on isolated barrier island beaches. In the fall and winter they can be seen doing aerial beach patrol, relentlessly diving for fish, or lounging about on area beaches.

Of the seven species of pelican found throughout the world, our brown pelican, with its seven-foot wingspan, is the smallest. This gives it a fishing option not available to its larger cousins. While American white pelicans fish from a sedate swimming position, brown pelicans engage in the highly entertaining activity of plunge diving. From a height of up to 60 feet, a pelican will scan the water for fish. Once the prey is spotted, the bird begins a steep dive. It enters the water

Brown Pelican afloat

Brown Pelican walking in the ocean

& Wildlife Service in 1970.

Among the factors contributing to the decline were turn-of-the 20th century plume hunters who killed pelicans, herons and egrets for their feathers. Then, during World War I, fishermen complained that the pelicans, eating as much as four pounds of fish apiece each day, were depleting the fishing grounds. A group of ornithologists led by T. Gilbert Pearson responded by making several thousand pelicans regurgitate what they had eaten. This smelly endeavor found only 27 fish that were deemed commercially valuable. The majority of the pelicans' diet consisted of "rough" fish such as menhaden, herring, mullet, pigfish, grass minnows, and silversides. The passage of the Migratory Bird Treaty Act in 1918 gave protection to pelicans and other birds and helped curb the illegal killing.

with an impressive splash – head first and wings stretched back. The flexible *gular pouch* may be filled with as much as three gallons of water that must be drained by tilting the bill forward. Then the head is tossed back to swallow the fish. Opportunistic gulls will wait nearby, sometimes even perching on the pelican's beak, hoping to steal the catch while the water is being drained.

Awkward and even downright comical on land, brown pelicans soar with effortless majesty.

In my mind, there have always been pelicans on South Carolina and Georgia beaches – perched atop dock pilings, flying formation along the water, or congregating on the sandbars at low tide. I don't remember the absence of pelicans – the population crisis of the 1950s and 1960s – that resulted in the brown pelican's being listed as an endangered species by the US Fish

By far the most serious threat to the pelican population came after World War II with the introduction of powerful pesticides such as DDT. These

Brown Pelicans together on a shell rake

Brown Pelican dives for his dinner

chemicals found their way into the water, then into the fish, and then to the pelicans, ospreys, bald eagles, and others. What resulted was a thinning of the eggshells, such that the eggs broke when the parents tried to incubate them. This reproductive failure caused the populations of these species to plummet.

With the ban on DDT in 1972 and the passage of the Endangered Species Act in 1973, all of the above species have shown significant signs of recovery. The brown pelican was the first to stage a comeback. In 1985, it was removed from the endangered list for the Atlantic coast portion of its range. On the Gulf and Pacific coasts it is still considered threatened.

Our National Wildlife Refuge system also owes a debt to the pelican. It was in 1903, in response to threats to this species, that President Theodore Roosevelt designated the three acres of Pelican Island, off the coast of Florida, as the country's first national wildlife refuge. Now, more than 100 years later, the refuge system encompasses some 93 million acres in more than 550 refuges.

One of my most memorable pelican experiences happened during a family beach vacation. Fishing in the surf one afternoon, we lucked into a school of small fish. My young nieces and nephews were thrilled to reel in two fish at a time. When we tired of fishing, my five-year old niece and I settled in to swim. We noticed that the pelicans also were drawn in by the fish. There was something magical about having these creatures, intent on their task, crash into the water barely six feet from us, and float there like giant aquatic rocking horses.

The next day, when we once again went swimming, my niece turned to me in puzzlement.

"But where," she asked, "are the pelicans?"

So, while many beach goers long to swim with the dolphins, I thank Teddy Roosevelt and Gilbert Pearson and Rachel Carson and many unheralded conservationists that here on the coast of the Low Country, we still have the opportunity to swim with the pelicans.

Brown Pelicans enjoying their meals

Tree Swallows & More Tree Swallows

There they were – a swirling mass of dark shapes hovering over the dunes on the north end of Tybee Island. I couldn't help thinking of a plague of locusts descending to exact biblical revenge. Or maybe I had unwittingly walked onto the set of Hitchcock's *The Birds*. The swooping, twittering cloud blackened the sky.

"Even if there are 10,000 of them," I told myself, "there is nothing to fear."

That is unless you happen to be a flying insect. Beware all ye mayflies, stoneflies, beetles, winged ants, spiders, and even sand fleas. You thought that with the purple martins, barn swallows, and chimney swifts well on their way to Central and South America, you'd be home free, kicking back, resting easy. Well, dream on. It's October, and

Tree Swallow acrobatics

Tree Swallows in flight

the tree swallows are back in town.

A casual observer might not notice the change. For most of the spring and summer, it is the stubby, dark chimney swifts that have chirped and twittered above us. Then in late summer, the occasional tree swallow puts in an appearance. By mid-October, the swallows will have claimed most of the airspace, with only a few lingering swifts to be seen.

A closer look shows that swifts have thin, pointed, sickle-shaped wings and short, stiff tails. Tree swallows, in contrast, have broader wings and longer, slightly forked tails. Adults in breeding plumage have steely blue-green backs and bright white underparts. Juveniles have dusky brown backs and faint breast bands.

They've been trickling in since late July, a few here and there. October and November bring the hordes and masses. 600,000 tree swallows were reported in McIntosh County in November 1998, while 500,000 tree swallows were tallied on Sapelo Island in October 2001. Many will treat this as a rest stop on the way to points south. However, a substantial number will make the Low Country their winter home.

Tree swallows are willing to become vegetarians when insects are scarce. They are particularly fond of bayberries, and can be found feasting in the dense stands of wax myrtle common on our barrier islands.

Tree Swallows flying over a pond

In a time when our technology changes almost daily, it is comforting to discover natural rhythms that remain constant. In his book *Georgia Birds*, published in 1958, Thomas Burleigh writes, *On the coast, this swallow has been noted at Savannah as late in the spring as May 26 (1909) and May 29 (1911), and as early in the fall as July 18 (1931) and July 23 (1908). I found it already plentiful there on August 6, 1929, hundreds being seen on telephone wires at the side of the road through a stretch of open salt marsh… It apparently winters commonly on the coast. I saw an occasional bird on Tybee Island, January 6, 1923, and a flock of possibly one hundred in the open salt marsh near the mouth of the Savannah River, January 30, 1924.*

By all accounts, tree swallows are doing well as a species and possibly even increasing in numbers. They are cavity nesters who have been quick to avail themselves of man-made housing. They have benefited from the popularity of the eastern bluebird. Bluebird nest boxes suit them perfectly, to the dismay of many a hopeful bluebird landlord. Thus far, tree swallows have not chosen

A flock of Tree Swallows in Sea Oats

Tree Swallows on a wire

to nest in the Low Country, though they are expanding their nesting range southward. A few pairs have been reported breeding in the mountains of north Georgia.

Tree swallows are active from dawn to dusk. They spend most of their time in the air, eating, drinking, and even bathing on the wing. Unlike chimney swifts, which must cling to vertical surfaces, swallows can be found perching on wires. Walking on the beach at the north end of Tybee Island, I was startled to find a host of tree swallows littering the beach. Some seemed to be simply resting. Others were picking at something in the sand.

Occasionally the tree swallows' habit of whirling about in large flocks leads to tragedy. I often see them swooping low over the Tybee road near the entrance to Fort Pulaski, directly into the path of oncoming traffic. Apparently tree swallow parents do not teach their children about the danger posed by cars, nor to look both ways before flying across the street.

Swallow watching can be an exhilarating, even dizzying experience. For those with diligence and a quick eye, it may yield unexpected rewards. Wait! That one looks different. Its breast is orange. Once in a blue moon, during the winter, a cave swallow can be found whirling among the tree swallows, a reminder to birders to keep their eyes open and pay attention to every bird.

> *Tree swallows are willing to become vegetarians when insects are scarce, feasting on wax myrtle berries during the winter.*

DANCE OF THE BLACK SKIMMERS

After countless fall hours spent staring into the tops of trees obsessing over the minute details of 30-plus species of warblers, it's a welcome change to watch a bird that is unique and unmistakable.

Standing out in the open on the beach, among multitudes of gulls and terns, is a bird with a black back, short red legs, long pointed wings that extend beyond its tail, and an astonishing beak. This beak, carmine red at its base and black tipped, has a lower mandible one third again as long as the upper. It belongs to *rynchops niger* – the black skimmer.

While black skimmers are year-round residents in the Low Country, during the fall and early winter they congregate on area beaches in huge numbers. Literally hundreds and even thousands of birds can be found sitting on the sand. At the least sign of trouble, the entire flock takes off in a ballet-like swirl of black, white and orange.

Now I generally don't have a memory for scientific names, but every now and then one catches my fancy. *Niger* is Latin for "black" while *rynchops* comes from two Greek words, *rynchus* for "beak" and *ops* for "face." I can just picture a laughing gull strolling up to a

Black Skimmers usually face the same way

skimmer to catch up on beach gossip. "Hey," he'd say, "what's up, Beakface?"

On land, skimmers seem to be natural comedians. Their gait on stubby, web-footed legs is part hop and part waddle. Since dawn, dusk, and night are their preferred feeding times, they often loll about on the beach during the day in large flocks, generally all facing in the same direction – into the wind.

Black Skimmers taking flight together

OCTOBER

Black Skimmers skimming the ocean waves

They chatter among themselves with low throaty barks – "kak, kak, kak" or "yap, yap, yap." Occasionally, as if they simply can't support the weight of their impressive beaks a moment longer, you see them stretched full length on the sand.

Once airborne, skimmers comport themselves with casual ease and elegance. They are buoyant flyers and while "skimming," their wing beats remain entirely above the plane of their bodies. Soggy wingtips just don't cut it for skimming! Skimmers show off the special abilities of their fancy beaks while feeding. As a skimmer glides low over the surface, its laterally compressed, knifelike lower mandible is inserted into the water. When it encounters prey, a skimmer ducks its head under its body, closes its beak, and then lightly tosses its prey upward to be grasped and eaten.

Skimmers favor shallow bays and estuaries where the water is calm.

There on the beach is a bird with a black back, short red legs, long pointed wings, and an astonishing beak – "rynchops niger" – the black skimmer.

Often a group will fly formation with the precision of a flight squadron, executing hairpin turns and multiple "skims" back and forth over the same patch of water. They feed entirely by feel, which allows them the freedom to feed at night when the water may be calmer and prey closer to the surface.

Another "skimmers only" feature is their eyes. Their fully dilated pupils are larger than those of diurnal birds, enabling them to feed in low-light situations. These large pupils narrow vertically, like the eyes of a cat, which helps shield their retinas from strong sunlight and reflections on the water.

When it comes to nest building, skimmers are minimalists. The female lays four to five variably colored eggs with dark splotches in a shallow, unlined scrape in the sand. Both parents incubate the eggs and both feed the chicks, regurgitating tasty morsels. Luckily for the chicks, they are born with mandibles of equal length so they can pick up the food from the sand. Not until they are almost full-grown and beginning to feed on their own does the lower mandible outgrow the upper.

Young skimmers are a mottled brown, black and tan, which helps them blend more easily with the sand. If danger threatens, they hollow out a hole in the beach to lie in, even flipping sand over their backs to aid in the camouflage.

There is one interesting variation in skimmer plumage. During breeding season, skimmer backs are solid black from stem to stern. In winter, a broad white collar cuts through the expanse of black. With practice, you may be able to sort out males from females. The males are generally larger, with longer, deeper bills.

In other parts of the world, skimmers have come by some interesting

Black Skimmer, aka "Cutta-water"

nicknames. In Guyana, they are known as the *Cutta-water*. In French, they have been called *bec de ciseaux* (scissor-bill). The Spanish word for skimmer is *rayador*, referring to their habit of skimming lines or *rayas* in the sand while hollowing out their nests.

Besides the black skimmer, found in both North and South America, there are only two other species of skimmer in the world – the African skimmer and the Indian skimmer. Only our North American black skimmer opts primarily for coastal beaches and barrier islands. The others can be found well inland around river systems and lakes.

So the next time you make a trip to a barrier island beach, keep your eyes open for this avian entertainer. The black skimmer is unarguably a delight to watch, whether lounging on the beach, or dazzling with aerial acrobatics.

Black Skimmer courtship offering fish

Black Skimmers resting on the beach

KEEP YOUR EYES ON THE SKIES FOR RAPTORS!

I walked out in the front yard one morning in early October and noticed that my feeders were oddly empty. All was quiet except for the strident "jay, jay, jay," coming from a tree on the lot next door.

"Strange," I thought, and walked over to investigate. Experience has taught me that when the blue jays, crows, chickadees or wrens call loudly and seem agitated, there is usually a

Red-tailed Hawk

Cooper's Hawk, juvenile

predator nearby. I scanned the tree branches until I found it – long barred tail, flattish head, hooked bill and talons which clutched a pigeon. Field guide in hand I assessed its size – similar to a crow but with a longer tail – and studied the fine barring on the chest. It was too small for a red-tailed hawk and not quite the right shape for a red-shouldered hawk. I finally identified it as a juvenile Cooper's hawk. As I watched, it sat barely moving until the

blue jays got bored and retreated. At that point it resumed its somewhat grizzly enjoyment of breakfast.

All across North America in the fall, hawk watchers flock to the tops of mountains, like Hawk Mountain in Pennsylvania or Mt. Tom in Massachusetts. They spend hours on specially constructed platforms at coastal sites like Cape May, New Jersey

Peregrine Falcon in flight

Red-shouldered Hawk, juvenile

...r Kiptopeke, Virginia. From dawn until dusk, binoculars are glued to the sky searching for soaring or flapping specks. All this concentrated activity is made possible by one simple fact: hawks, unlike songbirds, migrate during the day.

Cooper's Hawk in flight

It isn't necessary to trek to mountaintops or platforms to see birds of prey. Just keep your eyes and ears open in your neighborhood. You might find a red-tailed hawk perched atop a church steeple or an osprey perched on a cell phone tower.

One day in mid-October, a man called to report, with great excitement, that he was watching a peregrine falcon in his birdbath. "It's sitting under the dripper. I hope it's not hurt." I assured him that it was probably just tired and thirsty from migrating. His birdbath offered the equivalent of a highway rest stop. After about twenty minutes the bird took off, flapping strongly, and headed out over the marsh.

Raptors come in a variety of sizes and shapes, each filling a particular niche in the food chain. The crow-sized Cooper's hawk is classified as an accipiter. With slim body, long tail, and short, rounded wings, it is an agile flier, able to maneuver in wooded areas, urban streets, and suburban backyards. The slightly smaller sharp-shinned hawk, a winter resident in the Low Country, has similar habits. These two species dine mostly on small birds. For a hungry Cooper's or sharpie, a yard full of bird feeders makes a great fly-through for fast food.

Red-tailed Hawk

Buteos, sometimes referred to as soaring hawks, have broad wings and short, wide tails. When not circling in the sky, they frequently perch on poles, snags or branches and scan their surroundings in search of a meal. For the familiar red-tailed hawk, dinner consists of a squirrel, vole, rat, rabbit, snake, toad, insect or bird. The smaller red-shouldered hawk favors voles, mice, frogs, toads, snakes, small birds, and large insects. Buteos hunt more effectively in open areas, rather than the wooded habitat favored by accipiters.

With the arrival of fall, another small raptor can be found perched on roadside wires and snags. The American kestrel is our smallest North American falcon. It swoops down from a perch to capture an unsuspecting vole, mouse, grasshopper, beetle, frog or small bird. With streamlined bodies, pointed wings, and long tails, falcons are built for speed. The kestrel's larger cousin, the peregrine falcon, is a celebrated power-diver. Peregrines reach speeds of nearly 200 miles per hour, descending from great heights to grab an unlucky shorebird, duck, pigeon, gull or songbird in mid-air. The merlin, a medium-sized falcon, is compact and fast-flying. Merlins go for the daily catch, dining on whatever species of bird is locally abundant – house sparrows in urban areas or small shorebirds near the coast.

Specializing in fish, the osprey or "fish hawk," does not usually threaten birds at backyard feeders. You might regard it with disfavor if you raise catfish, stock a trout pond, or manage a fish hatchery.

The northern harrier, another fall-arriving raptor, spends its days flying relentless patrol over fields and marshes. Nicknamed "marsh hawks," harriers can be conclusively identified by the conspicuous white patch on the tops of

Merlin

their rumps. They dine on small rodents, rabbits, insects, lizards, frogs and the occasional bird, but rarely venture into the confines of suburban yards.

One excellent way to get close looks at birds of prey is to visit a raptor center. Oatland Island Wildlife Center in Savannah provides homes for many raptors that are unable to live in the wild due to injury. The Lamar Q. Ball, Jr. Raptor Center at Georgia Southern University has wonderful habitats to care for and display injured birds of prey, and has a regular flight show. The Center for Birds of Prey in Charleston, S.C., offers guided walks, environmental education programs and free-flight demonstrations.

By far the most fun is to travel to the top of a mountain or stake out a spot near the shore and simply keep your eyes on the skies for raptors.

Sharp-shinned Hawk

Raptors come in a variety of sizes and shapes, each filling a particular niche in the food chain.

American Kestrel

The Changing of the Guard

The shift from summer to fall to winter happens gradually, almost imperceptibly, here in the Low Country. With live oaks and evergreens dominating the landscape, there is no massive leaf fall, no dramatic emergence of bare limbs and trunks to signal the approach of winter. What we notice most are the shifts in the wind – the cool breezes blowing in from the north – bringing with them the next season's crop of feathered visitors.

Humans have long envied birds their freewheeling mobility. In fact, we now have our own "snowbirds" – folks that leave homes in Vermont or Michigan for the winter warmth of Florida, Georgia, or Arizona. Their migrations are complex, with suitcases and cars to pack, plane tickets to buy, or RVs to fill with fuel.

For birds, the movement is simple and instinctive. Days are getting shorter; temperatures are dropping; food is getting sparse; it's time to get a move on!

Yellow-bellied Sapsucker, female

With nothing but the feathers on their backs and no need to phone ahead for a reservation, they slip into our neighborhoods with little hoopla. One day in early November, I glanced at a bird that landed vertically on a tree trunk in classic woodpecker fashion. It was not the showy and abundant red-bellied woodpecker with his bright red mohawk, but a smaller, quieter relative – the yellow-bellied sapsucker – back in town for the winter.

Not visually showy, the sapsucker is still quite dapper in a variation of classic woodpecker red, white, and black. The creamy belly, tinted with yellow, is most often concealed against the trunk of the tree. More obvious field marks are the bold black and white facial lines, solid red cap, and white stripe running vertically down the side of a tree-clinging bird. The male also sports a bright red throat.

Sapsuckers announce themselves vocally with short, plaintive cat-like

Yellow-bellied Sapsucker, juvenile

...ounds, or with squeaks like those made by squeezing a plastic bathtub toy. They leave distinctive, neatly aligned rows of holes drilled in their favorite trees. Using brush-like tongue tips, they soak up oozing sap, also snacking on insects attracted to the syrup.

In addition to sapsuckers, late fall brings small flocks of tiny birds called kinglets. Even smaller than warblers, these birds come in two flavors, ruby-crowned and golden-crowned. They flit about incessantly, most often high in the treetops. The ruby-crowned kinglet flicks its wings and chatters softly, dis-

Golden-crowned Kinglet

Ruby-crowned Kinglet

playing its red crown patch only when agitated or showing off for a prospective mate. Golden-crowned kinglets have an extremely high-pitched, buzzy "zee-zee-zee" call. They often feed hanging upside down like nuthatches.

While most of the warblers head for points further south, we do have seven species that are regular fall and winter guests. With careful searching, birders can usually find yellow-throated, orange-crowned, and black-and-white warblers poking about in the oak leaves or Spanish moss in search of insects. Pine warblers actually do spend most of their time in pines, while palm war-

blers feed low to the ground, pumping their tails to display rich yellow undertail coverts. Yellow-rumped warblers have become increasingly plentiful, feasting on wax myrtle berries and coming to feeders for suet. Look for the bandit mask of the common yellowthroat in wet, marshy habitats.

Another bird that often hangs with the warblers is the handsomely understated blue-headed vireo. If you compare its head color to that of a bluebird, it would be more accurately called the "gray-blue headed" vireo. Look for

Palm Warbler, eastern race

Blue-headed Vireo

may visit a feeder for mealworms, fruit sunflower chips or peanuts.

Rose-breasted grosbeaks, great-crested flycatchers, Mississippi kites, indigo buntings, purple gallinules, and ruby-throated hummingbirds have all left for the Tropics. Coming in for the winter are sparrows, loons, gannets,

Hermit Thrush

wing bars, broad white "spectacles" around the eyes, and a habit of tilting its head to the side in the quizzical fashion characteristic of vireos.

The hermit thrush, a shy brown bird with spotted breast and rufous tail, is easy to overlook as it blends into the leaf litter while searching for worms and bugs. "Hermie" is a frequent bird-bath visitor, performing his bathing rituals with vigor and enthusiasm. He

waxwings, harriers, kestrels, snipe, meadowlarks, goldfinches, and ducks, ducks, and more ducks. This isn't Buckingham Palace, but if you keep your eyes and ears open, you just migh catch "the changing of the guard!"

A flock of winter-resident Semipalmated Plovers

What's So Purple About a Sandpiper?

I often wonder how certain birds get their names. Take the purple sandpiper, for example. Most of us remember mixing paints in school art class. Red plus blue equals purple – a deep, rich color good for royal robes, grapes, and the outer band of a rainbow. If you thumb through *Peterson's Field Guide to Birds* you may find that vibrant color on the crown of a violet-crowned hummingbird or on the breast of a purple gallinule. You certainly won't find it on a purple sandpiper! If you squint a little, in just the right light, you might convince yourself that there is a slight violet tinge to this small, plump, mostly gray shorebird. Or you might not.

All name speculations aside, the purple sandpiper is a regular winter visitor to certain Low Country beaches. It spends the summer months breeding in northernmost Canada and winters on rocky coasts and jetties from Newfoundland to northern Florida. It is often found in the company of ruddy turnstones that are only ruddy in the summer, and sanderlings, that are only sand-colored in the winter. Small mixed flocks of these birds can be found feeding on invertebrates that are common where ocean waves interact with rocks and rock jetties.

Purple Sandpiper & Ruddy Turnstone

A crowded rock full of Ruddy Turnstones and a lone Purple Sandpiper

NOVEMBER

Purple Sandpiper

My first looks at purple sandpipers came on the rocky coast of Cape Ann in Massachusetts. Standing atop a cliff looking down on an impressive assortment of mammoth rocks, I could just make out several small grayish shapes on the rock closest to the water. "Purple sandpipers," called out a nearby expert. Far be it from me to question this call, but all I ever saw – even through the spotting scope – were dark birds darting about on distant rocks. Getting a better look would have required the nimbleness of a mountain goat.

When I moved back to Tybee Island, I was thrilled to encounter the purple sandpiper in a more intimate venue. Walking along the sand, I could approach the rock jetty with binoculars to study the bird at leisure. There it was, just like the picture – a drooping, two-toned bill, yellow legs, grayish-brown on the breast that reached almost to the legs in front. With great concentration it poked and probed at a tasty morsel clinging to the rock. As the waves crashed onto the rocks, it would scurry or fly away to escape the spray.

The "purples" are one of the last shorebirds to leave their Arctic breeding grounds, usually appearing on Low Country beaches in mid-November. At high tide, when the rock jetties are covered with water, shorebirds can usually be found resting on the beach. The purple sandpipers generally hang with the turnstones and sanderlings, huddling together in flocks of ten, twenty, fifty, or even a hundred birds. With a little practice, you can pick them out. The turnstones have dark backs, white breasts, and orange legs. Sanderlings in the winter are the color of pale beach

> *Purple sandpipers are one of the last shorebirds to leave the Arctic in the fall, appearing on Low Country beaches by mid-November.*

Purple Sandpiper avoids ocean spray

Country is that I don't usually have to suffer through single digit temperatures, freezing toes, and watery eyes to get my purple sandpiper fix.

It is easy to take for granted the people, things and birds that we see every day. How quickly we grow blasé about that which is abundant, remarking dismissively, "Oh, it's just another ruddy turnstone." Birds that visit only rarely or in small numbers get a special welcome. That's how it is with purple sandpipers. They may not really be *purple*, but finding one on the beach in late fall or winter is always a treat.

land. If you spy something gray with yellow legs, you've got yourself a "purple."

Another wonderful thing about watching purple sandpipers in the Low

THE YELLOW-RUMPS ARE BACK!

As the fall songbird migration draws to a close in October, I have been heard to exclaim, "Oh no! It's a yellow-rump!" The rump in question belongs to a small warbler – the aptly named yellow-rumped warbler. In spring the male is showy with a black and white face pattern, yellow markings on the sides and a diagnostic yellow patch at the base of the upper

Yellow-rumped Warbler, front view

Yellow-rumped Warbler, rear view

side of the tail. In the fall the birds revert to a drab grayish-brown, losing all but the barest smudge of their yellow side patches. They do, however, retain their yellow rumps.

I greet the arrival of the first yellow-rump with dismay and regret because it generally means that my Neotropical friends – the painted buntings, summer tanagers, and most of the warblers – have departed for warmer climes. Where there is one yellow-rump, there

NOVEMBER

NOVEMBER

Yellow-rumped Warbler

will soon be many. They leave their nesting grounds up north but migrate only to southern North America. Their fondness for berries and ability to digest the waxy berry coating enables them to find food even when insect populations decline in the colder weather. They make themselves right at home in the stands of wax myrtle, bayberry, juniper, and even poison ivy that abound in the southeastern United States. In fact, many people still refer to this bird by its former name – the myrtle warbler.

I sometimes wish they had kept the name "myrtle warbler." Saying "yellow-rumped warbler" over and over gets tiresome. That's why, out in the field, they are commonly referred to as "yellow-rumps" or even "rumps."

Long time Ogeechee Audubon member John Stafford tabulated the census data collected over thirty years for the annual Harris Neck Christmas Bird Count. In 1970, eight observers recorded a total of 39 yellow-rumped warblers. In 2000, 17 observers recorded 1283 of the now seemingly abundant songbird. Counts have ranged from a low of 20 birds in 1974 to a high of 2786 birds in 2002.

It's funny how things that are abundant quickly lose their value. "It's the law of supply and demand," an economist would say. The showy northern cardinal is always fun to watch but does not usually inspire birders with the thrill of the chase. Seeing a bald eagle while they were endangered was an uncommon treat. Now that our successful conservation efforts have resulted in an increase in

> *Yellow-rumped warblers make themselves right at home in the stands of wax myrtle, bayberry, and juniper that abound in winter in the Low Country.*

Yellow-rumped Warbler, spring plumage

the eagle population and they are becoming a regular sight throughout the Low Country, will we value them as highly? Similarly, it is easy to lose interest in "just another 'rump.'"

Yellow-rumps are obliging birds in several ways. They regularly announce their presence with a distinct chip note that reminds me of a waitress asking for her "tip, tip, tip." You might notice them visiting your birdbath, enjoying the spray of a mister, or snacking at a suet feeder. They are also particularly responsive to *pishing*.

Pishing is one activity that distinguishes avid birders from regular people who just look at birds. It's the fine art of making a variety of strange hissing, whistling, smacking or kissing noises in the hopes of arousing the curiosity of nearby birds and inspiring them to come closer or pop out into the open. Those who risk looking and sounding foolish in order to attract birds have surely earned a special birder's merit badge.

Yellow-rumps *do* respond to *pishing*. When I tried it recently at the Savannah National Wildlife Refuge, a grove of seemingly empty trees came alive with fluttering, "tipping" birds. They hopped and flew, emerging from the leaves to check out the disturbance but disappearing again before I could take a photograph. I tried to look at every bird, hoping for something different, like an orange-crowned warbler or a blue-headed vireo. I did see two ruby-crowned kinglets – tiny winter visitors that flick their wings incessantly and communicate with a scolding chatter. But mostly what I saw were yellow-rumps.

If they didn't return, we'd miss them. Alarmed, we'd worry, "What's happening? Where are the yellow-rumps?" We'd do studies and print T-shirts and have campaigns to save them. So maybe I have been guilty of under-appreciation. I'll try to do better. I'll strive to treat every yellow-rump with wonder and respect. After all, if

Yellow-rumped Warbler in wax myrtle

the Neotropical birds didn't leave for the winter, what would we have to look forward to? Only four more months until spring migration!

Has Anyone Seen My *Icterid*?

If you spend any time watching birds, you have surely asked the question "what *is* that bird?" Unless you happen to have an expert handy, you have probably reached for a field guide, only to discover there are a lot of birds in North America and many of them look way too much alike.

If you consult your field guide often, you'll begin to notice the way that certain birds are grouped together. *Ornithologists* (scientists who specialize in the study of birds) have spent a lot of time trying to figure out these relationships. They study appearance, behavior, and even genetics to figure out which birds should be part of which families.

The scientists decided that in order to communicate clearly with other scientists around the world, they would name everything in Latin. Now if I

Red-winged Blackbird, female

Red-winged Blackbird, male

memorized all those Latin names, I would probably forget a lot of other important stuff, like my name, age and social security number. However, I do find that knowing the family groupings can come in handy when trying to find birds in the field guide.

For example, it helps to know that orioles are related to meadowlarks and blackbirds, and are members of the family *Icteridae*. The *icterids* are medium-sized to large songbirds with strong, straight, pointed bills. The name is derived from Greek and means "jaundiced" or "yellow" – in spite of the fact that many *icterids* are black. They are thought to be relatively recent in origin, are found only in the New World, and are located almost at the end of the field guide.

Icterids prefer open habitats, ranging from urban parks to grasslands, marshes, and agricultural fields. They seem to thrive in areas that have been altered by humans. One unique adaptation shared by most *icterids* is that they can open their beaks with great strength. This behavior, called "gaping," allows them to pry open bark, soil, mud or grass to find tasty treats inaccessible to other birds.

In North America, the main *icterid* groupings are the orioles; the meadowlarks and their allies, the bobolink and yellow-headed blackbird; and the grackles, blackbirds and their allies, the cowbirds. I'm still puzzling over the notion of birds having "allies." Does it mean that if there were a battle of the birds, the bobolinks would rush to the aid of the meadowlarks, while the cowbirds would back the red-winged blackbirds?

By far the most popular *icterids* are the orioles. These are colorful birds, patterned in bright orange or yellow and black. They have rich, whistled songs, and dine on insects, fruit and nectar. Of the two species common in

Bobolink in rice field

coastal Georgia, the rusty orange and black orchard oriole nests here but winters in the tropics. The more vivid orange and black Baltimore oriole continues further north to nest, but occasionally can be found wintering in our area, visiting feeders for nectar, fruit, and jelly.

Eastern Meadowlarks in flight

Gang of Boat-tailed Grackles

The icterids are medium-sized to large songbirds with strong, straight, pointed bills. The name is derived from Greek and means "jaundiced" or "yellow."

Baltimore Oriole, male

The eastern meadowlark is another well-loved *icterid* that favors open fields and frequents the Low Country in the winter. These birds hang out in flocks on the ground, using their brown streaked backs to almost disappear against the background of dirt and grass while they search for insects with their strong, straight beaks. Only when the meadowlark stands erect, or perches on a fence post or wire, does it reveal a glorious yellow breast adorned with a distinctive black "vee." Its call, described as "see you, see yeer" is pleasantly sweet and melodic.

In spring and fall, another showy meadowlark ally, the bobolink, stops over in the Low Country during migration. In the spring, male bobolinks are richly patterned in buff, brown and white. Female and post-breeding males are a rich buffy color, and look like large pointy-beaked sparrows. Bobolinks are sometimes known as "ricebirds," due to their fondness for chowing down in the rice fields.

Of course, the *icterids* that I see most often are not the showy orioles or the sweet-singing meadowlarks. I get their rowdy cousins, the boat-tailed grackles and red-winged blackbirds. These backyard bullies descend on my yard in flocks of ten, twenty, fifty, a hundred – filling the air with a cacophony of squawks and whistles. They puff up their feathers, flutter their wings, empty my feeders and muddy my birdbaths.

I'm thinking that whoever wrote that nursery rhyme had it right – four and twenty of these would make the perfect pie. Excuse me, but would someone please take my *icterids*?

IN YOUR YARD

ATTRACTING BIRDS TO YOUR YARD

Northern Cardinal, male

While most avid bird watchers spend time traipsing about in the field in search of birds, there's a lot to be said for sitting comfortably at home while the birds come to you. Warning! Read this at your own risk. Studies have shown that feeding and watching birds may be habit-forming. You may find yourself joining the more than 55 million Americans

Blue Jay with peanuts

who are hooked on feeding birds in their backyards.

It doesn't really take a rocket scientist to figure out how to attract birds to your yard. Like most other creatures, they're in the market for food, water, shelter and places to raise their families. Offer these four things in abundance, and the birds will come and bring their friends. If you're really successful, you'll soon be complaining that they are eating you out of house and home.

Let's start with food. You can offer this by planting bushes, shrubs and trees that will provide birds with berries, nuts and seeds. Or, for more immediate gratification, there's offering food in bird feeders.

What kind of feeder? What kind of food?

One simple solution is to put up an open tray or platform, fill it with a seed mixture that includes black oil sunflower seed, striped sunflower seed, safflower seed, white millet, and peanuts, and wait to see who shows up. Stay away from lends that contain oats, red milo, sorghum or cereal grains, as these are fillers that birds toss aside in search of the good stuff.

Feathered friends who might come calling include the always popular "redbirds" or northern cardinals that hull sunflower seed with large orange beaks; tiny Carolina chickadees patterned in black, white, and gray; raucous blue jays with a fondness for peanuts; muted gray tufted titmice; twittery groups of house finches (reddish males and brown streaked females); downy, red-bellied and red-headed woodpeckers; round-bodied mourning doves scratching about for whatever falls on the ground; and plump, bushy-tailed gray squirrels.

"Wait a minute," you say. "Squirrels? I thought we were attracting birds!"

That's the bad news. The challenging art of feeding birds is figuring out what to do about the squirrels.

Female Downy Woodpecker on suet feeder

One solution is to mount your platform on a pole or post, about five and a half feet from the ground, and eight feet from any tree, fence or roof edge. Add a guard or baffle below the feeder, and, with luck you may be able to feed birds, not squirrels.

Of course, just when you get this problem solved, you look out at your feeder to discover that it has been taken over by a large, noisy flock of boat-tailed grackles.

"Aargh," you think. "I didn't really want to spend a fortune feeding grackles."

One solution is to change the food on your platform and just offer safflower seed. Grackles are not fond of safflower, but cardinals, chickadees, titmice, house finches and mourning doves all find it quite tasty.

Then you can add another feeder for your mixed seed. A tube feeder inside a cage will offer the small birds a place to

Female Red-bellied Woodpecker with nut

IN YOUR YARD

eat, undisturbed by squirrels, large birds, hawks or cats. Another option might be a feeder engineered to close under the weight of a squirrel or large bird.

After the initial rush that comes from attracting those first birds to your yard, you'll probably find yourself thinking "more, how I can get more?"

One solution is to add other kinds of food. Birds such as mockingbirds, brown thrashers, bluebirds, Carolina wrens, and warblers eat mostly insects and fruit. They may, however, be enticed to feeders with suet (a preparation of rendered beef fat), hulled sunflower seed, raisins, grapes, peanut butter or mealworms.

Then you'll need a nyjer feeder in the winter to attract the goldfinches, a millet feeder for painted buntings in the spring and summer, and a nectar feeder for hummingbirds.

At the moment, in my yard, I have one tube feeder with safflower seed, one suet feeder, two hummingbird feeders, three nyjer feeders, four caged feeders, five assorted other feeders, two birdbaths with drippers, two birdhouses, and a purple martin condo on the dock. Now if I could just get a partridge to roost in my non-existent pear tree, I'd be all set for Christmas. No wonder the sign next to my front door reads "This place is for the birds!"

Painted Bunting, male

> *Like most other creatures, birds are in the market for food, water, shelter, and places to raise their families.*

Carolina Wren with mealworm

In Your Yard title page features a male Northern Cardinal, Brown-headed Nuthatch and a pesky Gray Squirrel, pictured top to bottom.

Which Birds Eat Which Foods?

Note: Over the course of twelve years spent working at Wild Birds Unlimited, I have learned that there is a good deal of variation in the way birds behave in different yards. One customer reports that birds devour their suet, while another complains that no birds will touch it. The following table is intended to offer general guidelines, not gospel truth.

Key:
Orange = Preferred
Green = Will also eat

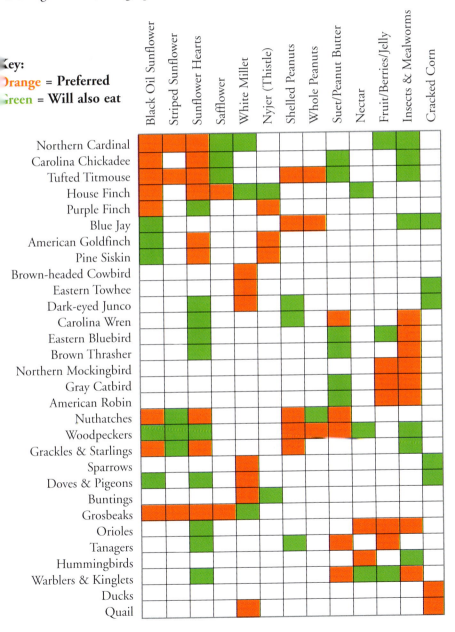

THE PLEASURES OF THE BATH

Few things in life equal the simple pleasure of a good bath. Immersion in water seems to freshen our spirits as well as our bodies, and this holds true for our feathered friends. Clean, fresh water can be scarcer than food in many environments, and birds will fly several miles to obtain it. They'll come for a drink and stay for a bath, in the same water. They're not as picky as humans, and they don't use soap.

Water is of particular importance during the heat of the summer. Since birds do not have sweat glands, they must cool their bodies by breathing more rapidly to increase evaporation in the lungs. As a result, birds - particularly small ones - are prone to dehydration on hot days. If your backyard offers a reliable source of water, you are likely to attract a wide variety of birds, many of which would not come to a bird feeder.

Here are some things to consider in choosing a birdbath.

• Size: less than a foot in diameter will be good for drinking but not bathing. Two to three feet in diameter

Blue Jay sunning after his bath

means several birds may bathe at the same time.

• Slope: even more important than size. Recommended depth is three inches at the center with a gradual slope to the edge, so a bird can wade to its preferred depth. Pebbles or rocks can be added to make a deep birdbath more attractive to birds. One day I counted twelve goldfinches enjoying a group bath in the largest of my birdbaths.

• Footing: a rough, textured bottom provides a better grip for tiny feet.

• Location: Place your birdbath in an open area with some cover nearby, enough for the birds to retreat to, but not enough to make it easy for a marauding cat to make a sneak attack.

Moving water seems to hold a particular fascination for birds. A pump that circulates the water will create the

Great Blue Heron bathes

Tufted Titmouse bathing

wonderful gurgling sound, while a dripper, hooked up to an outside spigot, will replenish the water lost to evaporation. Both will disturb the surface tension of your bath, making it less likely to become a breeding site for mosquitoes. Birds will perch on the dripper and drink from the spout.

Then there's the task of keeping the birdbath clean. Use a mild ten percent bleach solution and a good brush to get rid of the inevitable green slime. Rinse well and change the water often.

Small songbirds, such as warblers, hummingbirds, and vireos, take special delight in leaf bathing. Instead of total immersion, they prefer the greater privacy of perching among the foliage and rubbing against the wet leaves. By attaching tubing equipped with a mist nozzle to a leafy tree, you may attract a bevy of bathing beauties.

If you happen to live near a pond, lagoon, creek, or ditch, you may be lucky enough to watch the bathing rituals of larger birds. I watched mesmerized one day as a great blue heron walked into a pond up to its belly. It quickly began to rock and plunge, glancing around to make sure no predators were lurking nearby.

Every so often the osprey takes a break from patrolling for fish to visit the sandbar for a quick dip. Afterwards, it looks for a perch to complete the

> *If your yard offers a reliable source of water, you are likely to attract a wide variety of birds.*

Brown Thrasher

the shy hermit thrush slipping in during the winter for a quick splash, the brown thrasher hopping up for a drink and dunk, the green heron taking a sip from the dripper, and a group of yellow-rumped warblers popping in and out for an evening communal bath.

Give them water and they will come. Good bathing!

grooming ritual. For a bird, proper feather maintenance is crucial. Preening is required to make sure barbs and barbules are properly interlocked. Regular oiling keeps feathers from getting brittle. Well-tended feathers provide insulation against the cold, waterproofing, and trouble-free flight.

I keep a separate yard list of birds seen bathing. Special treats have been

Red-winged Blackbird, male

BECOMING A BIRDLORD

"If at first you don't succeed, try, try again"…and again…and again. Thursday, March 4, 2004 was a red-letter day on Chimney Creek. On that day, as I got into my car to head into town, I glanced over at my cedar nest box, properly mounted on a pole with a raccoon baffle, and saw a chickadee emerge from the entrance hole.

Now that may not seem particularly memorable, but I had been putting up nest boxes for five years with no success. Year One, I bought a kit, assembled my own box, and waited eagerly for tenants. No luck. Year Two was more of the same. I noticed bluebirds in my parents' neighborhood and moved the box to their back yard, where a pair of Carolina chickadees

Carolina Chickadee nest in birdhouse

immediately moved in. Year Three I bought a different style of box, fancy with a copper roof, but still built to open on the side for easy monitoring and cleaning. Again, none of the usual small cavity nesting birds (chickadees, titmice, wrens, bluebirds and nuthatches) gave it a second glance. When I observed bluebird/nuthatch wars at my brother's house on Wilmington Island, I took the box to his yard where the brown-headed nuthatches rushed to sign a two-month lease.

Year Four, I went for the basic bluebird house, adding a metal portal around the entrance hole to keep woodpeckers from enlarging the hole. Once again, there were no takers.

That's why March 4 of Year Five was a day of celebration. At long last, I was a birdlord.

I had been hearing stories about other people's nesting birds for years. But just like with children, everything changes when you finally have your own. I watched Mrs. Chickadee bring in an assortment of moss, pine straw, grass, and plant fibers, until the nest was about five inches high. For years, I have suggested to people that they put out soft material for the birds to use as nest lining. I don't have pets, but my mother is a weaver, so I begged a small quantity of fleece from her. I put it in a mesh bag, and hung it from a branch near the birdhouse. Sure enough, when I checked on the nest a couple of days later, it was nicely fleece-lined. Now if there is an April cold snap, my chickadee babies will stay warm and toasty.

On March 18, I tapped on the box and got no response. When I opened it to inspect the nest, Mrs. Chickadee hissed at me. I hastily closed the box and began to speculate. Was she laying eggs? Just enjoying her new home? When I checked the box again two days later, she flew out, but I couldn't see any eggs.

It's funny how, now that the birds are in my yard and my box, I feel an urgent

Tufted Titmouse collecting fluff

need to know every detail of chickadee nesting behavior. I found lots of information at the Cornell Lab of Ornithology Birdhouse Network web site – www.birds.cornell.edu/birdhouse. Their data indicates that chickadees are monogamous and may actually mate for life. Carolina chickadees lay five to eight speckled white and reddish brown eggs at the rate of one a day. At six-tenths of an inch, the eggs are barely larger than jellybeans. Before the clutch is complete, she will cover the eggs with nesting material whenever she leaves the nest. Could that be why I didn't see any?

Incubation starts when the next-to-last egg has been laid, and continues

Carolina Chickadee nestlings

for 11 to 14 days. Mr. Chickadee doesn't sit on the eggs, but he faithfully brings food home during that time, as well as for several days after the eggs hatch. For the subsequent two weeks, both Mr. & Mrs. will spend their days in unrelenting pursuit of larval insects with which to feed the begging babies.

Of course, as a new birdlord, I have responsibilities. By monitoring the box at least once a week, I can record the number of eggs laid, when and how many hatched, and when they fledge. I'll need to stop monitoring a few days before the juveniles are scheduled to leave the nest, so I don't startle them into leaving too soon. I'll have to keep an eye on the pole and make sure no ants start climbing it. If they do, I can smear vaseline around the base of the pole.

I did feel a twinge of "nest box envy," when friends reported that they have chickadees in one box, bluebirds in another, and now brown-headed nuthatches in a third. However, with all the "birdlordly" duties involved, I think perhaps one nest of chickadees is just right.

Of course, now that the chickadees have a nest built, the Carolina wrens are hanging around the box and inspecting the hole. The real estate agents always say that a house sells better when it looks lived in. Guess I'll have to put up another box!

> *By monitoring a birdhouse once a week, you can keep track of how many eggs were laid, when they hatch, and when the young birds should fledge.*

OH, THOSE PESKY SQUIRRELS

It ought to be simple. I mean how hard could it be to feed a few birds? You make or buy a feeder, hang it from a tree, add some seed, sit back and enjoy. Ah, naiveté! Even the seemingly simple things in life can quickly acquire amazing layers of complexity.

Squirrel on suet feeder

You have just settled into your armchair in front of the window, prepared to enjoy the multitude of small, cute, red, blue, or gray-feathered friends who will rush to feast at your new feeder. Lights, camera, action – your first visitor has arrived! Only the creature has fur, not feathers. It's gray with a long bushy tail, and it is consuming vast quantities of birdseed. Congratulations! You are now the proud owner of a squirrel feeder.

Now, you can either decide that all along, you really wanted to feed squirrels, or you can join the rest of the bird-feeding world in pursuit of the elusive squirrel-proof bird feeder. After more than ten years of personal experimentation, as well as helping customers at Wild Birds Unlimited, I have come to a profound and familiar conclusion.

"You can beat some of the squirrels all of the time; you can beat all of the squirrels some of the time; but you can't beat all of the squirrels all of the time." I do have, however, a number of suggestions that could help in the goal of feeding more birds than squirrels.

1. Buy durable feeders made of metal and heavy-duty plastic. That way if the squirrels get to your feeder, at least all they can eat will be the seed.

2. Location, location, location! If possible, locate your feeders away from trees, roof edges, fences, and other things that

Gray Squirrel at a "squirrel-proof" feeder

Raccoon family enjoying the feeder feast

squirrels can jump from. Since squirrels routinely jump eight to ten feet, this can be more difficult than it sounds.

3. Use baffles! They may not look pretty, but a well-designed baffle can be more effective than even the most sophisticated "squirrel-proof" feeder. In my yard, I have two pole systems. Each is located ten feet from trees or roof, and each is equipped with a metal cylinder that resembles a long stovepipe hat. It is infinitely satisfying to watch the squirrels crawl up into the "hat" and come out again looking puzzled. The one time I observed a squirrel on my feeder, I found that it was a long-distance leaper. I trimmed some branches, moved the pole slightly, and was entertained to see the squirrel leap and land on the ground.

Hanging baffles are designed to hang above a feeder. They are most effective when the feeder is hung away from a tree trunk or vertical surface, so the squirrel cannot jump sideways to the feeder. My favorite is a durable, clear plastic baffle shaped like an inverted funnel, that I call the "witch hat" baffle. In addition to discouraging squirrels, it also protects the feeder from rain.

Pole system with baffle

4. If you are hanging a feeder in a location where you cannot prevent the squirrels from getting to it, try a caged feeder or one engineered to exclude squirrels. A number of companies have designed feeders with weighted bars that close when squirrels or large birds sit on them. However, there is usually one squirrel that figures out how to beat the system – even if it means hanging by its back paws and doing chin-ups to reach the seed in the feeder.

5. Try using a different seed. Squirrels tend not to prefer safflower seed, nyjer (also called thistle), or white millet. This does not mean that no squirrel will ever eat these seeds. Sometimes, squirrels just seem to get frustrated and chew up whatever they can get their teeth into!

6. Feed your squirrels at a site away from your feeders. I put out an ear of corn each morning that seems to placate the squirrels. If I forget their corn, they start to make mischief and go for the bird feeders.

Of course, just when you are congratulating yourself that you have successfully outwitted the squirrels, you wake up one morning and notice that all your feeders have been mysteriously emptied during the night, and a couple of them are on the ground. You get out your flashlight and detective's badge, determined to catch the crook. Sure enough, that evening you watch a furry, masked bandit traverse the line to your feeder, hang by its hind paws, and use agile hands to shovel your precious bird seed into its mouth.

And you thought feeding birds would be easy. Cheer up. Things could be worse. At least here on the coastal plain we aren't yet blessed with bears.

Gray Squirrel

A well-designed and strategically placed baffle can be more effective than the most sophisticated "squirrel-proof" feeder.

Gray Squirrel inspects the baffle

Birds in Your Yard – Quick Reference Guide

Year-Round Seed Eaters

Northern Cardinal m.

Northern Cardinal f.

Carolina Chickadee

Tufted Titmouse

House Finch m.

House Finch f.

Brown-headed Nuthatch

White-breasted Nuthatch

Blue Jay

Mourning Dove

Eurasian Collared-Dove

Rock Pigeon

Red-bellied Woodpecker m.

Red-bellied Woodpecker f.

Downy Woodpecker m.

Downy Woodpecker f.

 Red-headed Woodpecker
 Northern Flicker
 Eastern Towhee m.
 Eastern Towhee f.

 Red-winged Blackbird m.
 Red-winged Blackbird f.
 Brown-headed Cowbird m.
 Brown-headed Cowbird f.

 Boat-tailed Grackle m.
 Boat-tailed Grackle f.
 Common Grackle
 European Starling

 House Sparrow m.
 House Sparrow f.
 American Crow
 Fish Crow

BIRDS IN YOUR YARD

YEAR-ROUND INSECT & FRUIT EATERS
Visit birdbaths or feeders for suet, mealworms, sunflower chips

Carolina Wren | Brown Thrasher | Northern Mockingbird | American Robin

Eastern Bluebird m. | Eastern Bluebird f. | Pileated Woodpecker m. | Pileated Woodpecker f.

FALL & WINTER SEED EATERS

American Goldfinch breeding m. | American Goldfinch non-breeding | Purple Finch m. | Purple Finch f.

Pine Siskin | White-throated Sparrow | Chipping Sparrow | Song Sparrow

ALL & WINTER INSECT, FRUIT & NECTAR EATERS
visit birdbaths or feeders for suet, mealworms, sunflower chips

 Hermit Thrush
 House Wren
 Yellow-bellied Sapsucker, m.
 Ruby-crowned Kinglet

 Yellow-rumped Warbler
 Pine Warbler
 Yellow-throated Warbler
 Orange-crowned Warbler

 Baltimore Oriole m.
 Baltimore Oriole f.
 Gray Catbird
 Cedar Waxwing

RING & SUMMER SEED EATERS

 Painted Bunting m.
 Painted Bunting f.
 Indigo Bunting m.
 Indigo Bunting f.

BIRDS IN YOUR YARD

SPRING & SUMMER SEED EATERS

 Blue Grosbeak m.
 Blue Grosbeak f.
 Rose-breasted Grosbeak m.
 Rose-breasted Grosbeak f.

SPRING & SUMMER INSECT, FRUIT & NECTAR EATERS

 Ruby-throated Hummingbird m.
 Ruby-throated Hummingbird f.
 Orchard Oriole m.
 Orchard Oriole f.

 Summer Tanager m.
 Summer Tanager f.
 Purple Martin m.
 Purple Martin f.

 Great Crested Flycatcher
 Eastern Kingbird
 Northern Parula
 Blue-gray Gnatcatcher

WETLANDS BIRDS

Great Blue Heron

Little Blue Heron

Little Blue Heron, Juvenile

Tricolored Heron

Green Heron

Great Egret

Snowy Egret

Cattle Egret

Black-crowned Night-Heron

Yellow-crowned Night-Heron

White Ibis

Wood Stork

Anhinga f.

Double-crested Cormorant

Belted Kingfisher

Osprey

LOW COUNTRY BIRD WATCHING LOCATIONS

This list is intended to provide a brief introduction to Low Country birding locations. For more detailed information, directions, maps, etc., please consult the following resources.

BOOKS
Birding Georgia ©2000 by Giff Beaton
Finding Birds in South Carolina ©1993 by Robin Carter
Birding South Carolina: A Guide to 40 Premier Birding Sites
 ©2009 by Jeff Mollenhauer
Birder's Guide to Hilton Head Island, S.C. and the Low Country 5th edition
 ©January 2011 revised by Nan Lloyd. Originally compiled by the late Graham C. Dugas, Jr.
Bird Finding in Coastal Georgia's Golden Isles by Lydia C. Thompson

WEB SITES
http://www.wingsoverga.com/
http://www.birding.com/wheretobird/georgia.asp
http://www.georgiawildlife.org/node/1356
http://www.carolinabirdclub.org/
http://www.birding.com/wheretobird/southcarolina.asp
http://www.midnet.sc.edu/audubon/calendar.html
http://www.crbo.net/Charleston.html

GEORGIA - SAVANNAH AREA

SAVANNAH NATIONAL WILDLIFE REFUGE
15 minutes from downtown Savannah on SC170. A stop at the Visitor Center on U.S. 17, six miles north of the Talmadge Bridge, will provide a helpful introduction to the Refuge's habitat and birdlife.

Laurel Hill Wildlife Drive is a four-mile loop trail that takes you through **tidal freshwater wetlands**, originally created as rice plantations.

   All seasons: herons & egrets, ibises, Common Gallinules, raptors
   Winter: ducks, raptors, sparrows, American Bitterns
   Spring: migrating songbirds, shorebirds, wading birds, nesting Anhingas, rails
   Summer: Least Bitterns, Purple Gallinules, Mississippi & Swallow-tailed Kites
   Fall: migrating songbirds, raptors, shorebirds
   Fee: Free   Phone: 843-784-2468   Web: http://www.fws.gov/savannah/

Forsyth Park

Downtown Savannah, bordered by Gaston St. on the north, Whitaker St. on the west, Park St. on the South, and Drayton St. on the east. **Urban park** with variety of trees and grassy lawn.

- All seasons: resident songbirds
- Winter: Yellow-bellied Sapsuckers, winter warblers, Ruby-crowned Kinglets
- Spring and Fall: migratory songbirds
- Summer: resident nesters - woodpeckers, Brown Thrashers, Northern Mockingbirds, American Robins, Chimney Swifts

Fee: Free

Lake Mayer

Southside Savannah at the intersection of Montgomery Crossroads and Sallie Mood Drive. **Suburban park and lake**. Although Lake Mayer has a resident population of domestic ducks and geese, there are a variety of other birds that live and visit here.

- All seasons: Ospreys, gulls, Anhingas, herons and egrets, Eastern Bluebirds
- Winter: ducks, including Ruddy Ducks, Northern Shovelers & Ring-necked Ducks; Loggerhead Shrikes; American Coots
- Spring & Fall: migratory songbirds

Fee: Free   Phone: 912-652-6780
Web: http://parks.chathamcounty.org/Parks/CommunityParks/LakeMayer.aspx

Skidaway Island State Park

5 miles southeast of Savannah on Diamond Causeway
Maritime forest, salt marsh, freshwater pond, tidal creeks

- All seasons: herons and egrets, Bald Eagles, Ospreys, Eastern Bluebirds
- Winter: ducks, loons, grebes, marsh sparrows
- Spring: migrating songbirds, Wood Storks, nesting herons & egrets
- Summer: nesting songbirds, including Painted Buntings, Summer Tanagers, Orchard Orioles
- Fall: migrating songbirds, sparrows, raptors, shorebirds

Fee: $5 Phone: 912-598-2300
Web: http://www.gastateparks.org/SkidawayIsland

Fort Pulaski National Monument

12 miles east of Savannah on Cockspur Island off Georgia Highway 80
Open fields, pine woodlands, salt marsh, coastal scrub, tidal creeks

- All seasons: herons & egrets, Clapper Rails, Marsh Wrens, Brown-headed Nuthatches, Pine Warblers
- Fall and Winter: marsh sparrows, raptors,

Eastern Meadowlarks, Yellow-rumped Warblers,
Sedge Wrens, Forster's Terns, Brown Creepers
Spring: American Robins, Cedar Waxwings, migratory songbirds
Summer: Barn Swallows, Killdeer
Fee: $5   Phone: 912-786-5787   Web: http://www.nps.gov/fopu/index.htm

TYBEE ISLAND, GA

15 miles east of Savannah on US Highway 80. One of three barrier islands accessible by road. Very developed. Little remaining maritime forest. Best birdwatching is at north and south ends. Access north end from Fort Screven parking lot or walking path at end of Polk Street. **Sandy beach as well as dunes, salt marsh and coastal scrub**

All Seasons: herons, egrets, pelicans, gulls, Ospreys, terns
Winter: shorebirds, ducks, raptors, loons, Northern Gannets.
   One of few areas in Low Country to find wintering
   Purple Sandpipers
Spring: migrating songbirds, shorebirds
Summer: gulls, terns, Black Skimmers, Wood Storks,
   Painted Buntings
Fall: Tree Swallows, Caspian Terns, migrating songbirds & shorebirds
Fee: Parking Meters   Phone: 912-786-5444   Web: http://tybeevisit.com/

LITTLE TYBEE ISLAND, GA

Undeveloped barrier island immediately south of Tybee Island that is accessible only by boat. Many area tour companies offer trips to Little Tybee by motorboat or kayak. **Sandy beach, salt marsh, tidal creeks, sand bars, marsh hammocks**

All Seasons: herons, egrets, pelicans, gulls, Ospreys, Marsh Wrens, terns
Winter: marsh sparrows, Piping Plovers, Bald Eagles, ducks, loons, grebes
Spring: migrating songbirds, shorebirds
Summer: gulls, terns, American Oystercatchers, Wilson's Plovers,
   Whimbrels
Fall: migrating songbirds, shorebirds, raptors

WASSAW ISLAND NATIONAL WILDLIFE REFUGE, GA

Barrier island south of Little Tybee, southeast of Savannah; accessible only by boat. Area tour companies offer trips to Wassaw by motorboat or kayak. **Maritime forest, coastal scrub, tidal creeks, salt marsh, sandy beach**

All seasons: herons, egrets, pelicans, gulls, Ospreys
Winter: Bald Eagles, loons, grebes
Spring: migrating songbirds, shorebirds & raptors
Summer: Painted Buntings, Summer Tanagers,
   Yellow-throated Warblers
Fall: migrating songbirds, shorebirds, raptors
Fee: Free   Phone: 843-784-2468   Web: http://www.fws.gov/wassaw/

SAVANNAH-OGEECHEE CANAL MUSEUM & NATURE CENTER
.2 miles west of I-95 on Georgia 204. Boardwalks and trails through
bottomland hardwood forest with cypress and tupelo trees.
> All seasons: Red-shouldered Hawks, Barred Owls, resident songbirds
> Winter: Ruby- & Golden-crowned Kinglets, Blue-gray Gnatcatchers, Winter Wrens
> Spring and Fall: migratory songbirds
> Summer: Prothonotary and Hooded Warblers, Acadian Flycatchers, Yellow-billed Cuckoos, Mississippi Kites
> Fall: migratory songbirds

Fee: $2   Phone: 912-748-8068
Web: http://www.savannahogeecheecanalsociety.org/

J. F. GREGORY PARK, GA
miles east of I-95 on GA 144 in Richmond Hill. Turn left on Cedar Street to reach Park entrance. Three mile walking trail around what once was a 00-acre rice field and is now a **wooded wetland**.
> All seasons: wading birds, raptors, resident songbirds
> Winter: waterfowl, rails
> Spring & Fall: migratory songbirds, raptors, shorebirds
> Summer: Orchard Orioles, Northern Parulas, Yellow-throated Warblers

Fee: Free   Phone: 912-756-3345

GEORGIA – MID-COAST AREA

HARRIS NECK NATIONAL WILDLIFE REFUGE
One hour south of Savannah at Exit 67 off I-95. Go south one mile on U.S. 17 and then turn left on Harris Neck Road. Continue 7 miles to Refuge entrance on ft. **Salt marsh, tidal creek, woodland, freshwater ponds**
> All Seasons: wading birds, raptors, resident songbirds
> Winter: sparrows, wading birds, ducks, raptors
> Spring: migrating song birds, wading bird rookery at Woody Pond
> Summer: Painted Buntings, Summer Tanagers, Yellow-throated Warblers, Acadian Flycatchers
> Fall: migrating songbirds, ducks, sparrows

Fee: Free   Phone: 843-784-2486   Web: http://www.fws.gov/harrisneck/

BLACKBEARD ISLAND NATIONAL WILDLIFE REFUGE
Barrier island in the middle of the Georgia coast; accessible only by boat. Area our companies offer trips to Blackbeard. **Maritime forest, coastal scrub, tidal creeks & salt marsh, sandy beach**
> All seasons: herons, egrets, pelicans, gulls, Ospreys

Winter: Bald Eagles, loons, grebes
Spring: migrating songbirds, shorebirds & raptors
Summer: Painted Buntings, Summer Tanagers, Yellow-throated Warblers
Fall: migrating songbirds, shorebirds, raptors

Fee: Free   Phone: 843-784-2486
Web: http://www.fws.gov/blackbeardisland/

Altamaha Waterfowl Management Area, GA

About 3 miles south of Darien, GA on Highway 17. **Former rice fields, impoundments, ponds, forested dike area, fields, wooded roads**

All seasons: wading birds, raptors, resident song birds
Winter: sparrows, ducks, grebes, raptors, rails, American Bitterns
Spring: migrating songbirds, raptors, ducks, wading birds, rails
Summer: Painted Bunting, Barn Swallows, Least Bitterns, Black-bellied Whistling-Ducks

Fee: Free   Phone: 912-262-3173
Web: http://www.georgiawildlife.org/node/1338

Georgia – Brunswick Area

St. Simon's Island, GA

1 1/2 hours south of Savannah. Exit 38 off I-95 to U.S. 17. South to the F. J. Torras Causeway, then east 4 miles to St. Simon's Island. One of three Georgia barrier islands accessible by road, somewhat developed. Public areas to bird include: Christ Church/Ft. Frederica; St. Simon's Village/Pier; Gould's Inlet/East Beach. **Maritime mixed pine/hardwood forest, coastal scrub, grassy fields, salt marsh, tidal mud flats, beach, ocean, ponds**

All seasons: wading birds, gulls, terns, Clapper Rails
Winter: sparrows, ducks, shorebirds, gulls, terns
Spring: migrating songbirds, raptors, shorebirds including Marbled Godwits, Red Knots, Whimbrels
Summer: Painted Buntings, Reddish Egrets, Gray Kingbirds

Fee: Free   Phone: 912-265-0620   Web: http://www.comecoastawhile.com

Andrews Island Causeway, GA

4.2 miles east of I-95 on GA 341 (Exit 36). Turn right on Homer L. Wilson Wa Andrews Island, a dredge spoil island, is closed to the public but the causeway ca be good for shorebirds, wading birds, marsh sparrows, and ducks. **Salt marsh, tidal creeks, coastal scrub, tidal mudflats**

All seasons: wading birds, Clapper Rails
Winter: ducks, marsh sparrows, Marsh Wrens, American Avocets, Loggerhead Shrikes

Spring: migrating shorebirds, occasional songbirds
Fee: Free   Phone: 912-262-3173
Web: http://www.n-georgia.com/wildlife.htm

FAULK'S PASTURE WILDLIFE MANAGEMENT AREA, GA

miles east of I-95 on GA 341 (Exit 36), entrance on left. Main road is open seasonally. At 0.2 miles in, wet cut area below power lines is spot to look for elusive Henslow's Sparrows in winter. **Pine forest, floodplain forest, weedy fields, cypress-tupelo swamp**

- All seasons: White-breasted Nuthatches, resident songbirds
- Winter: sparrows including Henslow's, Song, Swamp; Sedge Wrens
- Spring & Summer: Prothonotary Warblers, Yellow-crowned Night-Herons

Fee: Free   Phone: 912-262-3173   Web: http://www.n-georgia.com/wildlife.htm

JEKYLL ISLAND STATE PARK, GA

Causeway to Jekyll Island is located 5.4 miles east of I-95 at Exit 29 on U.S. 17. Turn right on causeway and proceed six miles to Jekyll. The causeway itself goes through salt marsh and tidal creek habitat and offers good birding for shorebirds and wading birds. **Maritime forest, mixed pine/hardwood forest, coastal scrub, salt marsh, tidal flats, beach, ocean, freshwater ponds**

- All seasons: wading birds, gulls, terns, pelicans, Anhingas, resident songbirds
- Winter: sea ducks, sparrows, shorebirds, loons, Northern Gannets
- Spring: migratory songbirds, shorebirds
- Summer: Painted Buntings, Gray Kingbirds
- Fall: migratory songbirds, shorebirds, raptors

Fee: $5   Phone: 912-635-3636   Web: http://www.jekyllisland.com/

SOUTH GEORGIA

CUMBERLAND ISLAND NATIONAL SEASHORE, GA

Access by Ferry from St. Mary's, GA. Take Exit 3 off I-95 and go 9 miles east to St. Mary's. Advance ferry reservations recommended. **Maritime forest, coastal scrub, freshwater marsh, weedy fields, salt marsh, tidal creeks and mudflats, beach, pond, ocean**

- All seasons: gulls, terns, Brown Pelicans, American White Pelicans, Common Ground-Doves
- Winter: shorebirds, waterfowl, sparrows
- Spring & Summer: migratory songbirds, Painted Buntings
- Fall: migratory songbirds, shorebirds, raptors

Fee: $20 Ferry $4 Park User   Phone: 877-860-6787 or 912-882-4335
Web: http://www.stmaryswelcome.com/cumberlandislandV2.html

LOW COUNTRY BIRD WATCHING LOCATIONS

OKEFENOKEE NATIONAL WILDLIFE REFUGE, GA
Access is at Suwannee Canal Recreation Area on the east side or Stephen C. Foster State Park on the west. Suwannee Canal is only area in coastal Georgia with public access for red-cockaded woodpeckers. **Pine forest, mixed pine/hardwood forest, cypress-tupelo swamp, floodplain forest, freshwater marsh, weedy fields, ponds**
    All seasons: wading birds, Brown-headed Nuthatches, Pine Warblers, Wood Ducks, Red-cockaded Woodpeckers, Bachman's Sparrows
    Winter: Sandhill Cranes, ducks, sparrows, American Bitterns
    Spring & Summer: Prothonotary Warblers, Least Bitterns, Northern Parulas, Mississippi and Swallow-tailed Kites
    Fall: migratory songbirds, shorebirds, raptors
Fee: $5 for 7 day pass   Phone: Okefenokee NWR Visitor Center
Phone: 912-496-7836
Web: http://www.fws.gov/okefenokee/
Suwannee Canal Recreation Area Concessionaire Phone: 866-843-7926
Web: http://www.okefenokeeadventures.com/
Stephen C. Foster State Park   Phone: 912-637-5274
Web: http://www.gastateparks.org/StephenCFoster

SOUTH CAROLINA - HILTON HEAD ISLAND AREA

PINCKNEY ISLAND NATIONAL WILDLIFE REFUGE, SC
Entrance to parking area located on US 278 westbound 1/4 mile from Hilton Head Island, SC, between the two causeway bridges across from the public boat ramp. 4 mile gravel road - foot and bicycle traffic only. 4,053 acres, 14 miles of nature trails; **salt marsh, forest, brushland, fields, freshwater ponds**
    All Seasons: wading birds, raptors, resident song birds
    Winter: sparrows, ducks, loons, grebes, raptors
    Spring: migrating songbirds, wading bird rookery at Ibis Pond
    Summer: nesting birds, including Painted Buntings, Yellow-throated Warblers, Northern Parulas.
    Fall: migratory songbirds, shorebirds, raptors

SEA PINES FOREST PRESERVE, SC
605 acre preserve located within Sea Pines Plantation on southern end of Hilton Head Island. From the entrance to Hilton Head Island drive on SC 278 and turn right onto the Cross Island Parkway ($1 toll). Continue to the traffic circle on Palmetto Bay Road and turn right onto Greenwood Drive. The Sea Pines gate is 0.2 mile and the preserve is 1 mile from the gate on the left. $5 entrance fee for non-residents. Trail map available at kiosk.
Mixed pine forest, swamp, grassy fields, freshwater lakes

All seasons: wading birds, resident songbirds, owls
Winter: ducks, sparrows, kinglets, rails, American Bitterns
Spring & Fall Migration: warblers, thrushes, vireos
Fee: $5   Web: http://www.exploreseapines.com/forest-preserve.asp

Fish Haul Creek Park, SC

City park at north end of Hilton Head Island. From the high bridge over the Intracoastal Waterway at the northwestern edge of Hilton Head Island keep going on US 278 for about 4 miles. Ignore the turnoff for the Cross Island Parkway (toll road) and keep on the old, free US 278 Business route. Shortly after the turnoff for the toll road turn left (north) onto Beach City Road. Continue north on Beach City Road for 1.9 miles to a four-way stop. Keep going straight ahead to the park entrance on the right. **Oak forest, salt marsh, tidal flats, beach, ocean**

All seasons: Clapper Rails, Seaside Sparrows, gulls, terns, Black Skimmers
Winter: ducks, shorebirds, sparrows, Northern Gannets
Spring & Fall: migratory songbirds, shorebirds, raptors
Summer: terns, gulls, Reddish Egrets, Painted Buntings
Fee: Free   Phone: 843-361-4600
Web: http://www.carolinabirdclub.org/sites/SC/fishhaul.html

South Carolina - Southern Area

Hunting Island State Park, SC

5000 acre park which fronts on the Atlantic Ocean. From Beaufort, SC follow US 21 east for about 18 miles to the park entrance on the left. **Salt marsh, freshwater marsh, maritime forest, beach, mudflats, ocean**

All seasons: herons, egrets, American Oystercatchers, pelicans, Marsh Wrens
Winter: shorebirds, sea ducks
Spring & Fall: migratory songbirds, shorebirds, raptors, rails
Summer: Painted Buntings, Least Bitterns, Yellow-throated Warblers
Fee: $5   Phone: 843-838-2011
Web: http://www.southcarolinaparks.com/park-finder/state-park/1019.aspx

Donnelly Wildlife Management Area, SC

Access is from US 17, about 100 yards NE of intersection of US 17 and SC 303, approximately 2 miles east of Green Pond, SC. Office and kiosk located about 1/2 mile down gravel road. Donnelly WMA consists of 8048 acres located in the heart of the ACE Basin (the collective basins of the Ashepoo, Combahee, and Edisto Rivers). *Note:* Check calendar for specific hunting-related closures. Boynton Nature Trail is closed Nov. 1 until Feb. 9 to protect waterfowl. **Salt marsh, managed rice fields, freshwater marsh, swamp, river, mudflats, mixed** pine/hardwood forest, fields, farm land

All seasons: Red-headed Woodpeckers, Brown-headed Nuthatches, Pine Warblers, herons, egrets, Wood Storks, Wood Ducks, Anhingas

Winter: Blue-headed Vireos, Orange-crowned Warblers, Fox Sparrows, ducks, sparrows, American Bitterns

Spring & Fall: migratory songbirds, shorebirds, raptors

Summer: Prothonotary Warblers, Northern Parulas, Black-bellied Whistling-Ducks, Purple Gallinules

Fee: Free   Phone: 843-844-8957
Web: https://www.dnr.sc.gov/mlands/lookup/

BEAR ISLAND WILDLIFE MANAGEMENT AREA, SC

From the intersection of SC 303 and U.S. 17 in Green Pond go northeast (towards Charleston) for about 3 miles. Here turn right (south) onto Road 26, Bennett's Point Road. Follow Bennett's Point Road south for about 13 miles. The main entrance to the area is located on the left (east) approximately 1 mile after crossing the Ashepoo River. *Note:* Bear Island WMA is closed from Nov. 1 until Feb. 9 to protect waterfowl and for hunting-related activities. You may still bird along Bennetts Pond Road and at Marys House Pond. **Pond, river, salt marsh, freshwater marsh, mudflats, maritime forest, fields, farm land**

All seasons: Wood Storks, Mottled Ducks, King Rails, herons, egrets

Winter: Tundra Swans, American White Pelicans, Bald Eagles, ducks, sparrows, rails, American Bitterns, Bonaparte's Gulls

Spring & Fall: migratory songbirds, shorebirds, raptors

Summer: Least Bitterns, Roseate Spoonbills, Orchard Orioles, Black Terns, Black Rails

Fee: Free   Phone: 843-844-8957
Web: https://www.dnr.sc.gov/mlands/lookup/

ERNEST F. HOLLINGS ACE BASIN NATIONAL WILDLIFE REFUGE, SC

This area is also known as the Grove Plantation. From U.S. 17, take SC 174 south. Stay on SC 174 through Adams Run (174 will make a right turn in Adams Run). At the intersection with the flashing light, turn right onto Willtown Road. Go approximately 2 miles, entrance road will be on the left. Office is located in the Plantation House approximately 2 miles down gravel road.

Pine forest, hardwood swamp, ponds, old rice fields, freshwater marsh

All seasons: Brown-headed Nuthatches, Pine Warblers, King Rails, Barred Owls, herons, egrets

Winter: Northern Harriers, Sedge Wrens, Chipping, Song, Savannah & Swamp Sparrows, Virginia Rails, Soras

Spring & Fall: migratory songbirds, shorebirds, raptors

Summer: Painted Buntings, Acadian Flycatchers, Prothonotary Warblers, Yellow-throated Warblers, Summer Tanagers,

Mississippi Kites
Fee: Free   Phone: 843-889-3084   Web: http://acebasin.fws.gov

Edisto Island, SC

Barrier island about 45 miles southwest of Charleston. Birding areas include Edisto Beach State Park as well as a couple of other spots near the town of Edisto Beach. From U.S. 17, take Hwy 174 28 miles to entrance of the town of Edisto Beach. As you enter the town limits, the entrance to the park will be on your left.

Salt marsh, beach, dunes, maritime forest, mudflats

All seasons: herons, egrets, Pine Warblers, Brown-headed Nuthatches, gulls, terns

Winter: loons, sea ducks, Northern Gannets, Yellow-rumped Warblers, Blue-headed Vireos, Ruby-crowned Kinglets, Yellow-bellied Sapsuckers

Spring & Fall: migratory songbirds, shorebirds, raptors

Summer: Yellow-billed Cuckoos, Eastern Wood-Pewees, Northern Parulas, Summer Tanagers, Orchard Orioles

Fee: $5 State Park   Phone: 843-869-2156
Web: http://www.southcarolinaparks.com/park-finder/state-park/1298.aspx

SOUTH CAROLINA - CHARLESTON AREA

Dungammon Heritage Preserve, SC

From the intersection of US 17 and SC 162 in Rantowles, follow 162 west toward Hollywood. After 3.9 miles, turn right into small dirt parking lot. This 643 acre preserve was acquired by South Carolina DNR primarily to protect one of the state's largest colonies of nesting wood storks. Boardwalk closed during summer months to protect nesting storks.

Swamp, pond, maritime forest

All seasons: Wood Ducks, Pileated Woodpeckers, Black-crowned Night-Herons, Red-shouldered Hawks, Anhingas, herons, egrets

Spring & Summer: migratory songbirds, Wood Storks, Summer Tanagers, Chuck-will's-widows, Prothonotary Warblers, Acadian Flycatchers

Fall: migratory songbirds including warblers, thrushes, orioles, vireos

Fee: Free   Phone: 843-546-3226
Web: https://www.dnr.sc.gov/mlands/lookup/

Caw Caw County Park, SC

From the intersection of US 17 and SC 162 in Rantowles, follow 17 south. After 6 miles turn right into the entrance to Caw Caw County Park. This 654 acre park contains more than 8 miles of well-maintained hiking trails. Open 9-3

Wed.-Fri. & 9 to 5 on Sat. & Sun. Closed Mon. & Tues.
Swamp, pond, freshwater marsh, salt marsh, maritime forest
    All seasons: Anhingas, herons, egrets, ibis, King Rails, Pileated Woodpeckers, Barred Owls, Red-shouldered Hawks, Wood Ducks
    Winter: Yellow-bellied Sapsuckers, Hermit Thrushes, ducks, sparrows, wrens
    Spring & Summer: Painted Buntings, Least Bitterns, Wood Storks, Prothonotary Warblers, Acadian Flycatchers, Mississippi & Swallow-tailed Kites
    Fall: migratory songbirds, raptors, shorebirds
    Fee: $1   Phone: 843-889-8898   Web: http://www.ccprc.com/

MAGNOLIA PLANTATION & GARDENS, SC

Take exit 33, US 17 north to Charleston. Watch for the town of Rantowles and Rantowles Creek. Just after the creek, turn left onto Bee's Ferry Road and follow this road approximately 4 miles until it dead ends into SC 61. Turn left onto SC 61. Magnolia Plantation is 3 miles up Highway 61 on the right. 500-acre plantation with one of most easily accessible heron rookeries in South Carolina.

Swamp, pond, river, freshwater marsh, maritime forest
    All seasons: Wood Ducks, Red-shouldered Hawks, Anhingas, Barred Owls, herons, egrets
    Winter: ducks, sparrows, rails, Northern Harriers, Bald Eagles, Sedge Wrens
    Spring & Summer: herons, egrets, night-herons, Prothonotary Warblers, Least Bitterns, migratory songbirds
    Fall: migratory shorebirds, songbirds, raptors
    Fee: $15 Basic Admission. Other attractions such as Historic House, Nature Train, Nature Boat cost $8 each. Audubon Swamp Garden only – $8
Phone: 800-367-3517   Web: http://www.magnoliaplantation.com/

JAMES ISLAND, SC

Fort Johnson: From US 17 go south on SC 171, Folly Road, until you reach Fort Johnson Road, which is about 2.5 miles south of the intersection with SC 30. Turn left (east) onto Fort Johnson Road and follow it for about 5 miles to its end.

James Island County Park: Drive south on SC 171 toward Folly Beach. After 3.2 miles, turn right on Camp Road. In 0.8 mile, turn right on Sunderland Drive. Park entrance is 0.2 miles down road on left. Continue 0.6 miles to parking area for dog park on right.

Sunrise Park: Take the James Island Expressway to Exit #2 and go southeast on Harbor View Road for 3 miles until the road ends. Turn left onto Fort Johnson Road and go northeast 0.5 mile, then turn left onto Wildwood Road. Follow Wildwood Road to the end, and turn left onto Wampler Drive. Stay on Wampler Drive until you see the parking area for Sunrise Park on the right.

salt marsh, beach, mudflats, ocean, maritime forest, early successional
- All seasons: pelicans, American Oystercatchers, gulls, terns, Ospreys, Clapper Rails
- Winter: Red-breasted Mergansers, Bald Eagles, Great Black-backed Gulls, Northern Gannets, Forster's Terns, sparrows
- Spring: migrating songbirds, shorebirds, raptors
- Summer: Painted Buntings, Wood Storks, Yellow-crowned Night-Herons, White Ibis, herons, egrets
- Fall: migrating warblers, vireos, thrushes, raptors, shorebirds

Fort Johnson: Fee: Free   Mon.-Fri. 8:30 am – 5:00 pm
James Island County Park: Fee $1   Phone: 843-795-7275
Web: http://www.ccprc.com/
Sunrise Park: Fee: Free
Web: http://www.scgreatoutdoors.com/park-sunrisepark.html

FOLLY ISLAND, SC

miles southeast of Charleston at the end of SC 171 (Folly Road). Birding locations include Folly Beach County Park at the southern end of the island, Folly each Fishing Pier mid-island, and the Lighthouse Inlet Heritage Preserve (old Coast Guard Station) at the north end of the island.

salt marsh, beach, mudflats, ocean, maritime forest
- All seasons: wading birds, pelicans, American Oystercatchers, Eurasian Collared-Doves, Seaside Sparrows
- Winter: loons, grebes, gannets, scoters, Piping Plovers, marsh sparrows
- Spring & Fall Migration: songbirds, shorebirds, raptors
- Summer: Sandwich Terns, Least Terns, Black Skimmers, Wilson's Plovers, Common Nighthawks

Fee: County Park $5   Phone: 843-588-2426
Web: http://www.ccprc.com/index.aspx?nid=61
Fee: Lighthouse Inlet Heritage Preserve: Free   Phone: 803-734-3893
Web: https://www.dnr.sc.gov/mlands/managedland?p_id=26

HARLESTON HARBOR EAST, SC

irding locations include Patriot's Point, the Pitt Street Causeway, and Fort oultrie.

Patriot's Point: From the southern terminus of I-26 in Charleston go north U.S. 17 and take the first exit after crossing over the high bridge, West oleman Boulevard. Go about 0.2 miles and then turn right (south) onto atriot's Point Boulevard.

Pitt Street Causeway: Follow West Coleman Boulevard southeast for about 6 miles. Shortly after crossing Shem Creek turn right on Whilden Street and go out 0.4 miles. Turn right onto Morrison Street. Go one block and turn left nto Pitt Street. Follow Pitt Street for 1.5 miles to its end.

Fort Moultrie: From Charleston take U.S. 17 north, towards Mount Pleasant.

Take the first exit after crossing the high bridge, SC 703 or West Coleman Boulevard. At 2.5 miles from U.S. 17 bear right on Ben Sawyer Boulevard to continue on SC 703. At about 6 miles from U.S. 17 turn right onto Jasper Boulevard and go 1.5 miles to the Visitor Center.
Salt marsh, beach, mudflats, ocean, maritime forest
>All seasons: herons, egrets, Wood Storks, Clapper Rails, Common Ground-Doves, Marsh Wrens
>Winter: loons, grebes, mergansers, Bald Eagles, Piping Plovers, Purple Sandpipers, marsh sparrows
>Spring & Fall Migration: songbirds, shorebirds, raptors
>Summer: Yellow-crowned Night-Herons, Reddish Egrets, Least Terns, Sandwich Terns, Black Skimmers, Painted Buntings

Fee: Ft. Moultrie $3   Phone: 843-883-3123
Web: http://www.nps.gov/fosu/index.htm

SOUTH CAROLINA - COASTAL PLAIN

WEBB WILDLIFE MANAGEMENT AREA, SC
From Hardeeville, SC, take US 321 north for 25.6 miles to the small town of Garnett. Turn left onto Augusta Stage Coach Road, cross railroad tracks and continue 2.6 miles to entrance to Webb WMA on your left.
Pine forest, longleaf pine forest, maritime forest, early successional, field, freshwater marsh, swamp
>All seasons: Anhingas, Red-shouldered Hawks, Northern Bobwhites, Red-cockaded Woodpeckers, Brown-headed Nuthatches, Bachman's Sparrows
>Winter: Ruby- & Golden-crowned Kinglets, Blue-gray Gnatcatchers, Hooded Mergansers
>Spring & Summer: Swallow-tailed & Mississippi Kites, Purple Gallinules, Prothonotary Warblers, Kentucky Warblers, Summer Tanagers, Blue Grosbeaks, Indigo Buntings, Painted Buntings, Yellow-breasted Chats
>Fall: migratory songbirds

Fee: Free   Phone: 803-625-3569   Web: https://www.dnr.sc.gov/mlands/lookup/

GLOSSARY OF BIRDING TERMS

Altricial: Used to describe a bird that is born naked, immobile, with closed eyes and totally unable to feed itself.

Baffle: In the world of bird feeding, a device used to prevent squirrels and raccoons from getting access to feeders. May also be called a predator guard.

Call: Shorter and less complex vocalizations used throughout the year by birds to communicate specific messages.

Cavity Nester: A bird that nests within an enclosed area such as a hollow tree, an old woodpecker hole or a bird house provided by humans.

Crown: The top of a bird's head.

Coverts: Small feathers around the base of quills on the wing or tail of a bird.

"Eclipse" plumage: A cryptic plumage similar to that of females, worn by some male ducks in fall when they molt their flight feathers and are unable to fly.

Fledge: To grow the first full set of feathers, enabling a young bird to leave the nest.

Fledgling: A bird that has left the nest, but may still be receiving care from the parents.

Field mark: An obvious visual clue to a bird's identification. Field guides are based on describing these marks.

Irruption: A sporadic mass migration of birds into a non-customary range.

Juvenile: Refers to a bird that has not yet reached breeding age.

"LBJs": "Little brown jobbies." Expression used to refer to all the confusingly similar small brown sparrows.

Lores: The area between a bird's bill and its eyes.

Migration: The act or process of moving from one region to another.

Migrant: A bird that travels from one region to another in response to changes of seasons, breeding cycles, food availability, or extreme weather.

Mimic: A term used to describe birds that imitate other sounds and songs.

Molt: The periodic shedding and regrowth of worn feathers.

Neotropical Migrant: Refers to migratory birds of the New World, primarily those that travel seasonally between North, Central and South America.

Nestling: A bird that is still being cared for by its parents in the nest.

Peeps: A term used to refer to groups of confusingly similar small sandpipers.

Pelagic: Open ocean habitat very far from land.

Pishing: Sounds made by bird watchers to attract curious birds into the open. Most often made by repeating the sounds "pshhh" or "sphhh" through clenched teeth.

Precocial: A bird that is relatively well developed at hatching. Precocial birds usually have open eyes, extensive down, and are fairly mobile.

Raptor: A bird of prey; a carnivorous (meat-eating) bird; includes eagles, hawks, falcons, owls and vultures.

Resident: A non-migratory bird species – one that is present in the same region all year.

Rookery: A breeding or living area for large numbers of birds that come together in colonies to build nests and raise offspring.

Rufous: Reddish-brown, or brownish-red, as of oxidized iron. Used as an adjective in the names of some birds to describe their color.

Song: Refers to the longer and more complex vocalizations of birds, most often used to establish territories and attract mates.

Suet: Large chunks of hard, white fat that form around the kidneys of beef cattle. It is rendered and combined with corn, oats, peanuts and seed, then formed into cakes to provide a high-energy food for birds. Popular in the winter or in spring and summer when birds are feeding babies.

Vagrant: A bird that wanders far from its normal range.

Wing bars: Obvious areas of contrasting color, usually whitish, across the outer surface of a bird's wings.

Resources

What you need to get started:

Binoculars: 8 x 40 is standard these days. The first number denotes magnification and the second the diameter in millimeters of the objective lens. Compact binoculars – 8 x 25 or 8 x 21– offer small size and portability but sacrifice light gathering. 10x offers more magnification, generally a smaller field of view and greater possibility for image shake.

Field Guide: Sibley, Peterson, Stokes, National Geographic, Golden, or Kaufman are all good choices. Often beginners will choose a field guide that is organized by color – all blue birds together, all white birds together, etc. This is good when you want to sort by the bird's most obvious field mark. Once you are more familiar with the birds, you will want to shift to a guide with birds organized by family so that all the wading birds are together, all the terns are together, etc.

Birding Checklist & Notepad: Helps keep track of what you see in the field.

Tide Chart: Since birding in the Low Country is greatly affected by the tide, having an up to date tide chart is essential. Check a local boating store or marina. You can also find tides on-line at www.saltwatertides.com.

Later you might add:

Spotting Scope: Offers 20 to 60 power magnification. Must be used on a tripod. Particularly helpful for ducks and shorebirds.

Recordings of bird calls: The "Identiflyer" and its big brother, the "iFlyer" are handy gadgets, while hi-tech birders are using iPods, MP3 players, and even smart phones to take recordings into the field. For learning the calls, the Peterson's *Birding by Ear* and *More Birding by Ear* 3 CD sets by Richard Walton and Robert Lawson are invaluable.

Note: Use of recordings in the field is a sensitive topic. Such use is discouraged or prohibited on all national wildlife refuges. Please check on any posted guidelines and use discretion in heavily birded areas.

Organizations:

One of the best ways to learn about birds is to go out in the field with experienced birders. Many of these organizations offer field trips, most of which are free to the public. They also offer evening programs, and even classes to help you learn about birds.

RESOURCES

Georgia Ornithological Society
http://www.gos.org

Ogeechee Audubon Society
P.O. Box 13424
Savannah, GA 31416
http://www.savogeecheeaudubon.org

Coastal Georgia Audubon Society
http://www.coastalgeorgiabirding.org

Hilton Head Audubon Society
P.O. Box 6185
Hilton Head Island, SC 29938
http://www.hiltonheadaudubon.org

Sun City Bird Club
http://www.suncitybirdclub.org

Carolina Bird Club
1809 Lakepark Drive
Raleigh, NC 27612
http://www.carolinabirdclub.org

Savannah Coastal Refuge Complex
694 Beech Hill Lane
Hardeeville, SC 29927
Telephone: 843-784-2468
FAX: 843-784-2465
http://www.fws.gov/savannah

Friends of Savannah Coastal Refuges
PO Box 16841
Savannah, GA, 31416
843-784-2468 ext. 301
http://coastalrefuges.org

Oatland Island Wildlife Center
711 Sandtown Road
Savannah, GA 31410
912-395-1212
http://www.oatlandisland.org

Swampgirls Paddle Club
843-784-2249 Office
843-247-9191 Mobile
http://www.swampgirls.com/

Avian Conservation Center
The Center for Birds of Prey
4872 Seewee Road
Awendaw, SC 29429
843-971-7474
http://www.thecenterforbirdsofprey.org

The Center for Wildlife Education
The Lamar Q. Ball Raptor Center
P.O. Box 8058
Statesboro, GA 30460
912-478-0831
http://welcome.georgiasouthern.edu/wildlife

RETAIL STORES
Wild Birds Unlimited
8108 Abercorn St. Suite 210
Savannah, GA 31406
912-961-3455
http://savannah.wbu.com/

45 Pembroke Dr # 130
Hilton Head Island, SC 29926-2282
843-681-4461
http://hiltonheadisland.wbu.com

21 Pier Rd
Jekyll Island, GA 31527
912-635-3933
http://www.jekyllisland.wbu.com

975 Savannah Highway
Charleston, SC 29407-7868
843-571-3771
http://charleston.wbu.com/

BOOKS

Birds of North America ©1983, 1966 by Chandler S. Robbins, Bertel Brun, & Herbert S. Zim

A Field Guide to the Birds of Eastern & Central North America 5th Ed. ©2002 by Roger Tory Peterson & Virginia Marie Peterson

National Geographic Field Guide to the Birds of North America 5th Ed. ©2006 Edited by Jon L. Dunn & Jonathan Alderfer

The Sibley Guide to Birds ©2000 by David Allen Sibley

The Sibley Guide to Birds of Eastern North America ©2003 by David Allen Sibley

Birds of North America ©2000 by Kenn Kaufman

Stokes Field Guide to Birds: Eastern Region ©1996 by Donald W. Stokes & Lillian Q. Stokes

The Stokes Field Guide to the Birds of North America ©2010 by Donald W. Stokes & Lillian Q. Stokes

Common Birds of Coastal Georgia 2nd ed. ©2011 by Jim Wilson

Birds of the Carolinas ©2004 by Stan Tekiela

Birds of Georgia ©2002 by Stan Tekiela

Birds of Georgia ©2006 by Parrish, Eaton & Kennedy

The Annotated Checklist of Georgia Birds ©2003 by Georgia Ornithological Society

Lives of North American Birds ©1996 by Kenn Kaufman

The Sibley Guide to Bird Life & Behavior ©2001 Illustrated by David Allen Sibley, Edited by Chris Elphick, John B. Dunning, Jr. & David Allen Sibley

The Birder's Handbook ©1988 by Ehrlich, Dobkin and Wheye

The Low Country, A Naturalist's Field Guide to Coastal Georgia, the Carolinas, & North Florida ©2010 by Mallory Pearce

100 Birds & How They Got Their Names ©2002 by Diana Wells

Dictionary of Birds of the United States ©2003 by Joel Ellis Holloway

A Neotropical Companion ©1997 by John Kricher

RECORDINGS

Peterson Birding by Ear ©1989 by Richard Walton and Robert Lawson

Peterson More Birding by Ear ©1994 by Richard Walton and Robert Lawson

Stokes Field Guide to Bird Songs ©1997 by Donald Stokes, Lillian Stokes & Lang Elliott

Bird Songs of Georgia ©2007 by Georgann Schmalz

RESOURCES

FOR A GUIDED EXPERIENCE

Bull River Cruises
Coastal Georgia & Savannah River
Captain Michael Neal
912-898-1800
www.bullriver.com/

Coastal Georgia Adventures
Captain Wild Bill
912-429-0237
www.captainwildbill.com

Dunham Farms
Meredith Devendorf
912-880-4500
www.dunhamfarms.com

Lydia Thompson's Jekyll Island Bird Rambles
912-634-1322
artworksbylydia@bellsouth.net
www.coastalgeorgiabirding-lydia.blogspot.com

Moon River Kayak Tours
Waters of Skidaway Island State Park and Wormsloe Historic Site
45 Diamond Causeway, Savannah GA
912-344-1310
www.moonriverkayak.com

SaltyDawg Adventures
Coastal Georgia
Captain Roy Hubbard & Peach Hubbard
912-657-3927   912-657-3929
http://www.saltydawgadventures.com

Savannah Canoe and Kayak
414 Bonaventure Road
Savannah, GA 31404
912-341-9502
www.savannahcanoeandkayak.com

Sea Kayak Georgia
1102 Highway 80
Tybee Island, Georgia 31328
888-529-2542 or 912-786-8732
www.seakayakgeorgia.com

Skimmer Nature Charters
Captain Howard Costa
Shelter Cove Marina, SC
843-842-9447
www.skimmercharters.com/

Southeast Adventure Outfitters
St. Simon's Island and Brunswick
912-638-6732 / 912-ME-TO-SEA
Kayak@SouthEastAdventure.com
www.southeastadventure.com/

Sundial Nature Tours
Captains Rene & David Heidt
Tybee Island, GA
912-786-9470
www.sundialcharters.net/

Tybee Island Charters
Captains Cecil & Elizabeth Johnson
Tybee Island, GA
912-786-4801
www.fishtybee.com

Water-dog Outfitters
Kayaking & Biking Center
Hilton Head Island, SC
843-686-3554
www.waterdogoutfitter.com

Wilderness Southeast
A non-profit 501(c)3 organization
Savannah, GA
Phone: 912-236-8115
www.wilderness-southeast.org/

Checklist

Key:

Season	Abundance
W Winter	U Uncommon
S Summer	C Common
F Fall	R Rare
M Migration	L Local
Y Year-round	

Species	Season	Abundance
Red-throated Loon	W	U
Common Loon	W	C
Pied-billed Grebe	W	C
Horned Grebe	W	U
Eared Grebe	W	R
Northern Gannet	W	C
American White Pelican	Y	UL
Brown Pelican	Y	C
Double-crested Cormorant	W/S	C/U
Anhinga	Y	C
American Bittern	W	U
Least Bittern	S	U
Great Blue Heron	Y	C
Great Egret	Y	C
Snowy Egret	Y	C
Little Blue Heron	Y	C
Tricolored Heron	Y	C
Reddish Egret	S/F	U
Cattle Egret	S/W	C/R
Green Heron	S/W	C/R
Black-crowned Night-Heron	Y	C
Yellow-crowned Night-Heron	Y	U
White Ibis	Y	C
Glossy Ibis	Y	U
Roseate Spoonbill	S	U
Wood Stork	Y	C
Black Vulture	Y	C
Turkey Vulture	Y	C
Black-bellied Whistling-Duck	Y	UL
Greater White-fronted Goose	W	R
Snow Goose	W	U
Canada Goose	Y	UL
Tundra Swan	W	UL
Wood Duck	Y	C
Gadwall	W	U
American Wigeon	W	U
American Black Duck	W	U
Mallard	W	C
Mottled Duck	Y	U
Blue-winged Teal	W	C
Northern Shoveler	W	C
Northern Pintail	W	U
Green-winged Teal	W	C
Canvasback	W	U
Redhead	W	U
Ring-necked Duck	W	C
Greater Scaup	W	U
Lesser Scaup	W	C
Surf Scoter	W	U
White-winged Scoter	W	U
Black Scoter	W	C
Long-tailed Duck	W	R
Bufflehead	W	C
Common Goldeneye	W	UL
Hooded Merganser	W	C
Red-breasted Merganser	W	C
Ruddy Duck	W	C
Osprey	S/W	C/U
Swallow-tailed Kite	S	CL
Mississippi Kite	S	CL
Bald Eagle	Y	C
Northern Harrier	W	C
Sharp-shinned Hawk	W	C
Cooper's Hawk	Y	C
Red-shouldered Hawk	Y	C
Broad-winged Hawk	M	U
Red-tailed Hawk	Y	C
American Kestrel	W	C
Merlin	M	U
Peregrine Falcon	M	U
Plain Chachalaca	Y	RL
Wild Turkey	Y	U
Northern Bobwhite	Y	U
Black Rail	Y	RL
Clapper Rail	Y	C
King Rail	Y	CL
Virginia Rail	W/M	UL
Sora	M/W	C/U
Purple Gallinule	S	UL
Common Gallinule	Y	C
American Coot	W/S	C/R
Sandhill Crane	Y/M	RL/U
Black-bellied Plover	W/M	C
American Golden-Plover	M	U
Wilson's Plover	S/W	U/R
Semipalmated Plover	M/W	C
Piping Plover	M/W	U
Killdeer	Y	C
American Oystercatcher	Y	U
Black-necked Stilt	S	CL
American Avocet	Y	UL

224

CHECKLIST

Species			Species		
☐ Greater Yellowlegs	M/W	C/U	☐ Whip-poor-will	M/W	U/R
☐ Lesser Yellowlegs	M/W	C/U	☐ Chimney Swift	S	C
☐ Solitary Sandpiper	M	C	☐ Ruby-throated Hummingbird	S	C
☐ Willet	Y	C	☐ Black-chinned Hummingbird	W	R
☐ Spotted Sandpiper	M/W	C/U	☐ Rufous Hummingbird	W	U
☐ Upland Sandpiper	M	R	☐ Belted Kingfisher	Y	C
☐ Whimbrel	M/W	C/R	☐ Red-headed Woodpecker	Y	U
☐ Long-billed Curlew	M/W	R/R	☐ Red-bellied Woodpecker	Y	C
☐ Marbled Godwit	M/W	U	☐ Yellow-bellied Sapsucker	W	C
☐ Ruddy Turnstone	W/S	C/R	☐ Downy Woodpecker	Y	C
☐ Red Knot	M/W	C/U	☐ Hairy Woodpecker	Y	U
☐ Sanderling	W/S	C/U	☐ Red-cockaded Woodpecker	Y	R
☐ Semipalmated Sandpiper	M	C	☐ Northern Flicker	Y	C
☐ Western Sandpiper	W/S	C/U	☐ Pileated Woodpecker	Y	C
☐ Least Sandpiper	W/S	C/U	☐ Eastern Wood-Pewee	S	C
☐ White-rumped Sandpiper	M	U	☐ Acadian Flycatcher	S	C
☐ Baird's Sandpiper	M	R	☐ Eastern Phoebe	W	C
☐ Pectoral Sandpiper	M	C	☐ Great Crested Flycatcher	S	C
☐ Purple Sandpiper	W	UL	☐ Eastern Kingbird	S	C
☐ Dunlin	M/W	C	☐ Gray Kingbird	S	RI
☐ Stilt Sandpiper	M/W	U/R	☐ Loggerhead Shrike	Y	C
☐ Buff-breasted Sandpiper	M	U	☐ White-eyed Vireo	S/W	C/
☐ Short-billed Dowitcher	M/W	C	☐ Yellow-throated Vireo	S	U
☐ Long-billed Dowitcher	M/W	U/R	☐ Blue-headed Vireo	W	U
☐ Wilson's Snipe	M/W	C	☐ Red-eyed Vireo	S	C
☐ American Woodcock	Y	U	☐ Blue Jay	Y	C
☐ Laughing Gull	Y	C	☐ American Crow	Y	C
☐ Bonaparte's Gull	W	U	☐ Fish Crow	Y	C
☐ Ring-billed Gull	W/S	C/U	☐ Purple Martin	S	C
☐ Herring Gull	Y/S	C/U	☐ Tree Swallow	M/W	C/
☐ Lesser Black-backed Gull	F/W	U	☐ N. Rough-winged Swallow	S	C
☐ Great Black-backed Gull	F/W	U	☐ Bank Swallow	M	U
☐ Gull-billed Tern	S	UL	☐ Cliff Swallow	M/S	U/
☐ Caspian Tern	F/Y	C/U	☐ Barn Swallow	S	C
☐ Royal Tern	Y	C	☐ Carolina Chickadee	Y	C
☐ Sandwich Tern	S/W	C/U	☐ Tufted Titmouse	Y	C
☐ Common Tern	M	C	☐ Red-breasted Nuthatch	W	R
☐ Forster's Tern	W/S	C/R	☐ White-breasted Nuthatch	Y	U
☐ Least Tern	S	U	☐ Brown-headed Nuthatch	Y	C
☐ Black Tern	FM	C	☐ Brown Creeper	M/W	U
☐ Black Skimmer	Y	C	☐ Carolina Wren	Y	C
☐ Rock Pigeon	Y	C	☐ House Wren	W	C
☐ Eurasian Collared-Dove	Y	UL	☐ Winter Wren	W	U
☐ White-winged Dove	Y	R	☐ Sedge Wren	W	U
☐ Mourning Dove	Y	C	☐ Marsh Wren	Y	C
☐ Common Ground-Dove	Y	UL	☐ Golden-crowned Kinglet	W	U
☐ Yellow-billed Cuckoo	S	C	☐ Ruby-crowned Kinglet	W	C
☐ Barn Owl	Y	RL	☐ Blue-gray Gnatcatcher	S/W	C/
☐ Short-eared Owl	W	R	☐ Eastern Bluebird	Y	C
☐ Eastern Screech Owl	Y	C	☐ Veery	M	C
☐ Great Horned Owl	Y	U	☐ Gray-cheeked Thrush	M	R
☐ Barred Owl	Y	U	☐ Bicknell's Thrush	M	
☐ Common Nighthawk	S	U	☐ Swainson's Thrush	M	C
☐ Chuck-will's-widow	S	C	☐ Hermit Thrush	W	C

Species			Species		
Wood Thrush	M/S	C/U	Henslow's Sparrow	W	U
American Robin	W/S	C/U	Le Conte's Sparrow	W	R
Gray Catbird	S/W	R/C	Nelson's Sparrow	W	UL
Northern Mockingbird	Y	C	Saltmarsh Sparrow	W	UL
Brown Thrasher	Y	C	Seaside Sparrow	Y	CL
European Starling	Y	C	Fox Sparrow	W	U
American Pipit	W	C	Song Sparrow	W	C
Cedar Waxwing	W	C	Lincoln's Sparrow	W	R
Blue-winged Warbler	M	R	Swamp Sparrow	W	C
Golden-winged Warbler	M	R	White-throated Sparrow	W	C
Tennessee Warbler	M	UF	White-crowned Sparrow	W	UL
Orange-crowned Warbler	W	U	Dark-eyed Junco	W	U
Nashville Warbler	M	R	Northern Cardinal	Y	C
Northern Parula	M/S	C/C	Rose-breasted Grosbeak	M	U
Yellow Warbler	M	U/C	Blue Grosbeak	M/S	C/U
Chestnut-sided Warbler	M	R/U	Indigo Bunting	M/S	C/U
Magnolia Warbler	M	U/C	Painted Bunting	S	C
Cape May Warbler	M	C/U	Bobolink	M	C/U
Black-throated Blue Warbler	M	U	Red-winged Blackbird	Y	C
Yellow-rumped Warbler	W	C	Eastern Meadowlark	W	C
Black-throated Green Warbler	M	R	Rusty Blackbird	W	U
Blackburnian Warbler	M	R/U	Brewer's Blackbird	W	R
Yellow-throated Warbler	S/W	C/U	Common Grackle	Y	C
Pine Warbler	Y	C	Boat-tailed Grackle	Y	C
Prairie Warbler	S	C	Brown-headed Cowbird	Y	C
Palm Warbler	M/W	C/C	Orchard Oriole	S	C
Bay-breasted Warbler	M	R/U	Baltimore Oriole	M/W	C/U
Blackpoll Warbler	M	C/R	Purple Finch	W	U
Cerulean Warbler	M	R	House Finch	Y	C
Black-and-white Warbler	M/W	C/U	Pine Siskin	W	U
American Redstart	M	C	American Goldfinch	W/S	C/R
Prothonotary Warbler	S	C	House Sparrow	Y	C
Worm-eating Warbler	M	U			
Swainson's Warbler	S	UL			
Ovenbird	M	C			
Northern Waterthrush	M	U/C			
Louisiana Waterthrush	M	U			
Kentucky Warbler	S	U			
Common Yellowthroat	Y	C			
Hooded Warbler	S	C			
Wilson's Warbler	M	R/U			
Canada Warbler	M	R			
Yellow-breasted Chat	S	C			
Summer Tanager	S	C			
Scarlet Tanager	M	U			
Eastern Towhee	Y	C			
Bachman's Sparrow	Y	CL			
Chipping Sparrow	W	C			
Clay-colored Sparrow	M	R			
Field Sparrow	W	U			
Vesper Sparrow	W	UL			
Lark Sparrow	M	R			
Savannah Sparrow	W	C			
Grasshopper Sparrow	W	U			

CHECKLIST

Acknowledgments

First, I would like to thank Kenn Kaufman for viewing this as a project worth supporting, and writing the Foreword for the book. His *Lives of North American Birds* has been my go-to reference throughout the years.

Writing articles is like running sprints. Putting together a book is a marathon. I am indebted to many people who have helped along the way, including friends no longer with me, Tanya Starzenski and Rachael Orr Schepkowski. Paula McCormick gave me the courage to pitch my first two articles to the *Savannah Morning News*. Editors Rexanna Lester, Susan Catron, Steve Corrigan and Bob Mathews supported my column for a host of years. Friend and fellow writer, Charles Coe, of Cambridge, MA, was my "running buddy," offering companionship and sound advice throughout the journey.

Special thanks go to my employers, and co-workers at Wild Birds Unlimited in Savannah – Bob and Ardie Simmons, Nicole and Craig Janke, Betsy Freeman, Pat Wolters, Sarah Lucas, Mark and Susan Peddy, and Craig and Nancy McEwan.

Joyce Murlless, executive director of Wilderness Southeast, helped me grow from a birder into a naturalist and educator.

Thanks to the birders in MA and GA – Bill Drummond, Linda Ferrarresso, Bob Stymeist, Lainie Epstein, Pat Young, Lydia Thompson, Steve Calver, Dot Bambach, Pat Metz, Steve Wagner, Russ Wigh, Brad Winn, John Parrish, Giff Beaton, and many more – who have inspired and taught me through the years, and to the dedicated staff of the Savannah Coastal Refuges Complex and the Georgia Department of Natural Resources.

Many people read drafts and offered suggestions, including Deirdre Kindthistle, Doris Grieder, Brenda Brannen, Pat Metz, Connie Sechrest, Wendy Perrotta, Giff Beaton, Steve Calver, Dr. Tom Williams, Ellen O'Leary, and Dot Bambach.

Kathy Bolch of Skipping Stones Designs worked with inspiration and diligence to bring beauty and order to the book. Jake Kawatski turned his considerable skills to creating the index. My brother, David Paddison, contributed marketing savvy.

For photographic support, I thank the members of Savannah Photographic Roundtable and Geechee Camera Club.

Lastly, I am grateful to my readers. Without your feedback and encouragement, I would not still be writing *Birder's Eye View*, nor would I have managed the sustained effort necessary to create this book.

Photo Credits
Nicole Janke: *Indigo Bunting (m)* p. 16, 202; *Indigo Bunting (f)* p. 202; *Purple Finch (m)* p. 42, 201; *Blue Grosbeak (m & f)* p. 203; *Summer Tanager (f)* p. 203
Bob Paddison: *Aerial view of Low Country* p. 3
Sarah Lucas: *Yellow-breasted Chat* p. 16
Giff Beaton: *Yellow-throated Vireo* p. 85
Dan Leger: *Yellow-bellied Sapsucker (m)* p. 202
Mary Hutson: *Least Bittern nestlings* p. 110

INDEX

Note: photos indicated in **bold**

A

Accipiters, 172, 173
Alligator, American, 6, **6**
Altamaha Waterfowl Management Area, GA, 209
Andrews Island Causeway, 209
Anhinga, 17, 27, 32, 109, **123–25**, **204**
Audubon, John James, 74, 114, 115–16, 130, 153
Avocet, American, 32, 142

B

Baby birds. *See* Nestlings
Banding, 50–51
Bear Island Wildlife Management Area, SC, 213
Beautyberry, American, **154–56**
Birding by Ear (Walton & Lawson), 80
Birds, in your yard, 188–204
  bird baths, 75, 191–93
  deterring squirrels, 187, 189, 195–97
  feeding, 187–90
  nesting boxes, 193–95
  reference guide, 199–203
Birds of the South (Green), 158
Bird song, 79–81
  Brown Thrasher, 114–15
  Vireos, 84–86
Birdwatching locations, 205–17
Bittern, 101
  American, 32, 69, **100**, 103
  Least, 18, 69, 103, 107, 110, **110**
Blackbeard Island National Wildlife Refuge, 208–9
Blackbird, Red-winged, 25, 26, 27, 32, 71, 109, 183, **183**, 184, 185, **193**, **200**
Bluebird, Eastern, **66**, 71, **87–89**, 111, 112, 155, **201**
  nesting boxes for, **72**, 82, **82**, 83–84, **107**, 108, 166
Bobolink, 69, 81, **81**, 149, 184, **184**, 185
Bobwhite, Northern, 27
Bottomland forests, 6–7, **13**
"Breakfast Club," 131–33
Bufflehead, 20, **20**, 29, 34
Buntings
  Indigo, 16, **16**, 42, 68, 109, 149, 177, 202
  Painted, 9, 10, **10**, 42, 68, 78, **96**, 96–98, **97**, 109, 149, **189**, **202**
Burleigh, Thomas, 166
Buteos, 147, 173
Buzzards. *See* Vultures

C

Canvasback, 29, 34
Cardinal, Northern, 25, 78, 79, **79**, 108, **186**, **187**, 188, **199**
Catbird, Gray, 10, 31, 80, 81, **154**, 202
Caw Caw County Park, SC, 214
Charleston Harbor East, SC, 216
Chat, Yellow-breasted, 16, **16**, 67, 148
Chickadee
  Carolina, 25, 40, **81**, **82**, 108, **108**, **112**, 188, 193, 194, 195, **195**, **199**
  nesting boxes for, **193–95**
Chuck-will's-widow, 69, 80, **98**, 98–100, **99**, 149
Coastal scrub habitat, 10, **10**
Coot, American, 17, 27, 32, **48**, 118, **118**, 119
Cordgrass, Smooth (*spartina alterniflora*), 4, **4**, 37
Cormorant, 124
  Double-crested, 26, 27, 32, **125**, 142, 152, **152**, **204**
Courting behavior, 76–78
  Bald Eagle, 46–47
  tern, **143**
Cowbird, 97, 98, 184
  Brown-headed, **200**
Crab
  Blue, **5**, 5–6
  Fiddler, 139–40, **140**
Creeper, Brown, 12, 31
Crow
  American, 25, 108, **200**
  Fish, 25, **200**
Cuckoo
  Black-billed, 149
  Yellow-billed, 13, 69, **69**, 109, 149
Cumberland Island National Seashore, GA, 210
Curlew, 32
  Long-billed, 32, 69, 150, 153 **153**

D

DDT, ban on, 46, 92, 163–64
Dolphin, Bottlenose, **5**, 5, 37
Donnelly Wildlife Management Area, 212
Dove
  Eurasian Collared, **199**
  Mourning, 25, 188, **199**
Dowitcher, 142
  Long-billed, 32, 69, 150
  Short-billed, 21, **21**, 32, 69, 150
Drives of a Lifetime, 3
Ducks, 33–35, 149
  American Black, 34
  Black-bellied Whistling, 29, 35
  dabblers *vs.* divers, 34
  Harlequin, 29
  Long-tailed, 29
  Mottled, 29
  Ring-necked, 29, 34
  Ruddy, **28**, 29, 34
  Wood, 17, 27, 29, **29**, **35**
Duerling, Richard J., 155–56
Dungannon Heritage Preserve, SC, 214
Dunlin, 32, **69**, 142, 150

E

Eagle, Bald, 26, 31, **31**, 45–48, **46**, **47**, **48**, 181
Early successional shrub, 16, **16**
Edisto Island, SC, 214
Egrets, 76–77, 101
  Cattle, 25, 70, 76, 102, **103**, 110, **204**
  Great, 25, **66**, 70, 72, **72**, **76**, 77, 102, **102**, **104**,

228

110, 131, **204**
Reddish, **21**, 22, 141
Snowy, 25, 36, **37**, **66**, 70, 72, 102, 110, 131, **132**, **133**, **204**
Eider, Common, 29
Ernest F. Hollings Ace Basin National Wildlife Refuge, 213
Estuary habitat, 5

F

Falcons, 173, *See* also Kestrel; Merlin
Falcon, Peregrine, 31, 70, 147, 153, **171**, 172, 173
Fall, 146–85
  migration, 147–53, 175–77
  overview, 147–50
Finches, **40–42**
  See also Goldfinch
  House, 25, **41**, **42**, 87, 108, 188, **199**
  Purple, 31, 41, **42**, **201**
Fish Eagle. *See* Osprey
Fish Haul Creek Park, SC, 212
Fledglings, 111, **113**, **115**
Flicker, Northern, 25, 108, 120, **121**, 121–22, **122**, **200**
Floodplain forests, 6–7, 13, **13**
Floridan aquifer, 6
Florida's Wild Edibles (Duerling & Lantz), 155–56
Flycatchers
  See also Phoebe; Kingbird; Wood-Pewee
  Acadian, 13, 69, 109, 149
  Great Crested, 14, 69, 72, 81, **93–95**, 108, 149, 177
  Least, 69, 149
  Vermillion, 93
  Yellow-bellied, 69, 149
Folly Island, SC, 216
Forsyth Park, **14**, 206
Fort Pulaski National Monument, 206
Franklin, Benjamin, 45–46
Freshwater marsh habitat, 17, **17**

G

Gadwall, 29, 34
Gallinule, **117–19**
  See also Coot
  Common, 17, 27, **27**, 32,
109, 118, **118**, **119**
Purple, 18, 69, **106**, 107, 109, **117**, 118, 177
Gannet, Northern, 23, **23**, 24, 32
Geese, 30
  Canada, 30
  Greater White-fronted, 30
  Snow, 30
Georgia Birds (Burleigh), 166
Georgia state bird, 116
Gnatcatcher, Blue-gray, 9, **9**, 10, 31, 83, **83**, 108, **203**
Goatsucker, 98–100
  See also Chuck-will's-widow; Whip-poor-will
Godwit, Marbled, 21, **21**, 32, 69, 150, 153
Golden-Plover, American, 69, **160**, 161
Goldeneye, Common, 29
Goldfinch, American, 31, **40**, 40–42, **41**, 73, 87, 153, **201**
  song of, 79, 81
Grackle
  Boat-tailed, 25, 26, 27, 32, **73–75**, 109, 131, 185, **185**, **200**
  Common, 26, **73**, 75, 187, **200**
Grebes, 149
  Eared, 30
  Horned, 20, 30
  Pied-billed, 17, **17**, 30
Green, Charlotte Hilton, 158
"Grinches." *See* Goldfinch, American
Grosbeaks
  Blue, 16, 68, 109, 149, **203**
  Rose-breasted, 42, **68**, 78, 149, 177, **203**
Gulls
  Bonaparte's, 32, **32**, 150
  courting behavior, 77
  Great Black-backed, 32, 150
  Herring, 26, 32, 70, 141, 150
  Laughing, 26, 32, 70, 71, **72**, 108, 110, 141, 144, 150
  Lesser Black-backed, 32, 150, **150**
  Ring-billed, 26, **26**, 32, 70, 141, 150

H

Harrier, Northern, 31, **35**, 36, 70, 147, **149**, 173–74
Harris Neck National Wildlife Refuge, 208
Hawks
  See also Falcon; Kestrel; Kites; Osprey; Merlin; Harrier
  Broad-winged, 147
  Cooper's, 26, 70, 149, **171** 172
  Red-shouldered, 26, **172**, 173
  Red-tailed, 26, **171**, 172, **173**, 174
  Sharp-shinned, 31, 70, 149 171, **174**
Herons, 76, 101
  See also Night-Herons
  Great Blue, 25, 70, 101, **101**, 102, 109, **191**, 20
  Green, 17, 25, 70, 81, **101** 102, 103, 193, **204**
  Little Blue, 25, 70, 72, 10 102, **103**, 109, **204**
  Tricolored, 25, 70, 72, 101 **105**, 109, **204**
Hummingbirds, 83, 108, 126 134–36, 192
  Ruby-throated, 31, 69, 77–7 **78**, **106**, 108, **134**, **135 149**, 177, 203
  Rufous, **136**
  wintering, 31, 135
Hunting Island State Park, S(212

I

Ibis, 101
  Glossy, 25, **25**, 70
  White, 25, **25**, **36**, 70, 90, 104, **105**, 107, 109, 14 **204**
Icterids, 183–85
  See also Blackbird; Bobolin Grackle; Meadowlark; Oriole

J

James Island, SC, 215
Jay, Blue, 25, 108, **187**, **191**, 19
Jekyll Island State Park, GA, 210
J.F. Gregory Park, GA, 208

nco, Dark-eyed, 30

estrel, American, 31, 70, 147, 149, 173, **174**
illdeer, 15, 26, 107, 110, 150, **160**, 160–61, **161**
ingbird, Eastern, 69, 109, 149, **149**, **203**
ingfisher, Belted, **1–2**, 17, 26, 27, 32, 36, 90, **204**
inglet, 149, 176
  Golden-crowned, 31, **176**
  Ruby-crowned, 10, 31, **176**, **202**
te, 136–38
  Mississippi, 69, 107, 109, **136**, 137–38, **138**, 149, 177
  Swallow-tailed, 69, 107, 109, **136**, 137, **137**, 138, 149
ot, Red, 22, 69, **71**, 73, 78, 150, 152
oodsma, Donald, 115

ke, pond and lagoon habitat, 17, **17**
ke Mayer, 206
nier, Sidney, 35, 37
ntz, Peggy S., 155–56
wson, Robert W., 80
e and Death of a Salt Marsh (Teal), 132
tle Tybee Island, GA, 207
ve Oaks, 6, 7, **7**, 9
on, 38–39, 149
  Common, 20, 23, 30, **38**, 38–39, **39**
  Red-throated, 23, 30, **39**
w Country, 3–7, **3**
  alluvial rivers, 4–5, 7
  bird watching locations, 205–17
  crabbing in, 5–6
  habitats, 9–23
  rice growing in, 6
  tides in, 4, 6

agnolia Plantation & Gardens, SC, 215
allards, 34, 35
aritime forest, 9, **9**

"Marshes of Glynn, The" (Lanier), 35, 37
Marsh grass. *See* Cordgrass, Smooth
Marsh habitat, freshwater, 17, **17**
Marsh hawk. *See* Harrier, Northern
Marsh hen. *See* Rail, Clapper
Martin, Purple, **52**, 52–54, **53**, **54**, 67, 126, **203**
Meadowlark, Eastern, 15, **15**, 31, 73, 184, **184**, 185
Merganser
  Hooded, 17, 20, **20**, 29, **34**
  Red-breasted, 20, 23, 29, **34**
Merlin, 31, 70, 147, 149, 153, 173, **173**
Meyer, Ken, 138
Migration, 147–53, 175–77
Mockingbird, Northern, 14, 25, 31, **80**, 112, 157, **157**
  diet of, 61, 62, **63**, **154**, 155, 157, **201**
  fledgling, **113**
  mimicry of, 80–81
  nesting, 108
Moss, Spanish, 6, 7, 9, **9**
Mud Hen. *See* Gallinule
Mummichogs, 132–33

N

National Wildlife Refuge System, 164
Near-shore ocean habitat, 23, **23**
Nesting behaviors, 108–9
  Bald Eagle, 47
  Brown Thrasher, 115
  cavity nesters, 83, 108
  Chickadee, 193–95
  Chimney Swifts, 126–27
  Flycatcher, 95
  Kingfisher, 2
  Osprey, 92
  Oystercatchers, 41
  Purple Martins, 52–53, **54**
Nesting boxes, 82–84, 193–95
Nestlings (baby birds), **52**, 89, 110, 111–13, **126**, 195
Nighthawk, Common, 69, 149
Night-Herons, 103–4
  Black-crowned, 25, 70, **102**, 103, 110, **204**
  Yellow-crowned, 25, 70, 103, **104**, 110, **141**, **204**

Nightjar, 98–100
  See also Chuck-will's-widow; Whip-poor-will
Nuthatches, 72
  Brown-headed, 11, 12, **12**, 25, 27, 84, **84**, 88, 108, **186**, **199**
  White-breasted, 81, **199**

O

Okefenokee National Wildlife Refuge, GA, 211
Open field habitat, 15, **15**
Orioles, 68
  Baltimore, 31, 68, **146**, 149, 155, 184, **185**, **202**
  Orchard, 68, 109, 149, 184, **203**
Osprey, 26, 37, **90–92**, **204**
Ovenbird, 68, 148
Owls, 43–45
  Barn, 26, 44
  Barred, 13, **13**, 26, **28**, 43, **43**
  Great Horned, 26, 31, 43, **44**, **45**
  Screech-Owl, Eastern, 26, 43, **44**, **45**, 108
  Short-eared, 31
Oystercatcher, American, 20, 21, 32, 37, **49**, 49–51, **50**, **51**, 107, 110, 141, 153
  banding, 50–51

P

Park habitat, 14
Parula, Northern, 9, **67**, 72, 75, 108, 148, **203**
Paulk's Pasture Wildlife Management Area, GA, 210
Pelagic (open ocean) birds, 24, **24**
Pelican, Brown, 20, 23, 26, 32, 108, 110, 142, **162–64**
  White Pelican compared, 162
Phoebe, Eastern, 31, 80, **80**, 149, 153
Pigeon, Rock, 14, **199**
Pinckney Island National Wildlife Refuge, SC, 211
Pine Forest habitat
  Longleaf, 11, **11**
  Slash & Loblolly, 12, **12**
Pintail, Northern, 29, 34
Pipit, American, 15, **15**, 31

INDEX

Plovers, 158–61
  See also Golden-Plover; Killdeer
  Black-bellied, 21, 32, 69, 73, 78, **78**, 142, **152**, 153, **160**, 161, **161**
  Piping, 22, 23, 32, 69, 153, **159**, 159–60
  Semipalmated, 32, 69, 142, **159**, 160, **177**
  Wilson's, 22, 26, 32, 107, 110, **159**, 160

R

Raccoons, **197**
Rails, 140 *See also* Sora
  Clapper, 19, 26, 36, 109, **128–30**
  King, 18, 32, **106**, 109
  Virginia, 18, 32
Raptor Center, 47
Raptors, 69–70, 149, 171–74
  See also Eagles; Hawks; Owls
Redhead, 29
Redstart, American, 68, 148, **151**
Rice production, 6
Robin, American, 14, **14**, 31, 61–62, **62**, 108, **147**, 155, **201**
Rookeries, 100–105

S

Salt Marsh, 19, **19**
  low tide in, 139–41
  secrets of, 35–37
Sanderling, 22, **22**, 32, 69, 150, 153, 179
Sandpipers, 178–80
  Baird's, 150
  Buff-breasted, 69, 150
  Least, 15, 32, 69, 142, 150
  Pectoral, 15, 69, 150
  Purple, 22, 32, **178**, 178–79, **179**, 180
  Semipalmated, **67**, 69, 142, 150
  Solitary, 69, 150
  Spotted, 17, **17**, 69, 142, 150
  Stilt, 32, 69, 150
  Upland, 69, 150
  Western, 32, 69
  White-rumped, 150
Sandy beach habitat, 22, **22**
Sapsucker, 149

Yellow-bellied, 31, 121, **122**, 175, 175–76, **202**
Savannah Area Christmas Bird Count, 7
Savannah National Wildlife Refuge, 59, 182, 205
Savannah Ogeechee Canal Museum & Nature Center, 208
Scaup
  Greater, 29
  Lesser, 29, 34
Scoter
  Black, 23, 29
  Surf, 29
  White-winged, 29
Sea Pines Forest Preserve, 211
Shearwater
  Corey's, 24, **24**
  Greater, 24, **24**
Shorebirds, 32
  See also Plovers; Sandpipers
  feeding habits, 141–42
  migrating, 150, 153, **153**
Shoveler, Northern, 29, **34**
Shrike
  Loggerhead, 27, **27**, 31, **156–58**
  Northern, 156, 157
Singing Life of Birds (Kroodsma), 115
Siskin, Pine, 31, **41**, **201**
Skidaway Island, 47, 48, 206
Skimmer, Black, 26, 32, 70, 108, 110, 141, **146**, 150, **168–70**
Slash Pine Forest, 12
Snakebird. *See* Anhinga
Snipe, Wilson's, 32, 73, 150, **150**
Sora, 18, **18**, 32
Sparrows, 58–60, 73, 149
  Bachman's, 11, **11**, 27, 30
  Chipping, 15, 30, **58**, 59, **201**
  Clay-colored, 30
  Field, 30
  Fox, 30
  Grasshopper, 30
  House, 14, **14**, 25, 30, **58**, 88, 108, **200**
  Lark, 30
  Le Conte's, 30
  Nelson's, 19, 30, 37, **37**, 60
  Saltmarsh, 19, 30, 37, **60**, 153

Savannah, 30, **59**
Seaside, 19, **19**, 26, 30, 3●
  37, 60, 109
Song, 30, **60**, **201**
Swamp, **58**
Vesper, 30
White-throated, 30, 59, 5●
  201
Spoonbill, Roseate, 25, 70, 101, 104–5, 132, **132**
Spotting scope, 34, 220
Spring, 67–105
  overview, 67–70
Squirrels, gray, **186**, 187, 18●
  196–98, **196**, **198**
St. Simon's Island, GA, 209
Starlings, European, 88, **200**
Stilt, Black-necked, 18, **18**, ●
Stork, Wood, 25, 37, **70**, 10● **102**, 105, 109, 131, **133**, 141, **204**
Storm Petrel, Wilson's, 24, 2●
Suburban park habitat, 14
Summer, 107–45
  overview, 107–10
Swallows, 108
  Bank, 67, 148
  Barn, 67, 109, **109**, 148
  Cave, 148, 167
  Cliff, 67, 109
  Northern Rough-winged, ●
  Rough-winged, 109, 148
  Tree, 31, 32, 67, 88, 148, **165–67**
Swamp chicken. *See* Gallinu●
Swamp habitat, 6–7, 13, **13**
Swift, Chimney, 14, 69, 107● 109, **125–27**, 149, 165

T

Tanager
  Scarlet, 68, 78, 149
  Summer, 9, 68, 109, 149, 2●
Teal
  Blue-winged, 29, **33**, 34, ●
  Cinnamon, 29
  Green-winged, 29
Teal, John and Mildred, 132
Terns, 141, 142–45
  Black, 108, **144**, 145, 15●
  Bridled, 24
  Caspian, 32, 108, 143–4● **144**, 150
  Common, 70, 108, **145**, ●

courting behavior, 77
Forster's, 32, 70, 108, **143**, 144–45, 150
Gull-billed, 110, 145, **145**
Least, 70, 108, 110, **142**
Royal, 23, **23**, 26, 32, **66**, 70, **70**, **77**, 108, 110, **142**, 143, **143**, **144**, 150
Sandwich, 32, 70, 108, 110, **143**, 144, 150
Sooty, 24
rasher, Brown, 14, 25, 71, 80, 108, **111**, **114–16**, **193**, **201**
rush. *See also* Veery
Bicknell's, 69, 148
Gray-cheeked, 69, 148, 155
Hermit, 31, 69, 73, 148, 155, **177**, **202**
Swainson's, 69, 148, **153**, 154, 155
Wood, 69, 148, 155
dal creek and river, 20, **20**
dal sandbar and mudflat, 21, **21**
les, 4, 6, 36–37, 49, 129
salt marsh, 139–41
mouse, 72, 188
Tufted, 25, 108, **192**, **194**, **199**
whee, Eastern, 10, 25, 27, 30, 31, 109, **200**
rkey, Wild, 27, 46
nstone, Ruddy, 22, 26, 32, **67**, 69, 78, 150, **178**, 179
ee Island, GA, 207

an park habitat, 14, **14**

ry, 69, 148
eos, 84–86, 192
Blue-headed, 31, 84–85, **85**, 86, 148, 176–77, **177**
Red-eyed, 84, 86, **86**, 148, 155
Warbling, 148
White-eyed, 31, 84, **84**, 85, **86**, 148
ellow-throated, 84, **85**, 85–86, 148
tures, 64–65
lack, 26, **63**, 64–65, **65**
urkey, 26, 36, **64**, 65, **65**

W

Wading birds
  See also Egrets; Herons; Ibis; Stork
  feeding habits, 140–41
  rookeries, 100–105
Walton, Richard K., 80
Warbler, Myrtle. *See* Warbler, Yellow-rumped
Warblers, 192
  Bay-breasted, 68, 148
  Black-and-white, 9, 31, **55**, 57, 68, 148
  Blackburnian, 68, 148
  Blackpoll, 68, 148
  Black-throated Blue, 68, 155, **155**
  Black-throated Green, 68, 148
  Blue-winged, 68, 148
  Canada, 68, 148
  Cape May, 68, 148, **153**
  Cerulean, 68, 148
  Chestnut-sided, 68, 148
  Connecticut, 148
  Golden-winged, 68, 148
  Hooded, 67, 109, 148, **148**
  Magnolia, 68, 148
  Mourning, 148
  Orange-crowned, 31, 57, **57**, 68, 148, **202**
  Palm, 31, 57, **57**, 68, 148, **176**
  Pine, 11, 12, **12**, 16, 25, 27, 31, **56**, 57, 67, 85, 108, 148, 175, **202**
  Prairie, 10, 12, 16, 67, 148
  Prothonotary, 13, **13**, 67, 108, 148
  Swainson's, 67, 109, 148
  in winter, 55–57, 148
  Worm-eating, 68, 138
  Yellow, 148
  Yellow-rumped, 31, **55**, 55–56, 68, 148, 176, **180–82**, 193, **202**
  Yellow-throated, 9, **9**, 31, **56**, 56–57, 67, 108, 148, **202**
Wassaw Island National Wildlife Refuge, 207
Waterthrush
  Louisiana, 68, 148
  Northern, 68, **68**

Waxwing, Cedar, **28**, **61**, 62–63, **202**
Weaver Finch. *See* Sparrow, House
Webb Wildlife Management Area, SC, 217
Whimbrel, 69, **139**, 142, 150
Whip-poor-will, 69, 99, **99**, 149
Whistling-Duck, Black-bellied, 29, 35
Wigeon, American, 29, 34
Willet, 22, 26, 32, 69, 107, 110, **110**, **139**, 142
Wilson, Alexander, 52
Winter, 29–65
  overview, 29–32
Wolters, Pat, 112
Woodcock, American, 32, 150
Woodpecker, 71, 119–22
  Downy, 25, 108, 120, **120**, 121, **188**, **199**
  Hairy, 121
  Northern Flicker, 25, 108, 120, 121–22, **122**, **200**
  Pileated, 108, **120**, **121**, 122, **201**
  Red-bellied, 14, 25, 76, **76**, 108, **111**, 120–21, **121**, **146**, **188**, **199**
  Red-cockaded, 11, **11**, 27, 88, 121
  Red-headed, 25, 108, 120, **120**, **200**
  Yellow-bellied Sapsucker, 31, 121, **122**, 175, 175–76, **202**
Wood-Pewee, Eastern, 69, 109, **109**, 149
Wrens, 149
  Carolina, 25, 71, 79, **79**, **83**, 108, **113**, **189**, **201**
  House, 31, 81, **202**
  Marsh, 19, **19**, 26, **26**, 109
  Sedge, 31
  Winter, 13, 31

Y

Yellowlegs
  Greater, 32, 69, 142, 150
  Lesser, 32, 69, 142, 150
Yellowthroat, Common, 10, **10**, 18, 31, 55, **55**, 67, 109, 148

RECENT REVIEWS OF BIRDER'S EYE VIEW

I found this book to be a delightful read. Diana brings birding and nature to life. She shows a genuine love and understanding of the local birdlife that takes bird watching beyond just checking a bird off on a list.

Steve Calver, Biologist, Savannah, GA

Diana has a way with words that intrigues, entertains, and makes memorable her ever-growing body of birding knowledge. She can inspire non-birders as well as impress the experts. Her ability to communicate her passion for the feathered is beautifully enhanced by her fabulous photos. If a picture is worth a thousand words, this book is full of bonuses. Whether you want a guide that's useful and easy to use, or you're just looking for a good read, you'll find it here.

Joyce Murlless, Executive Director, Wilderness Southeast

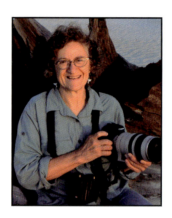

ABOUT THE AUTHOR

Diana Churchill grew up in Savannah and developed an early love of the beaches, marsh, tidal creeks, and birds of the Low Country. She attended Eckerd College in St. Petersburg, Florida where she majored in Spanish. She took one formal class in ornithology and spent a month riding around the state of Florida watching birds. After graduating from the Boulder School of Massage Therapy, Diana moved to Massachusetts where she had a private massage practice for 17 years. There, she joined the Brookline Bird Club and got seriously hooked on birds - particularly the spring migration of songbirds. She got her bird education in the field, attending walks led by expert birders.

In 1997, Diana embarked on a four-month mid-life adventure, traveling around Australia watching and photographing birds. This led, indirectly, to her return to Savannah in 1998, where she began working at Wild Birds Unlimited in February 1999. In 2001, she started writing "Birder's Eye View" for the *Savannah Morning News*. She has twice served as President of Ogeechee Audubon, and has led birding and natural history programs for Audubon, Georgia Ornithological Society, and Wilderness Southeast.

Diana started trying to photograph birds in 1996 with a Canon Rebel film camera and a 75-300 lens. In 2001, she upgraded to Canon's 100-400 IS lens, and in 2004, replaced her film camera with a Canon 20D. Currently, she uses a Canon 40D and the faithful 100-400 IS lens.

Photos of the author by Bob Paddison